Sourcebook of Language Learning Activities

Sourcebook of Language Learning Activities

Instructional Strategies
and Methods

William Justin Worthley, Ph.D.
Language, Speech, and Hearing Center
Central Washington University
Ellensburg, Washington

Little, Brown and Company

For all who work to bring some meaning into the lives of
those less fortunate

Contents

Preface   xi

I USING THE SOURCEBOOK: TECHNIQUES AND METHODS

1 Language Sets, Teaching Techniques, and the Criterion Placement Test   3
Title, Criterion, Levels of Production, Materials, Purpose, Demonstration Sequences, Teaching Techniques, Criterion Placement Test, Marking the CPT, Levels

2 Motivation and Reinforcement Techniques and the Cumulative Response Record   7
Definition, Reinforcers, Goals, Incorrect Productions, Schedules, Cumulative Response Record — Instructions

3 Sequence of Using the Language Sets   11
Transformations; Section A. Basic Skills; Section B. Receptive Vocabulary Building; Section C. Expressive Syntax — Words and Phrases; Section D. Expressive Syntax — Sentences; Section E. Communication Skills — Cognitive Analysis; Section F. Reading; Section G. Writing — Spelling

4 Behavioral Control   15
Controlling Tantrums, Hyperactivity, Distractability; Pretraining; Eye Contact, Behavioral Focusing, Remaining Quiet — Remaining Seated; Play Activity

5 The Natural Communicative Environment: Study at School, at Home, and at Play   17
At School and Play; At Home; Helping a Child to Talk; Language Interventional Techniques

6 Assessment   19
The Diagnostic-Therapeutic Principle; Language Learning Disabilities; The Language Sample — Instructions for Using the Sourcebook Language Script; Obtaining the Sample; Analyzing the Sample; Evaluating the Sample — Comparing Readministrations

II THE LANGUAGE SETS

A Basic Skills

A a   Becoming Aware of Sound — Attending to Sound   29
A b   Producing Rhythms   30
A c   Visual — Motor Organization: Cutting and Coloring   31
A d   Producing Nonmeaningful Sounds   32
A e   Following Directions Presented Verbally and/or Gesturally   34
A f   Producing Speech Melody Patterns   36
A g   Imitating Environmental Sounds: Onomatopoeia   37
A h   Matching Forms, Sizes, and Pictures   38
A i   Sorting Forms, Sizes, and Pictures   39
A j   Visual — Motor Association: Pairing According to Function   40
A k   Visual — Motor Sequencing: Completing an Action Sequence   41
A l   "Same" vs. "Different"   42

B Receptive Vocabulary Building

B a   Identifying Pictures and/or Objects by Pointing   45
B b   Associating Objects with Pictures   46
B c   Recognizing Objects or Pictures Presented Aurally   47
B d   Identifying Verbs by Pointing   48
B e   Making "Yes — No" Judgments   49
B f   Discriminating Nouns and Verbs by Pointing: Negation   50

C Expressive Syntax — Words and Phrases

C a   Naming Objects and Pictures: Nouns   53
C b   Producing Common Expressions   54
C c   Naming Pictures and Objects: Vocabulary Expansion   55
C d   Identifying Actions: Verbs   56
C e   Auditory Decoding and Listening: Recognizing Sounds   57
C f   Auditory Closure: Word Completion   58
C g   Sequential Visual Memory: Remembering Names — Nouns   60
C h   Arranging Words into Classes   61
C i   Learning Noun Phrases: Article plus Noun   63
C j   Visual — Motor Organization: Learning Numbers, Conceptualizing, Counting   64
C k   Conceptualizing Categories: Plurals   65
C l   Identifying Colors: Conceptualizing Adjectives   66
C m   Making Yes — No Judgments: Conceptualizing "Yes" and "No"   67
C n   Learning Noun Phrases: Noun plus Adjective, Adjective plus Noun   68
C o   Understanding Relationships: Prepositions   69

C p   Learning Verb Phrases: Subject plus Verb   70

C q   Learning Adverb Phrases: Verb plus Adverb   71

C r   Identifying Characteristics by Sight and Touch: Adjectives   72

C s   Learning Noun Phrases: Quantifier plus Noun, Plurals   73

C t   Identifying Persons: Pronouns "I" and "You"   75

C u   Learning Verb Phrases: Verb plus Object   76

C v   Using Nouns and Possessive Pronouns: Conceptualizing Possession   77

C w   Learning Verb Phrases: Verb plus Particle, Preposition, Pronoun   78

C x   Learning Predicative Phrases: Demonstrative plus Possessive Pronouns and Full- to Substitute-Form Transformations   79

C y   Learning Designative Phrases: Locator, Demonstrator, Identifier plus Noun, and Plurals and Interrogatives   80

D Expressive Syntax: Sentences

D a   Auditory Sequential Memory: Building Sentences   83

D b   Auditory Sequential Memory: Remembering Word Sequences   84

D c   Grammatical Closure and Sequential Memory: Sentence Completion   86

D d   Grammatical Closure: Sentence Completion   87

D e   Building Beginning Sentences   88

D f   Conceptualizing Negatives   89

D g   Learning "Is" in Present Indicative   90

D h   Learning "Is" with an Adjective   91

D i   Learning "Is" with "Ing"   92

D j   Learning to Use Pronouns with "Is"   93

D k   Learning "Is" and "Are" with Pronouns and Nouns   95

D l   Using Adjectives as Predicate Complements   96

D m   Expanding the Use of "Is"   97

D n   Coordinate Transformations: Making Two Sentences One Sentence or Making One Sentence Two Sentences   99

D o   Producing Expanded Sentences Using "Is" and Other Subjects, Verbs, Prepositions, and Objects of the Preposition   100

D p   Building Sentences: "Wh" Questions and Other Interrogatives   102

D q   Learning "Am, Are, Was, Were," Using Pronouns, Adjectives, and Verbs   103

D r   Learning to Use Pronouns with Verbs: Want — See — Have — Has   104

D s   Learning to Use Verbs: Past, Present, Future Tense   105

D t   Learning to Use Verbs: Actor — Action Sentences   106

D u   Learning "ed" Verb Endings plus Past Tense   107

D v   Learning to Use Verbs: Past Tense   108

D w   Learning Verbal Sentences   109

D x   Expanding Sentence Forms: Transformations of Order   110

E Communication Skills — Cognitive Analysis

E a   Using Sentences in Context: Conversation, Telling a Story   113

E b   Auditory Organizing: Word Associations   116

E c   Visual — Auditory Association: "Tell me all you can about . . ."   117

E d   Associating Words   118

E e   Associating Ideas Presented Orally: "What Is It?" "What Is Happening?"   119

E f   Using Auditory Memory: Answering Questions   123

E g   Auditory — Vocal Sequencing: Giving Directions and Instructions   127

E h   Associating Ideas Presented Aurally: Problem-Solving   128

E i   Making Mental Judgments: "Alike — Different"   130

E j   Associating Ideas: Alike — Different Comparisons   131

E k   Associating Words: "Which Doesn't Belong?"   133

E l   Auditory Decoding — Encoding: Associating Ideas Presented Aurally: "What's Wrong with It?"   134

E m   Verbal Association: Answering Questions   136

F Reading

F a   Visual Closure: Object — Picture Identification   139

F b   Visual Association: Consonant Recognition   140

F c   Visual Association: Combining Consonants with Vowels and Diphthongs   141

F d   Visual Organizing, Sound Blending, Word Building   142

F e   Visual Closure: Word Perception   144

F f   Visual Association: Word and Picture Identification   145

F g   Visual Association: Word Recognition   146

F h   Visual Association: Reorganizing Written Phrases   147

F i   Visual Association: Reorganizing Written Sentences   148

F j   Visual Organizing: Reading   149

G Writing — Spelling

G a   Visual — Motor Sequencing: Manually Duplicating an Ordered Sequence   153

G b   Visual Closure: Completing Form Drawings   154

G c   Visual Memory: Making Simple Drawings   156

G d   Motor Encoding: Draw a _____   157

G e   Writing the Letters of the Alphabet   158

G f   Visual — Auditory Sequential Memory: 159
        Spelling
G g   Writing Words   160
G h   Writing Sentences   161
G i   Writing Connected Sentences   163
G j   Writing a "Story"   164

APPENDIXES

Appendix I: Word Finder   167

Appendix II: Records   175
Order Form   176
Criterion Placement Test   177
Cumulative Response Record   185
Sourcebook Language Script   186
Certificate of Achievement   187

Appendix III: Materials   189

Appendix IV: Self-Originated Sets   191

BIBLIOGRAPHY

Nature of Language   195
Development of Language   197
Assessment of Language   200
Language-Related Tests   201
Nature of Aphasia   202
Aphasic Disorders   203
Assessment of Aphasia   203
Habilitation of Aphasia   204
Emotionally Disturbed   204
Cerebral Palsy   205
Mental Retardation   205
Therapeutics   206
General References   208

Preface

This *Sourcebook* grew from a deep concern for the often frustrated speech and language clinician and for the special education teacher who has insufficient language instruction alternatives. It may be used to teach verbal language, reading, and writing to the developmentally delayed, dysphasic, foreign-speaking, mentally retarded, and autistic, and to persons with other speech difficulties. It may also be employed at the pre-school level or in the normal classroom whenever a more specific and precise mode of teaching is indicated.

The activities presented throughout this book constitute a fund of therapeutics aimed directly at the learner. They occur first as imitative productions. When these productions are eventually linked together and sufficiently practiced, they become complex verbal, read, and written output using thinking and listening processes.

Activities are planned to occur as day-to-day language learning experiences with heavy emphasis on things to do.

The principal teaching tools are the sets (part II), which provide information on specific objectives, learning sequences, and examples of language items to be taught. These basic learning activities enable the therapist to teach various language elements in a series of coordinated, stimulus—response experiences. They are grouped in order of difficulty, with the simplest usually occurring first in any section.

The beginning sections in part II (A, Basic Skills; B, Receptive Vocabulary Building; C, Expressive Syntax — Words and Phrases; and D, Expressive Syntax — Sentences) teach language from an extremely low, nonverbal level up to orally produced sentences. Section E, Communication Skills — Cognitive Analysis, provides opportunities to apply vocabulary in a variety of listening, thinking, and communicating situations. Section F, Reading, begins with low level preparatory activities and proceeds, through a process of visual recognition of letter and word symbols, to actual reading tasks. Section G, Writing and Spelling, also begins at a low level and progresses to written expression.

Developmental language usage is taught up to and including the junior high school level. Words that occur most frequently have been chosen. The "Word Finder," for instance, contains vocabulary comprising 90 percent of the verbal usage of children and 70 percent of that used by adults.

The arrangement of materials in this book is based on two major considerations. The first is the essential premise that words and word symbols (pictures, spoken vocabulary, printed, and handwritten words) are the building blocks of our language. The second is that these words are learned, hence they should be taught from the standpoint of the psycholinguistic

abilities described by Kirk and McCarthy (1968). These include visual and auditory reception, visual and auditory organizing, verbal and manual expression, grammatical and visual closure, and auditory vocal and visual motor sequential memory. Impairment of any of these abilities creates disabilities in language learning or language use. This book is arranged so that language is taught from the standpoint of the student and his problems. As you plan and conduct therapy, you may thus choose tasks that best relate to your pupils' deficits and the disabilities that contribute to the problem.

Meanings of words and words themselves are probably learned most readily when they appear in normally occurring conversational exchanges. However, the persons for whom this *Sourcebook* is intended are not "normal," since they have special problems, hence special needs. An attempt has been made to combine drill on special points with "natural" situations so that neither method of learning is neglected. Some sets may be quite specific in artificially using pictures and objects as substitutes for their counterparts in the real world. Yet, any session will also include a spontaneous "natural" communication situation.

As you study the various sections and sets within the sections, you will observe that a variety of teaching choices are open to you. Your task is to select sets that are the most suitable for your pupil. For instance, one group of sets emphasizes imitative (sublinguistic) responses. Another is structured to teach the student to make a response following a nonimitative cue. Still others combine imitative and "cued" productions. Other sets place emphasis on the more cognitive "eureka" learning activity, in which the student forces the conceptual conclusion by providing spontaneous utterances.

The *Criterion Placement Test* (CPT), the *Cumulative Response Record* (CRR), and the *Language Script* (see Appendix II) have been developed especially for use with the *Sourcebook*. Their function is to assist in diagnostics, simplify record keeping, facilitate therapy planning, and provide a precise accountability check. Their purpose and their use is explained in detail in Part I, Chapters 1, 2, and 6.

The original development of these materials occurred through a three-year ESEA Title III grant (#1258) called the Modesto Program for Speech and Language Disabilities. A total of seven hundred children served as members of either experimental or control groups being treated for language and articulation deficits. The format and learning experiences contained in this *Sourcebook* now represent the most effective of those that were utilized in direct contact therapy.

W. J. W.

Using the Sourcebook: Techniques and Methods

I

All the chapters in Part I have to do with the use of the *Sourcebook* — in face-to-face student contact, in instructing family and assistants, as an assessment tool, and in other ways. The strategies and methods there should greatly assist you in conducting therapy. Maximum results cannot be expected if these are slighted. A minimum can be achieved by improvisation, but why be contented with imprecise, half-analyzed methods? Both the patient and the therapist deserve more than that. As therapist you should have materials with which to conduct solid, meaningful therapy. Part I is intended to provide a substantial beginning.

Language Sets, Teaching Techniques, and the Criterion Placement Test

Each set indicates the level of difficulty and degree of complexity of the activities contained in it. The level of difficulty appropriate for your student(s) will have been ascertained in advance by the administration, scoring, and interpretation of a language sample and other tests (see Chapter 6, Assessment).

A discussion of the form and function of the sets is essential to understanding how to employ them. This chapter will first explain the organization of the sets and the significance of the information given under the various labels within them. It will then suggest techniques of using the sets in therapy. Finally, it will explain how to use the *Criterion Placement Test* (CPT) as an ongoing progress record, therapy planning device, and diagnostic instrument.

Refer to Set C a in Part II. This will be used as the vehicle for illustrating the organization of the sets.

ORGANIZATION OF THE SETS

Title

The title describes the function of the set. It briefly designates the language activity and/or the psycholinguistic emphasis. Set C a is entitled *Naming Objects and Pictures — Nouns.* The capital letter "C" indicates the section in which the set occurs, and the lower case "a" indicates the individual set. For brevity, the sets will be referred to by these two letters.

Criterion

The Criterion note appears in the center portion of each set. It names the minimal number of correct productions required of the student in a "test" situation. The criterion has been met when he or she can, at any time, achieve that degree of accuracy. Meeting the criterion indicates that that particular language behavior is in the student's repertoire. In other words, if he can pass a particular criterion test, he probably does not need to continue with that set. The criterion does *not* mean that, until he passes it, a pupil may not work in another set. However, it does serve as a guide for clinical planning. With knowledge of the degree of accuracy that a pupil *can* achieve, you are better able to fit practice sessions into a framework of what he *should* achieve.

The set C a Criterion specifies that if a student can produce twenty consecutively correct identifications of objects and/or pictures at Level IV, he has "passed" that set and need not continue with it. This does *not* mean that he knows all the nouns he needs. Many more nouns will occur as newly practiced vocabulary in subsequent (more difficult) sets. All sets accumulate vocabulary and syntax complexity.

"Level" indicates the amount of stimulation required to obtain the productions of the Criterion. These levels will be

explained in detail at the end of this chapter. By way of introduction now they are as follows:

LEVELS OF PRODUCTION
I   Clinician models
    Student is physically assisted
II   Clinician produces
    Student produces simultaneously
III   Clinician models
    Student imitates
IV   Clinician cues
    Student produces
V   Student produces spontaneously

Refer again to C a. The right-hand column gives an example of the progressive use of Levels II, III, and IV. In this case your option is to practice the set at *easier* levels before attempting Criterion level. This principle holds true with all sets.

Materials
Recommended materials are indicated in the upper left-hand corner of each set. For a list of these, and suggestions as to obtaining and storing them, see Appendix III.

Purpose
Basic teaching objectives are identified as a Purpose statement immediately under the Materials list and Criterion statement. As semester objectives are identified, lesson plans constructed, and end-of-year reports written, these "purposes" may be listed on lesson plans and reports and related to the degrees to which they were achieved.

Demonstration Sequences
The Demonstration Sequences of each set are intended as a guide for the therapist's thinking and talking. They provide a series of ideas and suggestions which, when used one after the other, help you to fulfill the purpose of the set. These sequences serve to establish the initial activity, which needs to be further expanded by lesson plans and in actual use of the set. They are not complete within themselves but are to be used as deemed necessary. The left-hand column gives suggestions for the most effective way to present the set. The right-hand column provides a sample script. Remember that it is only a sample. It is not absolute, nor is it total. Tailor what you say to the instructions, using the script as brief cues for yourself. It also helps in teaching the use of the *Sourcebook* to an aide or to a parent or other family member. (See Chapter 5, The Natural Communicative Environment.) Whenever appropriate, a model sentence or phrase, suggested parts of speech, and a possible teaching sequence are provided. The order in which sets are taught and suggested combinations of them are identified in Chapter 3. However,

other concepts and alternatives will be presented here as a part of your fund of strategies and methods.

Frequently occurring massed responses acting as "practice" items form the prime ingredient in establishing an ever-increasing student repertoire. The therapist may think of this as boring "drill" that should not be used. It need not be boring at all, however. Plan for the inclusion of relevant reinforcement (see Chapter 2). Make "work" fun by demonstrating energy and enthusiasm. The student will quickly·become accustomed to frequent repetitions. He is willing to work hard if he has a reason. Regular and repetitive practice is a part of all learning and need not be militarily rigid or mechanical. It is reasonable to require five repetitions of each stimulus and response production. If you are more comfortable with fewer, however, maximize the number of stimuli. You will cover more items this way.

When you talk, it should be only to give a specific instruction or production to be modeled and imitated or to let the student know how he did. You should not ask "Can you...?" Always give instructions as though the student will follow them.

Therapy time should not be used for social conversation unless this is a planned part of the procedure. Your real function is to provide stimuli and cues to your pupil so that he knows he should say or do something. A "model" shows the student how you want him to say it, and a "cue" signals him to go ahead and say or do it. A simple signal may be a cue. For example, hold up a finger or tap the table to indicate the number of desired repetitions. Any verbal instruction which you give to signal for a response is a cue. It may be "Say," or a "Let's say it together," or it may be some part of the desired sentence followed by a pause.

TEACHING TECHNIQUES – GROUP ACTIVITIES
Many sets contain suggestions for specific group activities (in the left-hand column of the Demonstration Sequence). Some general methods to use in groups, applicable to all sets, will be mentioned here.

All students may be asked to produce the same response in unison. There may also be solo turns, while the other students listen. Any competition consisting of "how many can you do" may be exciting.

A competition may be arranged in which students are instructed to monitor each other's productions. Bonus points are awarded to the student who identifies mistakes. (See Chapter 2.) Winners of small "contests" should also be awarded bonus points. Tandem practice may be used: turn from student to student, providing separate stimulations for each person.

While it does not include a "group" which is assembled "together," the following is an activity for a number of students present in the classroom at the same time: Students are placed about the room with specific production assignments. The clinician or an assistant moves from one to the other and has

each one produce on cue. In between "visits" each person rehearses his assignment.

The following may be included in any logically applicable situation: Construct a flannel board which may be propped up and viewed by the group seated together, and make flash cards with any appropriate lettering which coincides with set activities. Include pictures. A slotted board at the bottom will provide a means of supporting the materials. A more elaborate means is to glue a medium-sized piece of sandpaper to the back of each card and/or picture. Sentence models, phrase models, letters, syllables, etc., can thus be made more readily usable. If possible, supply each child with a small flannel board and give oral assignments which match the visual components. Students may also practice directly at the large flannel board, singly or together. They may take turns acting as the "teacher." In lieu of a flannel board, any desk top or table top may be used. Audio stimulation may be used to augment an activity. The key term here is "augment." Earphones, records, and tape recorders should not replace the therapist. You and aides who may be assisting you should continually monitor the productions of the student as he proceeds orally with the recorded lesson. This might be accomplished by playing a record or one tape recorder briefly, turning it off, and cueing various students to respond to it.

Important activities in a set may be tape-recorded. Games may be placed on a tape if they correspond to any particular set. Any group of instructions may be tape-recorded. Also, any sequence of production may be recorded with the student instructed to follow along and "do what the recorder says." If more than one recorder is available with headset attachments, the lesson may be practiced with students "plugged in."

CRITERION PLACEMENT TEST
Refer to the Criterion Placement Test (CPT) in Appendix II. Study it carefully. Although it is not mandatory, there should be a current CPT kept for each student. The CPT shows all therapeutic activities from the initial meeting to the present. There is space for the name of the student, his or her age at the beginning of therapy, and the beginning date.

The Levels of Production list provides a ready reference point. Keep the CPT form out in plain sight and handy for marking during *each* session. You will find that a quick glance at the Levels list will be initially helpful as you conduct therapy. You will also be able to make any mark on the form as the necessity for it occurs. Pages 1-6 of the CPT provide spaces for marking those Levels that were practiced.

Page 7 may be copied as often as necessary. This makes it possible for you to produce new sets tailored specifically to the student.

Page 8 (Verbal Expression Output) is for posting data from the language sample. There is space for noting the results of test administrations at three different times. Chapter 6 examines in detail the method for obtaining a language sample.

MARKING THE CPT

Refer again to the front page of the CPT. Opposite each set is a group of Levels which can be marked with one or a number of Notations. Use the CPT each time you have occasion to indicate any of the following situations: work on a set has begun and is in process (√), criterion has been passed (√̄) or passed on a limited basis (√̄), or criterion has been failed (0).

Administer a test for Criterion anytime you feel the student can pass it, for example, when he has been operating at 80 percent correct or better for two consecutive days. If the test is passed at the designated level, that set need not be continued. It should be noted however, that the criterion for each set refers to one level alone. No assumption is made regarding whether or not that performance is in the spontaneous (Level V) production capabilities of the student. If you are interested in ascertaining this, create a structured conversational-play situation during which you provide a "rigged" opportunity for the desired spontaneous responses to occur. If they do, place the appropriate check mark in the Level V column.

Administer the criterion test for any set prior to using it for therapy. This may help you decide to eliminate the set because it is either too difficult or too easy. The decision as to where to begin in the sets should also be based upon which criteria the student is able to pass.

When you do begin, work at a point which is quite simple for the student. Proceed until the level of difficulty results in a logical therapeutic beginning place. This usually is at the point where more than 50 percent incorrect productions are occurring. This method might be referred to as "diagnostic therapeutics." More will be said of this in Chapter 6. As you begin, place a check mark (√) on the appropriate line of the CPT, opposite the set you start with and directly under the Level(s) (I, II, III, IV, or V) which you are using. On the same line write the date that you first practiced the set. Any time you make a notation on the CPT, be sure to date your entry, at any convenient place which works for you.

It is extremely important to note that the first work on any set need *not* be at the level specified in the Criterion. Your aim is to work up to it from easier levels. The CPT has space for marking any level. Write in a new check mark and date each time you move up to a new level. Find the level at which the pupil can work at better than 80 percent accuracy from the beginning. Success is very encouraging. Arrange your sessions so that there is a high frequency of correct responses. Stay at that level for as long as the pupil is below 80 percent correct. Once he moves beyond that, move up to the next level and work there. (See Chapter 2 and the Cumulative Response Record for instructions on figuring performance percentages.)

Select a combination of sets which realistically meets the needs of a person according to the form and severity of his deficits. Omit sets which are obviously beyond his capabilities. Work backward and identify all that the student CAN DO regardless

of Criterion. For example, in Set C a the normal requirement is twenty correctly produced different nouns at Level IV, but you may limit the criterion to three nouns correctly produced twenty times. Plan to return to the set and work on other nouns later. Interchange sets during each session to maximize interest and use of varying sense modalities. Some people may need a great deal of practice on one set and may be able to achieve only limited productions within that set. In this case, you may wish to revise the Criterion to limit the requisite target. Place a check mark with two dashes in the appropriate Level column (√̄) of the CPT, if you have used a limited-target criterion measure.

On the other hand, some students may move quickly through certain sets without needing any continued practice with them. You can then analyze the content of those "easy" sets and determine what it was about them or their subject matter which made them easy. You may discover a previously unidentified psycholinguistic ability in which the student is unusually strong in comparison to other areas.

LEVELS

Level I is intended to provide assistance for the severely involved mentally retarded or dysphasic patient. It may be combined with other levels in the case of work with the cerebral-palsied or similarly involved patient.

Level II is quite easy. It requires no linguistic choices. The pupil only matches the sounds he is making simultaneously with yours based upon your prompting. But he is saying *something*, even though it makes no real sense at the time to him. Use this level in the very early stages of therapy.

Level III will be employed quite often. The intention is to have the pupil echo whatever the therapist specifies. Imitation requires little or no language ability. But the frequent use of imitative responses provides very necessary rehearsal. If that rehearsal occurs under reinforcing conditions, it is more likely to be used spontaneously later.

Of prime importance is the difference between Levels III and IV. Level III is purely imitative. After you provide the stimulus, say nothing else until the student repeats the appropriate response. Normally, you require that he do so quickly, within one second. However, the difficulty of Level III may be increased by allowing a time delay between the stimulus presentation and the response of the student. He probably will not use the time to think of the right word. Rather, he will use the delay to forget it. Your job is to encourage him to do the former.

At Level IV you provide the stimulus and then request that the student say the word. There are several ways this may be done. You may say a word as a stimulus and place an intervening statement between that stimulus and the response you want. The intervening statement makes it different from an imitative Level III. As shown in Set C a, Level IV also provides for a verbal cue which does *not* include the desired response word. The cue for the response is a pause after an introductory statement: "This is a_____." Another Level IV function in C a is simply to point to the object or picture, selecting as many nouns as desired and having the student say each noun.

A more difficult form of Level IV is to provide a model for the desired response, wait a few seconds, and cue the student with only a portion of the first model. He is then to complete his task by producing the originally modeled stimulus in its entirety. You may gradually decrease the cue words until only one (i.e., the subject of the sentence) is sufficient to evoke the entire response. For example:

The topic sentence is: "The bird flies in the sky."
You say: "The bird flies in the sky."
Your cue: "Say 'The bird flies in the sky.'"
Student says: "The bird flies in the sky."

Topic: "The car went up the street."
Your cue: "Say the whole sentence. The car went up the _____."
Student says: "The car went up the street."

Topic: "The beach was hot today."
Your cue: "The beach was _____ _____."
Student says: "The beach was hot today."

Topic: "I love pretty trees in the forest."
Your cue: "I love pretty trees _____ _____ _____."
Student says: "I love pretty trees in the forest."

Topic: "Her dress is blue and green."
Your cue: "Her dress _____ _____ _____ _____."
Student says: "Her dress is blue and green."

Topic: "The package is big and heavy."
Your cue: "Package."
Student says: "The package is big and heavy."

The highest form of Level IV is to provide only visual cues, such as pictures or actions which you perform, and to have the student produce a sentence which describes them. Examine any set in terms of this nonverbal cue. When you are operating in this mode, say as little as possible. Establish the initial behavior at the easier level, then fade your instructions to zero while you continue to require that the student provide the appropriate sentence. For instance, your intention is to practice "is" with a variety of prepositional phrases and nouns. Accumulate pictures which show things on, under, above, and below other things ("The hat is on the head, the car is on the street, the cloud is in the sky, the plane is above the ground"). Practice initially at Level III, then say "You make up the sentences now." After this instruction, continue to hold up pictures and wait for the sentence. You may also say to the student, "Tell me what I am doing." Model some activity for which a descriptive sentence is provided. Select a group of objects and create the action ("The block is on the table, the plane is on the floor, the doll is on the chair"). This aspect of Level IV may be applied at any suitable time.

Level V is the ultimate toward which you are working. At this level responses and productions are "spontaneous," that is, they occur as a result of the situation and not as a previously modeled stimulus. Your role in this case is to plan the activities so that the appropriate type of response occurs. Few of the earlier sets have Level V as criterion. You are ahead if you do observe productions at Level V and note this on the *CRR*, *CPT*, or both (Appendix II). In order to achieve this, you may wish to tape-record or monitor a playtime activity. (See Chapter 5.)

The next chapter, on motivation and reinforcement techniques, provides further amplification of the variety of activities which may be employed with the *Sourcebook*.

This chapter describes a system of counting and reinforcing student output. The target in some instances is interpretation of single words. Later on, an entire sentence counts as one production.

It uses as a frame of reference the *Cumulative Response Record* (CRR) (Appendix II), instructions for which are given at the end of the chapter. All correct and incorrect output of productions required by the sets is noted on this form.

This method should not be dehumanizing. Its purpose is to provide a means of teaching in the most efficiently successful manner. Furthermore, if the CRR is used as suggested here, it will eventually result in a total therapeutic record, which is very convenient in these days of accountability requirements.

If at all possible, obtain volunteers or assistants who can help give reinforcement. You may then concentrate on stimulus sequences.

DEFINITION

The term *reinforcement* is used here to mean an action that lets the student know he is producing correctly. It is used as a motivational tactic to create a willingness to work. The extremely low level pupil (and others for that matter) requires a great deal of repetitive practice if he is to progress. Rehearsal is essential to learning. Reinforcement serves to ease the fatiguing effect of constant concentration and performance. Thus, a "reason" to work is superimposed upon the actual task. Reinforcement for the mentally retarded person, for instance, may be tangible (e.g., food, tokens, poker chips, styrofoam stars). These accumulate as points or filled vessels (cups), which are subsequently used to "purchase" a prize. The intangible compliment "Good" is given according to an established plan (see under next heading). It too serves as a strong motivator.

REINFORCERS

Intangibles

Of primary importance is the social intangible "Good." Say this only to signal a correct production. Never say it to acknowledge hard work. If you feel that your pupil needs praise for his efforts, talk about it at the end of the session when you are not actually attempting to teach. The regular use of the word "good" only following correct productions will create a state of expectation and a more receptive attitude.

The CRR is in itself a reinforcer. Although initially it gives no more reward than an accumulation of marks on paper, these are significant because they tell the student he is performing correctly, and they tell him so immediately. Knowledge of progress is satisfying.

Another intangible form of reinforcement is a special privilege at home, a small trip, or another greatly desired social activity. The student directs his efforts toward earning enough points to qualify for these. A parental or family conference is necessary to clear the way. These are "intangible" because the reward is deferred. They become tangible when an actual object is ultimately awarded.

Tangibles

In terms of clinical therapy, a tangible reinforcer is one which can be consumed on the spot (food) or taken home as recognition of a given level of achievement. The sets are not highly dependent upon such objective reinforcement. However, the teaching rate and amount of success will be higher if it is used. Severely involved aphasic, autistic, and mentally retarded pupils certainly do need it.

FOOD

Obtain permission from parent or family. Discuss your plan with them. Establish which foods are preferred and will be most effective. Your pupil should arrive hungry on therapy days. Some food reinforcers are the ever popular m & m's and Frosted Flakes. Snacks which are tasty but contain no sugar are also recommended: graham cracker bits, certain cereals, etc. All should be quickly consumable. Talking and chewing at the same time is not efficient. Be sure to have milk or another drink handy.

If the student becomes satiated with any food reinforcer, a new foodstuff is substituted. A point system may also be initiated. Analyze the situation. Find out if, in fact, the student was hungry when he came to the session.

"TAKE HOMES"

Obtain very small inexpensive toys or other objects. Arrange these visibly in order of their value and desirability. The degree to which you enter into such items will depend upon the finances of your district and parents. Establish the number of points, percentage correct per session, or other criterion which will be required to "earn" an item. The more desirable object should be more difficult to obtain.

The very delayed person should have something to take home each day, especially at the beginning of the school year. Thus, it should be fairly easy to earn something at first. For instance, have on hand a large number of styrofoam stars and clear plastic cups. Hold a star poised above the cup. As soon as the correct production occurs, drop the star into the cup. Do this in clear view of the student. If the production is incorrect, make no movement. Present another stimulus. The filled cups are counted at the end of the session. The desired toy may then be "purchased" with the cups. Poker chips or other tokens may function in a similar manner. In this instance, however, the actual number of chips will determine the value of the selection.

Another form of "take home" may be a Certificate of Achievement or one of a variety of stickers which are commercially produced and readily obtainable.[1] The Certificate of Achievement should contain a signature and some statement of the nature of the accomplishment. Stickers might say "Good Worker" or "I Know My____" or have a smiling face on them.

GOALS

Establish goals for each student. These may be the number of correct responses or the number of consecutive days of a predetermined percentage of correctness. The number of correct responses which the student produces will earn a special recognition or take-home item. There are many variables to consider — the degree of delay, the attitude of the learner, and family finances. Of course, the reward should be commensurate with accomplishment. At no time should tangible objects constitute bribery. On the other hand, a very small bit of language output might be worthy of considerable attention if it occurs in a relative framework of even lesser production.

Use any means of counting "points" at your disposal. The most obvious is to assign a numerical value to each correct response mark on the CRR. Each mark could be worth 100 points or one point. Decide which would be more attractive. Because each set has a basic criterion level, a special reward might be given as each set is passed at criterion. Although all levels of performance may enter into the reinforcement system, the successful completion of a set is a simple, longer-range means of recognizing achievement. You may wish to combine the two. Construct a thermometer chart with an ultimate point total at the top and any other in-between achievement notations along the way. Color the thermometer very bright red, or another highly visual color, as the points add up.

If you feel the need, tell the student what he is working toward. You may even discuss his goals. This may not be realistic for some, in which case simply proceed with your own plan. Use the schedules and system described below. Even the most severely involved patients realize that something desirable is happening when the reinforcement system is functioning.

When reinforcement tactics do not appear to be working, do not give up on them. Emotions vary. Some days nothing works. If you have analyzed and identified what truly interests your student, he will settle into achieving the objectives you have set up for him. This will occur regardless of fluctuations in both his and your moods. If nothing seems to be working, study the problem carefully. Talk with parents, other teachers,

---

[1]A Certificate of Achievement may be obtained from this writer. The stickers may be ordered from TEECH-UM Company, Box 4232, Overland Park, Kansas 66204.

family, and physician. Explore all possible alternatives as objects or privileges toward which your pupil might work. Somewhere there is something which will pique his enthusiasm.

INCORRECT PRODUCTIONS

Say *nothing* if the production is incorrect. If the student initially makes an incorrect production, then corrects himself, do not say "Good" or in any way count that as correct. He may get the idea that saying something wrong, then saying it right, is what you want him to do. Remain silent. If ten consecutive incorrect productions occur, take a careful look at what you are doing and revise it to regenerate a higher correct-to-incorrect ratio. A particular set may be totally beyond the student. On the other hand, he may simply be confused and not understand exactly what you want him to do.

You may encounter the rather frustrating situation of hearing the student make inappropriate responses no matter what you do. Continue. Analyze the situation as well as you can, but continue. It is extremely important for your student to know that, no matter what he does, you and he will be working together on an irrevocably regular basis. When this realization settles in, his productions should improve. Interestingly, he will not understand any better if you attempt to explain things. Continue to provide the stimuli as they appear in the set, at an easy level. Remember, you need *not* respond in any way to incorrect or partially correct productions. Simply remain silent, withhold the reinforcer, and mark the form with a zero for that particular production. You will soon find that your student will know very well that he got something "wrong." His eyebrows may go up and he will look at that zero, back at you, and frown.

SCHEDULES

A number of systems or "schedules" of reinforcement administration are presented here. The schedule is the plan whereby you decrease the frequency with which you call attention to correct responses. This way the occurrence of that production is less and less dependent upon reinforcement and is more firmly learned. The ultimate aim is to have the student producing because it is a form of reward itself. Using something newly learned is fun. One "Good" from you becomes more powerful the less it is used. It should come to be extremely valuable.

As you begin each set in Sections A, B, C, and D of Part II, use the first (Continuous) schedule. As you proceed, each set will be operating on its own schedule after the continuous schedule changes. Because of this, you may have varying schedules operating during the same session. Write this information as a cue to yourself in the Clinical Notes column of the CRR next to the relevant set.

Follow the sequence outline below.

Continuous

A verbal "Good" and a slash mark on the CRR follows each correct production. If you are using stars or food, give them immediately. Be enthusiastic and personable as you say "Good." However, do not embellish this with other words of praise. If you do, your pupil will require more, and you may find yourself doing more talking than he. You do not need the therapy talking time.

Fixed Ratio

When twenty consecutively correct productions occur at any given level, switch to a fixed ratio of 1:2 for that level. Thus, for every two consecutively correct responses, say "Good" only once. Mark the CRR with one dash (—) and one slash (/). The dash indicates that the production was correct but you did not say "Good." The slash indicates that you said "Good." If you are using them, also place the reinforcers in the cup for each correct response regardless of whether or not you say "Good."

Once twenty consecutively correct responses occur at the 1:2 fixed ratio, go to 1:5, reinforcing with a diagonal slash mark and verbal "Good" after every fifth correct response. After another twenty correct responses, proceed with a 1:10 ratio. Continue at the fixed ratio schedule in a progressive manner in each set even as you add new vocabulary and increase the performance levels.

When three consecutive days of better than 80 percent accuracy has been achieved, administer the Criterion test for that set. The fixed ratio system may be terminated and one of the schedules suggested below may be substituted for it. This can be done as the 1:5 ratio is reached.

Fixed Interval

Administer verbal and/or tangible reinforcement after a selected amount of time has elapsed. This form of reinforcement forces the visual or auditory memory to function if you also wait to signal the student to respond.

Variable Ratio or Interval

Give reinforcement at varying ratios of produced responses: 1:3, 1:5, 1:7. Each ratio remains constant for some period of time.

Intermittent

Intermittent reinforcement is the final schedule of the sequence and should be reached at about the time the more complex (conversation) sets are started. (See Part II, Section E, Communication Skills — Cognitive Analysis.) Reinforcement is administered in varying ratios after target productions. The actual intent is to fade the reinforcement until you are using only an occasional "Good." Your student may thus reach a "goal" of only ten "Goods" but receive his reward in this case.

CUMULATIVE RESPONSE RECORD — INSTRUCTIONS

The Cumulative Response Record (see Appendix II) provides a daily account of everything which has occurred during each session. This includes target counts, activities conducted, production accuracy, and any other clinical information of significance. The following instructions clarify various uses of the CRR.

At the top of the page enter the name of the student, the beginning date of therapy, the session length (Sn. Lth.), the number of times per week which you meet with the student (# Sns./Wk.), the number of persons in the group, and the page number.

Each CRR page consists of fifty boxes. Each box is intended to contain 10 response (student production) notations, or 2 notations which equal 10 responses (i.e., a 0 and a / equals 5 incorrect and 5 correct responses for *one* box), or 1 notation (i.e., one slash mark [/] which equals 10 consecutively correct responses which were reinforced verbally). Proceed across the page as responses accumulate. Mark the boxes (within one second if possible) as soon as the required number of productions have occurred. The total of cumulative responses on one page is 500. Many persons are strongly motivated to look at their CRR in an effort to monitor their progress. Do not discourage this. In fact, have the form in clear view as the session proceeds. Instruct the student that each box represents ten things he says (or does). The zero means wrong, the dash means right, and the slash means right.

Place the session number in the appropriate column (under "Sn. #"). At the conclusion of each session, draw a line across the center column vertical lines immediately adjacent to the last box in which you marked responses. You will then have a visual picture of the number of responses that have occurred, the set(s), and the percentage of correct data for that particular session.

Enter the capital and lower case designators for each set (e.g., "A a") in the center column under "Set(s)." Repeat this for each session as you work with the same or different sets.

Compute the percentage correct at the conclusion of each session and place that number in the center column under "%." Add the total responses together, both correct and incorrect. Divide the number correct by the total to obtain percentage correct. (For example, out of 375 total responses, 317 were correct. Divide 317 by 375 and you get 84.53 percent correct.) Round off to the nearest whole number. Thus, in our example, 84.53 would round off to 85. However, if research is being conducted, do not round off. Leave the numbers as they are. This will make data analysis more accurate.

Any written comments may be placed in the Clinical Notes column. Use the reverse side of the page if necessary. Identify any targets which warrant special attention, such as the identification of extremely limited language elements. Special individualized behavioral (deportment) notes are of great benefit for specialists who will work with the student in the future.

If structured play is occurring rather than rehearsal of a specific set, indicate that fact by placing the abbreviation SP (Structured Play) in the Set column.

Use the CRR as an adjunct to the *Criterion Placement Test,* writing all pertinent "can do's" and "cannot do's" in the Clinical Notes portion of the CRR. Enter the criterion test notations in the Set column. Make a zero mark if the test was administered but not passed (0). Make a check mark with two dashes intersecting it if a limited criterion was passed ($\mathcal{F}$). Make a check mark with one dash intersecting ($\mathcal{\sqrt{}}$) if the actual criterion was passed. Be sure to date the CRR any time a Criterion test for any set is passed. Place the date in the last response box which contains the recording of test administration data.

There may be persons whose progress will not be apparent from the standpoint of scoring. Place any comment pertaining to this in the Clinical Notes column.

An examination of the CRR will show that complete progress data is retrievable on a session-by-session basis. Because each set has a simple capital and lower case letter designator, the sequence of therapeutic activities is immediately apparent. The percentage of correct responses is computed for each set activity on an on-going basis. This makes it possible to evaluate the relative efficiency of therapy, the extent of the deficit, and the effectiveness of reinforcement strategies. Further, any data may be coded into computer data analysis systems. Thus, research may be conducted with whatever variables the investigator chooses.

Give the student the benefit of the doubt if he produces sounds of words with less than standard intelligibility. Accept a variety of misarticulations. The prime purpose of language sets is not to correct articulation but to teach the use of vocabulary with appropriate inflectional emphases. When a nongrammatical response is appropriate, this will be indicated by a note in the left-hand column of the instructions to the set.

Much that is meaningful in the verbal language of very young or very involved persons is not at all grammatically appropriate. Early language usage is often not syntactically correct. The sets in Sections A, B, and C (and one in D) of Part II have simple vocabulary building and small word choice objectives. They conform developmentally to this concept.

Word choice in Section C is not always taught as "correct" usage. The student is required to produce what is required within the limitations of that set. In the initial stages practice may appear to be ineffective because the student continues to use his confusing output in spontaneous talking situations. Be patient. Include currently taught activities from the sets in your informal, nonstructured work. Even if results do not appear immediately, much of what is practiced in formal therapy will subsequently show up, if you provide the opportunity.

The teaching of sentence production begins in Section D. If you are of the opinion that the pupil has adequate vocabulary, you may wish to *omit* Sections A, B, and C and begin with Section D. Or you may wish to omit *most* of Section C but select a phrase structure or specific part(s) of speech which should be emphasized because a test result showed that it was deficient.

Section D provides extensive practice with sentence usage. This section begins at the third to fourth year achievement level and moves through a variety of activities into Section E. Section E requires coordination of thought (problem solving—cognitive) processes and verbal language usage. Section E can be combined with D, but be careful not to frustrate the pupil by making tasks too difficult.

If the student is working well into D and E and, on the basis of test results, is first grade level or more, you may then begin work with F, Reading, and G, Writing—Spelling.

The utilization sequences which are listed in this chapter are only suggestions. They show what points are emphasized by which sets within a section. Use whatever sequence appears to meet the needs of the pupil. (See Chapter 6, Assessment.) The sets will be used most efficiently if you are not working unnecessarily at any juncture. If the pupil *can do* what a set requires, mark the CPT and terminate the set. Date the CPT any time this happens.

All sections of sets build and are arranged in terms of difficulty as well as grammatical choice combinations. Because of this, it may be convenient to work consecutively through each, starting at the beginning. The decision as to which sets to use is up to you. That is why this is a "sourcebook." It provides sources for teaching many language functions. Only the most frequently occurring transformations are planned into sections

as aspects which are identified as such. Sections D and E also contain numerous opportunities to use transformations. These, for the most part, remain unidentified, as this is not a text in structural linguistics. Sentence structure and other terminologies have been included only to guide the thinking of the user, *not* to teach linguistics.

TRANSFORMATIONS

Some clarification of the term *transformation* may, however, be of assistance at this juncture. Transformations derive from the principle that all sentences contain two levels of grammatical structure. One is a "deep" structure, which represents the way a sentence is understood. The other is a "surface" structure, which represents the way the sentence is said (Chomsky, 1965). As a child's language develops, phrases and sentences change their meaning. Some of the most frequently occurring transformations are presented below.

Examples

Order. "Give me the ball" to "Give the ball to me."

Positive to Negative. "I'm hungry" to "I'm not hungry."

Statement to Question. "That is John's toy" to "Is that John's toy?" or to any Wh question such as "Whose toy is that?"

Full to Substitute Forms. "Boy, girl, children" to "they."

Active to Passive. Active: The verb form whose subject is shown performing the action of the verb, "Lightning struck the tree." Passive: The subject as receiver of the action, "The tree was struck by lightning."

Coordinate. Combination of two sentences that are the same except that a particular portion is represented in one by "y" and in the other by "z": "The boy is sitting" (y). "The boy is playing" (z). "The boy is sitting and playing" (y + z). This is often referred to as a *binary transformation*, because a single sentence is created from a combination of two sentences.

Singular to Plural. Requiring subject-verb agreement. "This toy is mine" to "These toys are mine."

THE LANGUAGE SETS

If a session is brief and time is at a premium, you may wish to focus on only one set per session. On the other hand, if one objective is to maximize interest and the use of varying sense modalities, you might interchange sets during each session. Either choice is appropriate. The decision should be based upon priorities which most realistically meet the needs of the pupil.

Section A. Basic Skills

Section A is intended for the beginning pupil who ranks extremely low developmentally and who has need of easy practice. It serves as an initial behavioral control vehicle for the person who requires time to adjust to the new situation.

No communicative verbal productions are taught. However, certain sound production activities are interspersed among the visual—motor and manipulative ones. If the sets are taught consecutively, they provide a variety of language preparatory experiences. If they are used to emphasize a particular function or functions, one of the following sequences might be used.

Following directions. A b, c, e, f, g, h, i, j, k, l.

Listening, focusing attention. A a, b, c, e, f, h, i, k, l.

Organizing symbols visually. Visual perception—association. Preparation for reading. A c, h, i, j, l.

Producing interpretative movements. Visual—motor association. A e, j, k.

Using auditory memory. Preparation for learning sound—word sequences. A b, f, g.

Producing sounds. Preparation for talking. A d, f, g.

Beginning conceptualizations. Associations: A h, k. *Rhythms:* A b. *Functions:* A j. *Sizes:* A i. *Alike—Different:* A l. *Sounds:* A a, d, f, g. *Colors:* A i. *Shapes:* A i.

Section B. Receptive Vocabulary Building

If the student can speak at all, consider omitting Section B. It too is intended for the severely involved or dysphasic person. The emphasis is on building a recognition vocabulary of verbs and nouns, the two most frequently occurring parts of speech in the entire language. They are pivotal to all sentence usage in that they amount to almost 40 percent of spoken English words. (See the tables at the end of Chapter 6.) No verbal productions are required. The pupil either points, performs a "picking and putting" motion, or nods his head. Sets B a, b, and c are solely oriented to *nouns*. Set B d has a total *verb* emphasis.

Two "conceptual" sets set the stage for extensive practice in later sets. These are sets B e and B f "yes—no" and "no" (negation) by itself.

Section C. Expressive Syntax — Words and Phrases

Section C emphasizes the basic visual recognition and verbal vocabulary building of those parts of speech which occur most frequently. These are arranged as two-word expressions and phrases until the last few sets, which become more conceptually complex (C u, v, w, x, and y).

The use sequences listed here illustrate options. Any one set in reality fulfills a number of objectives. For instance, Set C s simultaneously provides practice in two-word expressions and

shows that certain words (quantifiers), when modifying a noun, can change that noun to plural. This constitutes a transfer from single to plural usage.

Certain conceptualizations and word classes, transformations, and other psycholinguistic activities are included in the lists below. These also are superimposed on the main objective of vocabulary building.

PARTS OF SPEECH

Nouns: C a, c, e, f, g, h, i, j, k, l, n, o, p, q, r, s, u, v, y.

Verbs: C c, d, e, p, q, u, w, x.

Pronouns: C s, t, u, v, w, x, y.

Adjectives: C j, l, n, r, s.

Adverbs: C q.

Prepositions: C o, w.

Conjunctions: C f.

Articles: C a, g, h, i.

TWO-WORD EXPRESSIONS

Stereotypes: C b.

Article plus noun: C i.

Pronoun or noun plus adjective: C n.

Adjective plus noun: C l, n.

Verb plus object: C u.

Subject plus verb: C p.

Quantifier plus noun: C s.

Verb plus adverb: C q.

Verb plus particle, preposition, pronoun: C w.

Demonstrative pronoun plus possessive pronoun: C x.

Locator, identifier, demonstrator, plus noun: C y.

CONCEPTUALIZATIONS AND WORD CLASSES

Contexts and categories: C g, h, k.

Counting numbers: C j, k, s.

Contrasts: C r.

Person's names: C t.

Possession: C u, x.

Relationships: C o, p, s, u, w.

TRANSFORMATIONS

Negation: C m.

Plurals: C k, s, x, y.

Interrogation: C y.

Full to substitute: C x.

Auditory closure decoding: C e, f.

Listening—sound source recognition: C e.

Sequential memory: C g.

Section D. Expressive Syntax — Sentences

The first sets (A, B, and C) form a nucleus around which it is possible to build a great number of vocabulary and syntactic experiences. However, you might begin directly with Sets D a, b, c, d, e, and g. Set D e, for instance, might be used to bridge the gap between two-word utterances and those of greater length. It offers practice with simplified (nongrammatical) constructions which relate particularly to the world of the pupil. Set D e was not put first in this section, because it was decided that another way of beginning sentence instruction was preferable, that is, to begin by teaching correct word order (Sets D a—D d).

It has been suggested that Sections A, B, and C may be omitted entirely if vocabulary building is not a major consideration. Enough vocabulary accumulates in Section D so that any lack of practice in sight recognition of nouns and use of verbs, for instance, will not become an especially serious problem.

Psycholinguistic disability states enter into therapeutic considerations with more frequency now. At the outset, sequential memory is a major teaching variable. A number of examples are provided which permit you to choose the "form" of sequential memory sentence building activity you will employ. Try various sentence building forms with your pupil. See which works best. Transpose this activity into any set format if you are having good results with it, or make up sets of your own, tailoring the syntactic choices even more to the needs of your pupils. (See Appendix IV, Self-Originated Sets.)

The third person singular, present indicative of the verb "be" — or "is" — ranks as the first or second most frequently used word in the vocabularies of 5-, 6-, and 7-year-olds (Wepman and Hass, 1969). It is of such pivotal importance that other words of the sentence naturally group themselves around it. In its broadest sense, the verb "to be" serves as the simplest expression of the act of relating one term or idea to the other. Heavy emphasis is placed upon "is" because of its natural frequency of usage, and because a great variety of sentences with phrases and clauses can be generated from it. For this reason, Set D g could also be a starting point in the *Sourcebook.* Try all approaches. Establish which works best for you.

Start

Begin with any of these sets, then combine them for greater beginning emphasis on basic word order: D a, D b, D c, D e, D g.

Proceed with the sequences listed below or one of your own selection. Emphasize the sentence models which meet the needs of your pupil.

SENTENCE BUILDING

Nongrammatical: D e.

Words in sequence: D a, b.

Sentence completion: D c, d, p.

Carrier phrase + complement: D h.

Carrier phrase + "ing" verb: D i, j.

Pronoun + "is" + verb: D j.

Pronoun + "is" + article + noun: D j.

Pronoun + verb ("is," "are") + possessive pronoun or person's name + noun or pronoun: D k.

Pronoun or article + noun + verb ("is," "are") + adjective complement: D l.

Noun phrase + verb ("is") + adverb, adjective, or prepositional or noun phrase: D m.

Article + noun object + verb ("is") + prepositional phrase: D m.

Person's name ("he," "she," "it") + verb ("is" + "ing") + prepositional phrase (direct object): D m.

Pronoun or adverb + verb ("is") + possessive or article + adjective + noun: D m.

Article + subject + verb + preposition + article + object of preposition: D o.

Pronoun + verb ("am," "are," "was," "were") + adjective, verb, or pronoun: D q.

Pronoun or person's name + ("want," "see," "have," "has") + noun phrase: D r.

Noun + verb + adjective phrase or adjective or adverb phrase or adverb (tenses): D s.

Actor—Action: D t.

Pronoun or person's name + verb (past tense "ed") + pronoun or adverb, preposition: D u.

Pronoun or person's name + verb (past tense) + adverb phrase: D v.

Verb + or — particle + noun phrase and/or prepositional phrase: D w.

Auditory sequential memory: D a, b, c, e, h, i, j, k, l, m, n, o, p, q, r.

Grammatical closure: D c, d, g, h, i, j, k, n, q.

TRANSFORMATIONS

Negation: D f.

Interrogatives: D p.

Plurals: D k, l.

Order: D x.

Coordinate: P l, n.

PARTS OF SPEECH

Noun: D a, b, c, d, e, h, i, j, k, l, m, n, o, r, s, t, v, w.

Verb: D b, c, e, h, i, j, k, l, m, n, o, p, q, r, s, t, v, w.

Adjective: D a, l, m, q, s, w.

Adverb: D d, h, m, s.

Pronoun: D c, e, h, i, j, k, l, m, n, q, r, s, u, v.

Article: D a, h, j, k, l, m, n, o, r.

Conjunction: D b, l, t.

Preposition: D a, c, m, o, t, w.

Section E. Communication Skills — Cognitive Analysis

Section E emphasizes a more spontaneous use of language.
Note that Set E a provides many contexts in which a "Tell us
about" or a "Make up a story about" activity may occur.
Previously practiced models provide a vocabulary basis for the
more flexible, natural sentences used in this set. Other sets
provide an opportunity for utilizing various cognitive functions
in relation to word usage.

Word association: E b, c, d, i, j, k.

Generating ideas: E b, c, d, i, j, k.

Generating cognitive analysis: E e, f.

Answering questions: E f, m.

Giving directions: E c.

Problem solving: E h.

Alike—Different: E i, j.

"Which doesn't belong?": E k.

"What's wrong with it?": E l.

Section F. Reading. Section G. Writing — Spelling

Sections F and G should be practiced in order. They may be
studied as separate entities, but their emphasis must be consecutive. In other words, start with *a* and work to Criterion.
Then go to *b, c,* and so on. A great deal of practice as often
as possible is as important in these sections as in any others.
The set sequences progress through various learning experiences
directed toward reading and writing — spelling. Do not neglect
any of the sets. Be patient. It will be difficult to arrange the
sets for 80 percent correct productions to occur. Many typewritten pages of visual practice stimuli (see Set F b, c, e) and
many flash cards (F f) are needed. Prepare them. Once completed, they may be used again and again.

The activities described in this section are not typical of the normal classroom. Severely involved students, however, may display response patterns that require special techniques of handling.

The beginning therapist is always concerned about what options are available when tantrums or other disruptions occur. New students are sometimes especially problematic. They display a great reluctance to leave their parents. Violent scenes are abhorrent to most of us, and the new student knows this. Furthermore, he is aware (through past demonstrations) that the more traumatized he appears to be, the more sympathy he will get from those around him. If you are inflexible, and insist from the first day that he go with you alone to the therapy room, you may lose totally. A combat of wills with a determined, spoiled, and powerful child is very tiring. There is a middle ground. If the pupil makes a tremendous "thing" of the situation and absolutely refuses to leave his parent, it is permissible to allow the parent to be present during the first sessions. After a couple of sessions, the mystery should have dissipated. The pupil may even express some interest in the proceedings. Whether or not he does, you must now concentrate in earnest upon the task of establishing yourself as one who is able to control his behavior.

Chapter 2 described reinforcement technique. If the first analysis of appropriate reinforcement methods and items was even partially accurate, your student should exhibit some desire to obtain the reinforcer. If so, you have come a considerable distance in getting control of him.

CONTROLLING TANTRUMS, HYPERACTIVITY, DISTRACTABILITY

Do not allow the parent in the therapy room after the second session. This should have been a "last resort" tactic in the first place. Gently but firmly steer your pupil away from the reception area. If you must carry him, do so.

The teaching environment should present limited possibilities for distraction. It should be quiet, painted a soft color, with an uncluttered appearance and little or no obvious outside traffic.

The following options are open to you:

1. Look away, withdraw, do nothing, wait out the tantrum.
2. Slap the table top loudly. Slap your knee. Call his name loudly.
3. Ask the questions or give the stimulus much more loudly or close to the child.
4. Hold his legs between your legs.
5. Wedge him in a corner of the room as he is sitting at a table. Face him.

6. Present yourself in close proximity to him.
7. Present your head at the same level as his.
8. Utilize the token economy system. Withdraw tokens or points for disruptive behavior. Do this with an obvious movement. Be sure he observes you doing this. Make the point withdrawal sufficiently penalizing so he will want to avoid it.
9. See that windows, etc., are masked, if necessary, to lessen outside interference from hallways, waiting rooms, and so forth.
10. Place the student forcefully but gently in a chair at a table quite near to you. If he is too active, push his chair closer to the table so he is physically restrained.
11. If he appears to be contemplating doing violence to himself, restrain him. BUT, do not pay him for his behavior by trying to talk him out of it. Do not attempt to "love" him out of it by making commiserating gestures.
12. Leave the room abruptly but remain nearby outside to be sure that the child does nothing to himself or damage to the room. For this reason, if tantrums are suspected, the room should be free of items which are destroyable.
13. As soon as the negative behavior subsides, renew the session as if nothing at all had happened.
14. When the tantrum begins, withhold reinforcement and have time out until he is ready to begin again.
15. Be calm, quiet, and friendly when he is *not* misbehaving. You will want the words which you do use to make a distinct impression.
16. Say "STOP!" Reinforce immediately if he does so.
17. Even if he is struggling, place him in a seated position and reinforce him immediately. Place his hands in his lap.
18. Gradually lessen any physical restraint and lengthen the "quiet" time interval prior to the administration of reinforcement. This should make him calm down.
19. Demonstrate the desired position. "Do this." If he does anything resembling the target position, reinforce immediately.
20. Do not let him get out of his therapy session. Giving in to his power struggle will only reinforce his undesirable behavior for the next time.

PRETRAINING

Deeply involved pupils may require some form of pretraining before actual language rehearsal begins.

Eye Contact

1. Gently grasp the face of the student with your head close to his. Or, with your head directly in front of his and at the same level, say "Look at me."
2. Point to an object or picture which you have placed nearby on the table. Say "Look at that." Change objects and

pictures as desired. Say also, "Look at me." Say his name, then "listen" before presenting *every* activity.

3. Discontinue saying his name when he looks at you on each occasion prior to the changing of the object or picture. He should regularly and consistently look from you to the other items when instructed or cued. If he does not, gently grasp both sides of his head and turn it in the desired direction. Remove the grip. If he does not turn away, reinforce immediately. Fade head placement gradually to requiring only a touch on the chin with one finger in order to retain the desired facial attitude.

4. Closeness is important. Maintain a position as near as possible to him.

5. Touch his arm or shoulder occasionally. A friendly squeeze feels good to anyone.

Behavioral Focusing

The purpose of behavioral focusing activities is to teach the student to persist at a motor repetitive task. This is intended, of course, for the person who is unable to maintain such a task. (Strong reinforcement administration is quite essential with this activity.)

1. Select any highly repetitive picking-up-and-putting-back or moving-from-one-place-to-another activity. Reinforce continuously.

2. Demonstrate the action desired, e.g., putting blocks in box, tongue depressors in can, toys away in storage cabinet.

3. Be sure that there is *much to do*. When the student completes the task have him repeat it or begin another like it.

4. As a higher level of activity, have the student repeat a series of large circle (or other shape) drawings on the blackboard until the entire board is full. An alternative is to do the same thing but on a piece of paper with a felt or other highly visible marker.

5. Have the student pursue the activity without interruption until the prescribed amount is obtained.

Remaining Quiet — Remaining Seated

1. Face the pupil in his chair. Reinforce him if he simply remains seated.

2. Reinforce also for gradually increasing seated time.

3. Have him get up from his position by gently taking him by his arm and saying "Stand up." Then say "Sit down," and gently return him to his seat. If restraint is needed, carry it out with the instruction "Sit still."

4. Repeat the eye contact activity number 2, exchanging pictures and objects.

5. Continue to shape sitting behaviors by delaying the administration of reinforcers for increasing lengths of time.

6. If during any activity he should leave his seat, he should immediately receive the instruction to sit down.

PLAY ACTIVITY

See Chapter 5, The Natural Communicative Environment. The student should be provided free time so that he may achieve a balance between control (in order that concrete progress may be made) and the feeling of release that comes with a break. Structure the play according to your intentions. You may wish to tape-record spontaneous productions during this time. To this end, provide toys and persons which will be most conducive to communicative interchange.

The Natural Communicative Environment: Study at School, at Home, and at Play

A child develops language best when he begins by hearing his mother speak in one-word expressions and short phrases. These brief units give him his first opportunity to scan and sample sound sequences. As other family members and friends introduce themselves into his world, he has increased opportunity to hear a variety of sounds that become words. These occur in varying loudness intensities, pitches, and inflectional patterns. They become more and more meaningful as they are shown to serve useful purposes. Those that get the best results are the ones that the child uses most, as he learns to employ the word choice which is successful in expressing his needs. One such need is to be a part of what those around him are saying. In order to achieve this, he will attempt to fit his utterances in with theirs. Syntax will develop as the "rules" for word choice turn into recurring small problems. Language advances as each solution (correct usage) occurs. This happens in the natural, real world of human relationships as a part of the communication that occurs between human beings in proximity to each other.

The importance of as natural a setting as possible for language learning activities cannot be overemphasized. The school— therapy environment in which this *Sourcebook* will be used will be more like "school" and less like the real world. Plans should be made to allow the student — child or adult — to hear and use language to the greatest possible extent at home, in play, or in other social situations.

AT SCHOOL AND PLAY

Practice during therapy will help. As the student learns more, he will use more. What he desperately needs is the opportunity to put these newly learned language combinations into his everyday communicative life.

Arrange a portion of each session so that it includes some time for nonstructured play. The last meeting of the week might be set aside as an entire play session. Of course, this play is not at all nonstructured. It only appears to be. Plan a group game, storytelling, building project, or other activity which is conducive to conversation. Refer to Section E and consult Set E a for possible topics.

AT HOME

If you can help to generate both informal and formal language activities in the home, you will have moved considerably closer to actually helping your student. A training workshop is an excellent vehicle for preparing parents and other volunteers to cooperate in the total effort. The principle of brief, concentrated periods of instruction interspersed with informal communicative activities applies at home as it did at school.

If at all possible, make frequent home visits. You will encounter a variety of discouraging experiences aimed at keeping you out of the home. But this one aspect of your work is so important that almost any hindrance should not keep you from making a sincere attempt.

Obtain copies of the *Sourcebook* and record forms. During the workshop, teach the participants how to use the forms, employ reinforcement, and select sets for practice. Choose sets in line with what is occurring in school. Show how to use sets as they pertain to the particular person. Discuss your evaluation and diagnosis results in order to clarify this.

Insist that the person who will be practicing the sets with the student at home count every response. During periodic meetings, ask to see the completed CRR forms. This will be your proof that your instructions have been carried out. Review progress at any time and be readily available for questions. Formal practice of sets at home should not last for more than a total of 15 minutes per day. Brief, 5-minute periods are preferable. This may appear to be an insufficient length of time in which to accomplish anything. But remember, the parent or family member has only so much willingness to participate. Make it easy for everyone. Those 15-minute daily totals quickly turn into a great deal of solid progress occurring in familiar surroundings where it is most needed. If the sets are confusing, write down a simplified version of them in your own words. Actually, any activity task may be outlined in this way. Break down each component as thoroughly as necessary.

Your workshop should certainly include information about language which will help in everyday situations. If you are not using separate copies of the *Sourcebook* for all participants, reproduce the following list of "Do's" and "Do Not's." (These rules apply equally well to adult students.) Discuss each statement. Follow this by examining the language interventional techniques (Muma, 1971) which come immediately after the list.

HELPING A CHILD TO TALK

Do

1. Let the child hear you describe the activity which you are performing in as few words as possible, e.g., "wash the dish, drink the milk, pick up the pencil."
2. Make use of *any* opportunity to use speech when the person is near you. Let him imitate your expressions such as "thank you," "good-bye," and "pardon me." Capitalize on voluntary utterances and work to expand them. A general rule is to retain the words in the order produced by the student and add those words which have been omitted. For example:
   Child says: Sat wall.
   Adult says: He sat on the wall.
3. Let the child hear you say the names of objects in his environment.

4. Have fun imitating sounds such as animal noises and fire engine sirens.

5. Accept as speech any sounds which the child makes, but do not use "baby talk" in his presence.

6. Try to understand what the child says to you so that he will not have to repeat it, but do attempt to encourage him to use the best words he knows.

7. Encourage the child to make noises and sounds as he plays.

8. Imitate the correct sounds the child makes and suggest others.

9. Read to the child if he appears to tolerate it well. Stress important words or actions.

10. Provide sound-making toys for use in group play.

11. Encourage *group* game activities which motivate verbal sound and word productions.

12. Give the impression that it is fun to say sounds and words, to look at pictures, and to hear stories. Make all speech enjoyable.

13. Listen for the thought the child is trying to express, although it may be confused through sound and syntax errors.

14. Encourage voluntary talking.

15. Provide opportunities for the child to "help" you in small tasks. Verbalize as these are performed.

16. Put into words the everyday actions which he performs. Use words which *center around his own activities.* For example: "We put on shoes," "We get a drink."

17. Point out noun objects in the environment, repeating their names several times.

18. Obtain blow toys. Play games which will exercise lips, jaw, and tongue.

19. Respond to the utterances of the child with any or all of the methods described by Muma (1971). These are language interventional techniques.

Do Not

1. Correct errors in the speech of the child by saying "no" and telling him he did it wrong.

2. Discuss the speech problem of the child in the presence of others.

3. Indicate facially or vocally that the utterances of the child are incorrect.

4. Withhold food, toys, etc., in an effort to make him talk, or place other penalties on incorrect speech.

5. Place the child in a communicative situation which is beyond his capabilities and may punish his speaking attempts.

6. Show frustration or anger at his incorrect speech attempts.

7. Continually urge the child to talk or make him feel that because he does not speak he is less acceptable to you.

LANGUAGE INTERVENTIONAL TECHNIQUES

Correction:	Child says:	He ate supper.
	You say:	*She* ate supper. She is a girl.
Expansion:	Child says:	Baby cry.
	You say:	The baby is crying.
Expatiation:	Child says:	Baby cry.
	You say:	The baby is crying. Let's feed the baby.
Completion:	Child says:	Crying.
	You say:	The baby is_____.
		(child completes)
		Hungry.
		The baby is_____.
		(child completes)
		Blue.
		The baby's blanket is_____.
		(child completes)
Replacement:	Child says:	My ball is red.
(All dimensions	You say:	The ball is red.
of the sentence		The tree is pretty.
are specified		The girl is pretty.
but one.)		The girl is happy.
		The boy is happy.
Combination:	Child says:	The ball is red.
(exploring		The ball is round.
syntactic		The ball can roll.
alternatives)	You say:	The red round ball is rolling.
Revision:	Child says:	My sister is little.
		She lives with us.
		She is five years old.
		She has a blue dress.
		Our house is big.
	You say:	My little five-year-old sister has a blue dress.
		She lives with me in a big house.

These techniques help you to use the productions of the student and expand them into utterances which have more complexity. Do not interject whatever *you* say in a "teaching" or "correcting" tone of voice. Be as conversational-sounding as possible. The drawback of frequent interventions on your part is that they invariably contain many more words than the child is saying. You do not need the practice. He does. If the method succeeds, he will fall into the habit of repeating your version just after you present it.

Except for Verbal Expression Output (p. 8 of the Criterion Placement Test — see Appendix II), language evaluation tests will not be discussed in detail here. Space does not permit an examination of the many which are in print. Under Language and Language-Related Tests in the Bibliography there is an annotated listing of tests that includes the publisher's address and a brief statement about the function of each test.

Entire volumes have been written about assessment. Almost any text which has anything to do with language disorders includes a section on tests. The Bibliography lists some of these along with articles pertaining to assessment particularly.

Should you obtain all these tests? If not, how do you select those you need? You have only so much time to conduct an evaluation and differential diagnosis. Numerous variables are intertwined with your student and his problems. Which should you consider relevant? Is his home situation a contributing cause? Is he mentally retarded? Is he emotionally disturbed? Does he have one or more learning disabilities? Exactly what about his language output is deficient? Which of these factors is remediable and which is not? Regardless of the multiplicity of factors which insinuate themselves into the problem, one major point remains. You as therapist are primarily interested in the most efficient means of helping your student achieve better expression. Therefore, whatever tests you do select should be aimed at pinpointing specific problems of syntax in one or another psycholinguistic disability area.

One outcome of testing should eventually be a measurement of student improvement. If a pretest is administered prior to therapy and the same test readministered at a later date, scores may be compared and any gain noted. An index of progress (reflected as test results) may then be made a matter of record.

The Diagnostic-Therapeutic Principle
Assessment need not be totally test oriented. The CPT is a device for constant monitoring of achievement during therapy. Because it coincides exactly with the *Sourcebook* sets, it furnishes a continuous record. Furthermore, it is possible to make a diagnostic check any time by selecting any set and including it in a session. The criterion level of the set will help determine the level at which the student is performing. You will then have that information to add to your fund of knowledge about him and the nature of his deficit. This evaluative function is accomplished during the conduct of therapy.

Language Learning Disabilities
You should have some awareness of the psycholinguistic language learning processes described by Kirk and McCarthy

(1968) and of which of these processes your student is having difficulty with. With the administration and scoring of the *Illinois Test of Psycholinguistic Abilities* (ITPA), you will have a means of better understanding deficient language formulation and production. The ITPA lists the following areas of language processes.

REPRESENTATIONAL: VOLUNTARY USAGE OF MEANINGFUL SYMBOLS
Receptive processes (decoding): Using language symbols through senses of perception.
  Visual — Deriving meaning from visually presented material.
  Auditory — Deriving meaning from verbally presented material.
Organizing process (associating): Using the mental processes whereby symbols are related and manipulated meaningfully.
  Visual — Relating concepts presented visually.
  Auditory — Relating concepts presented orally.
Expressive processes (encoding): Using verbal and/or manual symbols to present an idea.
  Verbal (vocal encoding) — Speaking. Expressing one's own "intentions."
  Manual (motor encoding) — Gesturing and writing. Expressing one's own "intentions" with body movements.

AUTOMATIC: LESS VOLUNTARY, YET ORGANIZED, USE OF LANGUAGE
Closure: The ability to fill in the missing parts of a picture or verbal statement. The ability to make a whole out of a number of single units.
  Grammatical — Auditory sound blending. Making use of habits for handling syntactic constructions as sound combinations.
  Visual — Identifying symbols presented visually. Reading. Recognizing objects.

Sequential Memory: An essential aspect of the syntactic process involving the ability to combine elements in sequence to form a whole.
  Auditory-vocal — Combining heard symbols one after the other in sequence.
  Visual-motor — Combining observed sequences of communicative gestures. Combining sequences of printed letter symbols into words. Combining words into sentences. Combining sentences which reflect a thought, story line, problem solutions, etc.

Once areas of strength and weakness have been identified, work in the area of strength initially, then ease into more deficient areas. Bear in mind that treatment of disabilities is inseparable from language instruction — "word training." One is the vehicle for the other. For this reason, certain set titles contain both a term which indicates words and word combinations and a psycholinguistic term borrowed from Kirk and McCarthy (1968).

Developmental ages for disability patterns are available in Kirk and Kirk (1971). This paperback book gives a brief but excellent background which should help in the interpretation of the *ITPA* scores and in the selection of sets for therapy in accordance with these scores.

THE LANGUAGE SAMPLE — INSTRUCTIONS FOR USING THE SOURCEBOOK LANGUAGE SCRIPT

(The Sourcebook Language Script is in Appendix II.) A 50-utterance sample will yield significant information about the language status of your pupil. It should always be included in the evaluative process. Since information is more meaningful if it can be placed in some perspective, it is recommended that the data from the language sample which you have obtained be compared to that of so-called normals. The tables at the end of this chapter give data on language samples obtained from normal children and arranged according to age. Compare the scores of the 50-utterance language sample (as recorded on page 8 of the CPT) with those in the tables. Match the age of the student with the corresponding age levels on the tables.

Obtaining the Sample

Obtain a sample of 50 utterances. These need not occur consecutively. You may wish to set aside a few minutes three days in a row just as therapy begins. If behavior is a problem, take a few sessions to resolve this first. (Study Chapter 4, Behavioral Control.) Without some cooperation from the student, a bona fide sample is virtually impossible to get. It is permissible (only for purposes of the sample) to allow a parent, or someone else whom the student knows, to be present, if this will help.

Previous to meeting the student, collect any pictures, toys, objects, etc., which will help produce spontaneous verbalizations. Set E a provides numerous conversational ideas. Plan to base your questions on Set E a or on the activities that are carried on during the meeting.

Tape-record the entire session and/or have an aide write down each utterance. Post the responses on the language script the *same day* they are obtained. Otherwise you will find it quite difficult to remember accurately what was said. Place each utterance on a separate line on the script (in the wide column to the left). Use as many pages as necessary. Number each response consecutively, but wait until ten have occurred before you begin. McCarthy (1954) cautions against counting the first ten productions. They are usually tentative and not fairly representative.

If part of a remark is lost, cross that one out and do not count it. Originate a shorthand of your own which will be more rapid than cursive writing. If part of a response is unintelligible, write what you heard phonetically. Continue until you have written 50 remarks as accurately as possible.

Utterances connected by "um," "er," "uh," and "and" should be considered as separate if they are part of an enumerative series, e.g., "the dog, uh, the cat, uh . . . and the mouse." A production is also separate if it occurs after a logical pause or full stop and is obviously a new sentence. If two simple sentences are produced one immediately after the other with no breath pause, they should be counted as one, e.g., "My dad, he's strong, he lifted a big rock." Or, "For Christmas I got a bike . . . no, my sister got one."

Analyzing the Sample

Analyze each utterance separately. First note into which category (A—E, as described below) the sentence type falls. Place the capital letter which represents this in the first vertical column, "Sentence Type."

SENTENCE TYPES

A. *Incomplete*
   Obviously grammatically incorrect productions are ranked here. These may be without subject, verb, pronoun, preposition, or conjunction. If one is without an article, or you were not sure you heard one, count it complete. Incomprehensible or fragmentary responses count as incomplete: "It . . . see . . . no, there." So do those which change form: "My mom and dad . . . we went to show," and those left unfinished: "Let's go to . . ." or "Mary wants . . ." or "This thing . . . ."

B. *Functionally Complete — Structurally Incomplete*
   Many commonly used sentences are not complete structurally. Normal conversation often contains brief word groups or simple words which imply a complete sentence. Johnson, Darley, and Spriestersbach (1963) point out that "if a response is adequate in the situation and the child is using the most complete form he has had the opportunity to *learn,* his response should be counted as functionally complete though structurally incomplete. This includes practically all single-word sentences; names; expletives (interjections); responses to questions where omitted words are implied; and other remarks, incomplete in themselves, which are clearly continuations of preceding remarks."

C. *Simple Sentence Without Phrase*
   This form does contain a subject and verb: "He's tired." "The door is shut."

D. *Simple Sentence with Phrase*
   This includes compound subjects, objects, predicates, or sentences which contain one phrase: "That is mine and David's." "Her house is big and old."

E. *Compound and Complex*
   Any elaborated, multiple clause, phrase, and/or subject sentence may be counted here.

Once the Sentence Type column is completed for the entire sample, add up the number of A's, B's, C's, D's, and E's on each page. Place this total on the bottom of each page of the script. The *last* page of the script should contain a *grand total* of all preceding pages. To keep the pages in order, fill in the upper lefthand portion of each with the page number and total number of pages in the sample. Place this grand total for *each* sentence type category on page 8 of the CPT. If you have a 50-utterance sample, your grand total for all combined will be 50. To fill in the "%" column, simply double the numbers in the "#" columns. You now have the percentage of each type of sentence that occurred in the sample.

STRUCTURAL COMPLEXITY SCORE

The Structural Complexity Score (SCS) consists of one number which reflects a level of linguistic maturity. Although general in nature, it does show gain when compared on a test—retest basis. Assign the following numbers to the capital letters in the Sentence Type column of the language script:

Sentence Type	Structural Complexity Value
A	0
B	1
C	2
D	3
E	4

Place one number next to each capital letter in the Sentence Type column. Add these and post the total on the bottom of *each* page. The *last* page of the script should contain a *grand total* from all pages. This is the structural complexity score. Post the SCS on page 8 of the CPT.

PARTS OF SPEECH, ETC.

Next, examine separate utterances for the presence of the various parts of speech, etc. (The "etc." refers to infinitive ("to") forms, negatives, and interrogatives to the script.) Add the number of occurrences of each part of speech and place it in the appropriate box. Count infinitives as verbs, and place the total for both infinitives and verbs in the verbs box. As each page is completed, add the part of speech columns vertically and post the totals at the bottom of the page. The *last* page of the script should contain the *grand total* of all parts of speech on that and all previous pages. Post these grand totals on page 8 of the CPT in the "#" columns under "Frequency of Occurrence as Parts of Speech, Etc." Add the "#" column. Divide the total into the number of occurrences of each separate part of speech to obtain their percentages of occurrence. For instance, out of a total 250 parts of speech counted, 44 were nouns. Forty-four divided by 250 is 17.6. Therefore 17.6 percent of the utterances of the student were nouns.

RESPONSE LENGTHS

Count the number of words in each utterance and place this count in the "Response Length" box on the script. You are now in a position to figure the Mean Length of Response (MLR), Number of One-Word Responses (N1W), and Mean of the Five Longest Responses (M5L).

MLR: Total *all* words in the 50 utterances. Divide by 50. Post the result on page 8 of the CPT.

N1W: Count the number of one-word responses. Post the result on page 8 of the CPT.

M5L: Identify the five longest productions in the entire sample. Add all the words together and divide by 5. Post the result on page 8 of the CPT.

Some consistent set of standards should be applied to the system of word counting. The following suggestions should help: Count any two-word proper noun, person's name, as one word, e.g., "Mary Jane." Count any multiple-word term as one word if it pertains to one object, e.g., "roller coaster." Count contractions as two words if they occur as shortened versions of the subject and verb: "it's," "you're." Words contracted to the negative are counted as one word: "don't," "can't." Repetitions of an enumerated series of statements are counted separately: "There's Jody," "there's Billy," "there's Linda." Repetitions of the *same* word or phrase, if apparently unintentional, are counted only once: "My, my, my, my foot hurts."

Evaluating the Sample — Comparing Readministrations

Refer again to the script. Study all sentence types, particularly "A," for incorrectly or inappropriately used words and/or grammatical constructions. Underline all grammatically incorrect words and phrases. Use a specially colored marker to call special attention to these. What parts of speech do these mistakes represent? Examine their functional place in the utterance. Are they out of place but basically correct? Is vocabulary apparently satisfactory but word order amiss? All this analysis will assist you in choosing set sequences and preparing reports.

Make a list of vocabulary words that you are sure the child uses correctly. These could provide a pivotal place for therapeutic expansion into set choices.

Page 8 of the CPT contains space for recording scores from readministrations of the language sample. Compare these with initial language sample data to ascertain if there has been any gain. If working in a school system, you will probably redo the sample near the close of the semester or school year when reports are due. Specifying areas of improvement for all data shown under Verbal Expression Output will be quite illuminating. This page will become a substantial part of your report. Other gains reflected by the readministration of other tests should also be included in the report.

Table 6-1. Mean Percentage of 50 Oral Responses Falling Within Each Category of Sentence Types, Arranged According to Age

Age (yrs.)	Incomplete A	Functionally Complete Structurally Incomplete B	Simple Sentence without Phrase C	Simple Sentence with Phrase D	Compound and Complex E
1.5	11.9	78.4	9.6	0.0	0.0
2.0	25.1	53.8	17.3	1.4	0.9
2.5	18.1	35.3	38.7	5.3	1.5
3.0	16.2–16.8	27.2–28.2	32.0–45.1	8.7–13.7	1.5–2.9
3.5	13.1–13.9	23.8–30.6	35.3–39.5	11.4–16.4	3.3–6.5
4.0	6.8–11.2	19.7–32.0	37.2–39.4	10.9–18.5	6.1–6.9
4.5	8.8–12.1	19.5–31.2	36.5–37.6	10.4–16.2	6.8–7.0
5.0	12.6	17.2	35.8	10.8	8.7
5.5	15.4	38.0–39.4	29.4–31.4	7.8	4.6
6.0	8.6	9.8	38.2	20.7	10.8
6.5	15.2–16.4	9.0	30.8–32.2	9.8–10.8	5.4–7.4
7.0	10.5	9.0	34.1	22.8	11.1
8.0	9.5	9.4	31.5	21.3	15.0

Source: Data from Templin and McCarthy (1954).

Table 6-2. Mean Length of Response, Median Number of One-Word Responses, Mean of the Five Longest Responses, and Mean Structural Complexity Scores, Arranged According to Age, from 50-Utterance Language Samples

Age (yrs.)	MLR	Median N1W Boys	Median N1W Girls	M5L Boys	M5L SD	M5L Girls	M5L SD	Mean SCS Boys	Mean SCS SD	Mean SCS Girls	Mean SCS SD
1.5	1.2	—	—	—	—	—	—	—	—	—	—
2.0	1.8	—	—	—	—	—	—	—	—	—	—
2.5	3.1	—	—	—	—	—	—	—	—	—	—
3.0	4.1	3.5	3.0	7.95	2.63	7.82	1.83	36.4	19.7	32.2	16.5
3.5	4.7	3.5	4.3	8.66	2.08	9.46	3.05	38.1	17.3	43.2	18.2
4.0	5.4	3.0	2.5	10.35	3.05	10.66	3.43	48.0	18.8	54.9	20.7
4.5	5.5	2.5	1.1	10.73	3.03	10.78	2.23	50.9	24.0	52.9	16.6
5.0	5.7	2.6	1.8	10.82	2.98	12.63	3.61	50.6	18.8	63.2	23.5
6.0	6.6	2.7	0.4	12.42	2.78	12.11	1.90	71.5	22.1	68.7	17.4
7.0	7.3	0.6	0.3	13.76	1.81	13.37	2.45	69.7	20.0	73.9	16.6
8.0	7.6	0.6	0.3	13.55	2.87	14.75	2.69	74.4	18.7	79.2	28.7

Source: Templin, M. C. Certain Language Skills in Children: Their Development and Interrelationships. (*Child Welfare Monographs*, No. 26.) Minneapolis, Minn.: University of Minnesota Press, 1957.

Table 6-3. Mean Percentage of Each Part of Speech, etc., from Total of 50 Oral Responses, Arranged According to Age

Age (yrs.)	Noun	Verb	Adj.	Adv.	Pron.	Conj.	Prep.	Art.	Int.	Misc.
3.0	17.7	22.6	6.3	10.0	19.4	1.5	6.5	6.8	2.1	7.1
3.5	17.1	23.0	6.9	9.9	19.2	2.3	6.9	6.5	1.8	6.5
4.0	16.3	23.1	6.7	10.1	20.3	2.8	6.9	6.8	1.3	5.7
4.5	16.5	23.6	7.7	10.0	18.9	2.5	6.8	7.3	1.2	5.6
5.0	16.1	23.5	7.5	10.6	20.0	2.6	6.7	6.7	.8	5.4
6.0	17.1	25.0	7.6	10.0	19.3	2.6	7.6	7.0	1.0	3.1
7.0	17.0	24.0	7.3	10.4	18.0	3.3	8.0	7.9	1.4	2.8
8.0	17.0	24.3	7.4	9.1	17.8	3.7	7.9	8.1	1.2	2.9

Source: Templin, M. C. Certain Language Skills in Children: Their Development and Interrelationships. (*Child Welfare Monographs*, No. 26.) Minneapolis, Minn.: University of Minnesota Press, 1957.

Becoming Aware of Sound – Attending to Sound

Materials. Noisemakers: whistles, triangle, horn, xylophone, percussion instruments, human voice, door slamming, etc.

Criterion. Level IV
Point to 20 consecutively produced sounds at various intensity levels out of eyesight range.

Purpose. To teach the person to *listen to* and *for* sounds out of eyesight range, and to indicate from which direction they come.

Demonstration Sequence

1. Seat the person in the center of the room. (An assistant will be needed to administer reinforcers and help at Level I.)

2. Produce the sound loudly, directly in front of the person. If the person does not point, the assistant may physically help him.

3. Continue presenting a variety of relatively loud sounds. Include your voice: make any vowel sound or onomato-poetic sounds. Vary *loudness* and sound source. Gradually produce sounds of less and less intensity.

Suggested Sources
Percussion instruments
Human voice(s) (singly or in conversation)
Marbles dropped in a can
Eating utensils on plates
Coins jingling
Squeaky toys
Doors opening and closing
Chair or table pulled along floor

4. Gradually move out of visual range as you produce sounds. Continue until all sounds occur from behind.

5. Continue until Criterion is passed.

1. LISTEN TO THE SOUND.

2. IT MAKES *THIS* SOUND. POINT TO THE SOUND.

3. IT MAKES *THIS* SOUND. POINT TO THE SOUND. I MAKE *THIS* SOUND. POINT TO THE SOUND.

4. FOLLOW THE SOUND WITH YOUR EARS. POINT TO IT WHEN YOU HEAR IT.

Producing Rhythms

Materials. Drum, sticks, other rhythm makers, fingers tapping, voice, etc.

Criterion. Level III
Ten different rhythmic productions with various time delays of up to 5 seconds between cue and response.

Purpose. To exercise auditory memory through the vehicle of varying rhythms with time delays between cue and response.

Demonstration Sequence

1. Student and clinician should have the same rhythm instrument(s).

   Produce the rhythm quite slowly and regularly.

2. If using the voice, repeat one sound (vowel or consonant) over and over in concert with the beat being produced.

   This is an excellent group activity.

3. Vary the rhythms. Once the regular beat is established, go to syncopations.

4. Produce the rhythm while the person listens. Allow up to a 5-second delay between your model and the response.

5. Once rhythms can be imitated at Level III, move out of visual range so that the student's only cue will be auditory.

1. DO THIS WITH ME.

   Examples
   hand clapping
   stick tapping
   drum beating
   finger pointing
   foot tapping
   head nodding
   body movement
   tambourine

3. *Examples of rhythms*

   — — — — — — — —

   — — — — — —

   — — —   — —

   —   —

   — —   — — —   —

4. WAIT UNTIL I GIVE YOU THE SIGNAL. THEN YOU DO IT. I'LL DO IT FIRST.

5. I'LL GO BEHIND YOU. MAKE THE SAME SOUNDS I DO.

Visual – Motor Organization: Cutting and Coloring Ac

Materials. Scissors, geometric form outlines, crayons, 8½" X 11" paper, felt pen, cut-out coloring book.

Criterion. Level IV
Ten consecutively correct geometric shapes, cut out and colored.

Purpose. To encourage the use of the visual—motor organizing process through practice in cutting out and coloring geometric forms and word pictures.

Demonstration Sequence

1. Assemble figure drawings. Draw a large geometric figure (e.g., square, rectangle, parallelogram, circle) on each piece of 8½" X 11" paper. The lines should be quite simple and easy to follow.

   Have the person color the shape first, then have him cut it out.

   Once geometric forms are colored and cut out, the person may move to a higher level of cut-out pictures (e.g., pictures from a coloring book and/or those which you prepare by tracing over word pictures).

   Practice at the highest level of which the student is capable.

COLOR THIS, THEN CUT IT OUT.
IT IS A_____.
BE SURE TO COLOR THE WHOLE THING.

Materials. Tongue depressor, flashlight, mirror.

Criterion. Levels specified in steps. Twenty consecutively correct productions per step.

Purpose. To evoke the production of voiced and voiceless phonemes on a non-meaningful basis. TEACH: All vowels and [m p w t d n f v k g]. Also teach these more difficult to produce sounds, if possible; if too difficult, exclude them: [r s l θ ð ʃ ʒ t ʃ dʒ].

Demonstration Sequence

1. Engage in any activity which results in the student's producing some sounds. Select those sounds and activities which are appropriate to the student's abilities.

   Practice at Level II.

Suggested Exercises for Lips

2. Model (Levels I and/or II).

   If the student is not able to follow modeling instructions, grasp his lips and manipulate them into the desired position. Demonstrate by exaggerating wide openings and closings.

   Levels I and/or II.

3. Produce a half smile.

   Levels I and/or II.

4. Shift rapidly from the lips rounded position to lips back.

   Levels I and II.

5. Round the lips as if to produce [o].

   Levels I and/or II.

6. Repeat the articulatory positioning for [p] continually.

   Levels I and/or II

7. Repeat the articulatory positioning for [m]. Include voicing. Place the fingers of the student on your throat. Model [m] as a form of humming.

   Level II.

8. Model by blowing with lips rounded, turning on the voice and broadening the lips to form [a] "ah."

   Level II.

Suggested Exercises for the Tongue

9. Model an exaggerated variety of tongue positionings against the inside cheeks, teeth, alveolar ridge, etc. If needed, a tongue depressor may be used to guide the tongue.

   Level II.

10. Model and/or direct the tongue to various positions and teach the concept of "hold it" for as long a duration as you indicate. Practice the standard articulatory positionings. Combine the maintained tongue position with voice-on voice-off phonation and expelled air.

    Level II.

11. Shift your tongue to any position inside or outside the mouth.

    Level II.

12. Open your mouth. Protrude the tongue without touching the lips, and hold that position.

    Level II.

---

2. CLOSE YOUR LIPS. CLOSE THEM TIGHTLY LIKE THIS.
   CLOSE YOUR MOUTH.
   OPEN YOUR LIPS WIDE.
   CLOSE YOUR LIPS.

3. SPREAD YOUR LIPS.

4. DO THIS.
   DO THIS.

5. DO THIS. PUCKER YOUR LIPS.

6. SAY "PUH, PUH" (or) "P, P, P, P."

7. SAY "M, M, M, M, M, M, M, M."

8. BLOW LIKE THIS. THEN TURN ON YOUR VOICE.

9. DO THIS. ROLL YOUR TONGUE AROUND WITH YOUR VOICE ON.
   KEEP YOUR MOUTH OPEN A LITTLE.

10. PUT YOUR TONGUE HERE.
    HOLD IT.
    PUT YOUR TONGUE THERE.
    HOLD IT.

11. DO THIS.

12. DO THIS.
    HOLD IT.

13. Model the following tongue tip control and movement exercises.

Point sideways in both directions back and forth with tongue protruding.

Point up toward the nose.

Point down toward the chin.

Flick the tongue repeatedly against the upper lip and teeth.

Push the tongue into each cheek and move it around.

Rotate the tongue around the entire circumference of the lips.

Raise the tip of the tongue and touch the teeth, hard palate, alveolar ridge, etc.

Rapidly move the tongue to the right and left outside the mouth, gradually withdrawing it until the student is producing the movement on the inside of his mouth. From the point of gross movement, diminish its intensity until you are able to look inside the mouth and see a slight back and forth movement.

Level II.

14. Hold up a tongue depressor. Have the student push against it.

Push tongue against inside surfaces of the teeth, inside of cheeks, etc.

Level II.

14. PUSH YOUR TONGUE LIKE THIS.

PUSH YOUR TONGUE LIKE THIS.

Following Directions Presented Verbally and/or Gesturally Ae

Materials. Objects, movement toys.

Criterion. Level III
Produce 20 consecutively correct
actions on command.

Purpose. To establish verbal and visual
control and attention focusing through
teaching imitative gestures presented as
verbal and gestural instructions (or
commands).

Demonstration Sequence

1. Once the basic imitative performance is established, proceed to utilize fewer and fewer repetitions until you demonstrate only once and the person repeats immediately. Begin by pointing the finger and/or performing any body movement.

2. You may also introduce objects. Select any object which can be manipulated; e.g., a *baby*, roll a *ball*, roll a toy *car* along the floor, put a *hat* on the head, etc.

   Proceed as in step 1.

1. LOOK AT ME. DO WHAT I DO. DO THIS.

   STAND UP
   SIT DOWN
   COME HERE
   LOOK UP
   GO TO THE WINDOW
   SIT DOWN
   CLAP YOUR HANDS
   CLOSE THE DOOR
   THIS BIG (spread your arms wide)
   THIS SMALL (hold your cupped hands about 4″ apart)
   OPEN THE DOOR
   SO HIGH (reach high overhead)
   SO LOW (reach toward the floor)
   ROW A BOAT (sit on the floor and perform rowing motions)
   SWEEP THE FLOOR
   BEAT THE DRUM
   COMB YOUR HAIR
   RAKE THE LEAVES
   ROCK THE BABY
   PUT THE APPLES IN THE PACKAGE
   ANSWER THE TELEPHONE
   KICK THE BALL
   THROW THE BALL
   CATCH THE BALL
   HOP ON ONE FOOT
   LIFT ONE ARM ABOVE YOUR HEAD

   WIGGLE YOUR HEAD
   PAT YOUR (HEAD, STOMACH, ETC.)
   TOUCH YOUR (ANY PART OF THE BODY)
   JUMP
   PUT YOUR ARM OUT (extend one arm directly in front of yourself)
   PUT TWO ARMS OUT
   SHAKE YOUR HEAD UP AND DOWN
   SHAKE YOUR HEAD BACK AND FORTH
   STIR THE SOUP (revolve arms in a clockwise direction)
   WASH YOUR FACE
   TOUCH THE_____(walk around the room touching anything)
   GO
   STOP
   STAY
   GO OUTSIDE THE DOOR
   STAND BESIDE THE_____
   WALK AROUND THE_____
   RUN AROUND THE_____
   GO BEHIND THE_____
   STAND IN FRONT OF_____
   JUMP
   SWING ARMS
   STAMP FEET
   TAKE A STEP FORWARD
   TAKE A STEP BACKWARD
   TAKE A STEP SIDEWAYS

3. The movements and postures of this step are of a higher performance level, because they either require finer movements or more concentration (in holding an attitude for a selected time duration).

3. LOOK AT ME. DO THIS.

   DIAL A TELEPHONE
   FINGER A TRUMPET
   PLAY A PIANO
   PLAY A VIOLIN
   PLAY A GUITAR

4. Place one foot forward.

   Touch the floor with the opposite knee.

   Pause and maintain that position for a number of seconds.

4. FOLLOW WHAT I AM DOING.

   HOLD IT.

5. Stand up.

   Place the other foot forward, touch the floor with the other knee.

   Pause and maintain that position for a number of seconds.

5. DO THIS.
   STAND UP.

6. Begin with one gesture and move slowly into another one.

   Level I will probably be needed for a number of trials before the student can perform from sequences of movements.

   Repeat with various two-movement sequences. Gradually increase the flow of imitative movements until the student can follow along at Level II, keeping up with whatever is performed.

   Attempt various sequences at Level III whenever that appears possible.

7. Assume any pose and hold it for a number of seconds. In a group session, a competition may be conducted to see how long members can retain any given position.

6. DO THIS.

7. BE A STATUE LIKE ME.

Materials. Word lists, phrases, and sentence lists.

Criterion. Level III
Twenty consecutively correct productions of sound target with vowel combinations in simulated speech melody patterns.

Purpose. To evoke the production of the standard melody patterns of speech through mass practice using a target consonant-plus-vowel as a vehicle.

Demonstration Sequence

1. Proceed with only one target throughout the remainder of this set, *or* intermix consonant with vowel combinations in keeping with the ability of the student to produce various sounds. If the target is only newly learned, you may wish to focus on that exclusively for an entire session.

1. SAY "EE" WITH ME.
   SAY (target sound, e.g. [**k**]) WITH ME.
   SAY "KEE" WITH ME.

2. Proceed with easy two syllable words or phrases.

   Say the word first, then produce the sound combination.

   Examples
   "Hello"
   "Goodby"
   "doorway"
   "I'm cold."
   "That's nice."

   Be sure to include any stress and inflection that seem to be warranted.

2. *Examples:* Two syllables.
   KEE – KEE
   KEE – KEE
   KEE – KEE
   KEE – KEE
   KEE – KEE

3. Go now to three-syllable utterances.

   Say the word first, then produce the sound combinations.
   "Good morning."
   "How are you?"
   "That's my toy."
   "Let's play ball."
   "Please come here."
   "Shall we walk?"
   "I am hungry."

3. *Examples:* Three syllables.
   KEE KEE KEE
   KEE KEE KEE
   KEE KEE KEE
   KEE KEE KEE
   KEE KEE KEE

4. Go now to four syllable utterances. Say the words first, then produce the sound combinations.
   "Hi, how are you?"
   "Please get my coat."
   "Shall we walk home?"
   "I am hungry."

4. *Examples:* Four syllables.
   KEE KEE KEE KEE
   KEE KEE KEE KEE
   KEE KEE KEE KEE
   KEE KEE KEE KEE

5. The number of syllables in productions is not mandatory. Utilize as many syllables as the student can manage as variably as possible after establishing steps 2, 3, and 4.

6. *Variable targets*
   "Pick up the phone."
   "Come with me."
   "Can you sing?"
   "I'm sleepy."
   "Let's go to the show."

6. *Examples*
   TAH TAH TAH TAH
   BOH BOH BOH
   GOH GOH GOH
   FEE FEE FEE
   MAY MAY MAY MAY MAY

7. An alternative means of presenting this set is to omit the vowel sound and produce only the target.
   "Hello"
   "Hello"
   "Hello"

7. *Examples*
   M – M
   V – V
   SH – SH

8. Another alternative is to include varying sounds to simulate speech melody patterns.
   "I'm going home."
   "Give me that."
   "Hi"

8. *Examples*
   KEE-GA-GA-SO
   BOO-TEE-PAH
   SEE

Materials. Objects, pictures, sound-producing toys.

Criterion. Level III
Twenty approximate productions of 20 different onomatopoetic sounds.

Purpose. To evoke the production of sounds which resemble those which may occur in the natural environment or which utilize the sound-producing apparatus in some general way.

Demonstration Sequence

1. Model the sound loudly. If an object or picture which represents the sound is available, use it.

2. Point to the object or picture, e.g., cat.

If any motion is associated with the item, make the movement along with the production of the sound. You are not interested in *exact* sound production. Many trials of the same sound and motion may be necessary. Use many varying pitch changes.

2. MEOW-W-W-W
   SAY IT WITH ME: MEOW-W-W-W

Examples

A-OO-GA	(An old fashioned car horn. It's fun to say.)
RINNNG	(Bell)
SQUEEK	(Mouse)
AH CHOO	(Sneeze)
HONK HONK	(Car)
BEEP BEEP	(Car)
HEE HAW	(Donkey)
WAA WAA	(Baby crying)
TICK TOCK	(Clock)
R-R-R-R-R	(Rooster)
ERRRRRRR	(Rusty hinge. Do this with a raspy voice.)
BOOM BOOM	(Drum)
MOOOO	(Cow)
QUACK — QUACK	(Duck)
CHOO CHOO	(Train whistle)
CHUGA CHUGA	(Train moving along)
WHOOOOO	(High-pitched whistle)
WOO WOO	(What one says when one sees a pretty girl)
BAAAAA	(Lamb)
SSSSS	(Steam)
ROAR	(Like a lion)
BUZZZZZ	(Like a bee)
HUMMMM	(Airplane. Pitch changes are good here as the plane performs maneuvers.)
DING DONG	(Doorbell)
PEEP PEEP	(Baby chicks)
PLUNK	(Something heavy, dropping)
SHHHHH	(Go to sleep)
OW!	(Being hurt)
WHOOOO	(Wind blowing)
ER-ER-ER-ER	(Sawing. Use a raspy voice.)
OOOOOO	(Ghost. Use pitch changes.)
HE-HE-HE	(Witch's laughter)
OWOOOOO	(Coyote's howl)
GRRRRR	(Dog growling)

Matching Forms, Sizes, and Pictures Ah

Materials. Construction paper, identical and similar object pictures, painted blocks, and geometric forms.

Criterion. Level IV
Twenty consecutively correct matchings of forms, sizes, and pictures.

Purpose. To generate the visual perceptual—associational function by matching various colors, forms, and sizes.

Demonstration Sequence

1. Demonstrate each activity by both explaining it and performing any activity associated with it.

2. Assemble a group of blocks of various solid colors and of the same shape. Place one block in front of the person. Place another block just like it on top of the first block. At this point you are not attempting to teach the name of the color; only that the blocks go together because they are the same color and shape. Continue to add blocks of various colors until color combinations can be matched.

3. Place a single geometric form in front of the person. Place the same form plus one other form on a neutral field. Instruct the person to match his form with one of the two. Continue with matching one form from a choice of two until success is reached at Level IV. Increase the choice of forms to three, then to four once three has been mastered.

4. Assemble three different sizes of squares on a neutral ground. Give the person copies of the identical squares of different sizes. Instruct the participant that he is to match the sizes. Continue with other shapes which are the same except for size. It is not necessary to tell which is "bigger" or "smaller."

5. Assemble pictures which are identical and also pictures which are not identical *but* are of the same topic, e.g., various pictures of horses.

   Begin with only two pictures. As soon as possible, go to as many pictures as the person can handle. Practice the identical pictures first. Continue with the similar pictures.

2. *Examples*

   Match geometric wood blocks.
   Level I: MATCH THIS BLOCK WITH ONE JUST LIKE IT.
   Level II: LET'S DO IT TOGETHER.
   Level III: I'LL DO IT, THEN YOU DO IT.
   Level IV: PUT THE BLOCKS WHICH MATCH TOGETHER.

3. *Match paper cut-out forms.*
   Level I: MATCH THIS SHAPE WITH THIS ONE.
   Level II: LET'S DO IT TOGETHER.
   Level III: I'LL DO IT, THEN YOU DO IT.
   Level IV: PUT THE SHAPES WHICH MATCH TOGETHER.

4. *Match forms for size.*
   HERE ARE THINGS OF DIFFERENT SIZES.
   Level I: MATCH THIS SIZE WITH THIS ONE.
   Level II: LET'S DO IT TOGETHER.
   Level III: I'LL DO IT, THEN YOU DO IT.
   Level IV: PUT THE SHAPES WHICH MATCH TOGETHER.

5. *Match pictures.*
   Level I: MATCH THE PICTURES.
   Level II: LET'S DO IT TOGETHER.
   Level III: I'LL DO IT, THEN YOU DO IT.
   Level IV: PUT TOGETHER PICTURES THAT MATCH.

Sorting Forms, Sizes, and Pictures

Materials. Balloons, objects of same colors, colored paper, identical and similar object pictures.

Criterion. Level IV
Twenty consecutively correct sortings of objects and/or pictures.

Purpose. To generate the visual perceptual—associational function by sorting various colors, forms, and sizes.

Demonstration Sequence

1. Demonstrate each activity by both explaining it and performing any activity associated with it.

2. Assemble a large number of objects which are the same except for their color. Group only two colors together at first. When the student can sort two colors, increase the number of colors to whatever number the person can handle.

3. Assemble three boxes. Paste one large cut-out geometric form (e.g., a triangle, square, or circle) on each box. Place a group of each form on a neutral ground in front of the student. Practice the sorting activity of placing correct forms in each box through Levels I, II, III, and IV.

4. Assemble two boxes marked "big" and "little." Give the person two objects which are alike but are of different sizes (e.g., a golf ball and a beach ball). Increase the number of objects as the ability to sort objects of various sizes increases.

2. *Sort colors.*
   Level I: PUT THESE COLORS TOGETHER.
   Level II: LET'S DO IT TOGETHER.
   Level III: I'LL DO IT, THEN YOU DO IT.
   Level IV: PUT THESE COLORS TOGETHER.

3. *Sort paper cut-out forms.*
   Level I: THIS GOES WITH THIS.
   Level II: LET'S PUT IT WHERE IT GOES TOGETHER.
   Level III: LET'S PUT THE THINGS IN THE BOXES TOGETHER. I'LL HELP YOU FIRST.
   Level IV: I'LL DO IT, THEN YOU DO IT AFTER I SIGNAL.

4. *Sort sizes.*
   Level I: PUT THE LITTLE BALL THERE.
   Level II: LET'S DO IT TOGETHER.
   Level III: I'LL DO IT, THEN YOU DO IT.
   Level IV: PUT THE BALLS WHERE THEY BELONG.

Visual – Motor Association: Pairing According to Function

Materials. Object pairs that have a use function.

Criterion. Level IV
Ten consecutively correct pairings of different functional object pairs.

Purpose. To teach the use of visual–motor association by pairing objects according to their use function.

Demonstration Sequence

1. Select which object pairs to employ in this activity. The examples provide only initial practice. Develop pairs of your own.

2. Decide which levels are most appropriate, I, II, III, or IV. Practice at any level until Criterion is reached. Proceed until terminal Criterion is obtained.

3. Be sure to ascertain if this set is necessary by first attempting the activity at Criterion.

4. The level of practice needed will establish the extent of difficulty of the associational function which is being practiced. You may select many pair groups, combine them in a random pile, and request that the person both sort and place them together as pairs and demonstrate their function. Or, you may choose only two or three pair groupings from which the child is to select. Again, the difficulty level of the activity should be consistent with the ability level of the student.

5. This may or may not be a verbal activity. If necessary, it could be performed at the non-verbal level.

1. *Example:* Shovel and bucket.

   Level III
   THIS IS A SHOVEL.
   THIS IS A BUCKET.
   WHAT DO THEY DO TOGETHER?
   SHOW ME WHAT THEY DO.
   LET'S DO IT TOGETHER.

   Level IV (Do not name the items)
   PUT THE THINGS THAT GO TOGETHER WITH ONE ANOTHER. SHOW ME WHAT YOU DO WITH THEM.

   LOOK CAREFULLY AT THE THINGS.

   Other examples of functional pairs
   Flowers and vase
   Lock and key
   Baseball and bat
   Pencil and paper
   Shoe and sock
   Yarn and knitting needle
   Lightbulb and lamp
   Ball and glove
   Camera and film
   Can of cola and plastic glass
   Pillow and sheet
   Plate and fork
   Plastic flower and flowerpot
   Cue stick and pool ball
   Comb and wig
   Scissors and paper
   Record and record player
   Picture and frame
   Cup and spoon
   Candle and holder
   Ruler and pencil
   Checkers and checkerboard
   Hammer and nail
   Cup and saucer
   Belt and pants
   Lampshade and lamp
   Bed and mattress (toy)
   Hotdog and bun
   Shirt and tie
   Buggy and doll (toy)
   Train and tracks (toy)
   Drum and drumsticks (toy)
   Toothbrush and toothpaste
   Chicken and egg (toy)
   Fish and fishbowl (toy)
   Horse and saddle (toy)
   Boat and sails (toy)
   Broom and dustpan
   Ashtray and cigarette
   Billfold and money (toy)
   Soap and washcloth
   Fish and water
   Pan and meat (toy)
   Tree and leaf (toy)

Visual – Motor Sequencing: Completing an Action Sequence

Materials. Objects requiring a performance of the sequenced activity.

Criterion. Level V
Ten consecutively correct sequence completions.

Purpose. To utilize the visual–motor association function by providing opportunities for an action sequence.

Demonstration Sequence

1. Select action sequences to practice. More than one activity per session may be planned.

2. Model the activity with as many repetitions of particular steps as necessary.

3. Begin at any appropriate level.

4. This is an excellent activity to practice at home. Refer to Procedures and Strategies in Chapter 5.

1. LET'S DRESS THE DOLL. THIS IS HOW WE DO IT.

   Examples of action sequences
   Dressing
   Going Shopping
   Setting the table
   Washing a window
   Cleaning a room (picking up)
   Washing hands and face
   Making a picture with colors
   Building a stack of blocks
   Making piles of things
   Making groups (rocks, wood, etc.)
   Taking a trip (e.g., walking a predesignated course around the room)
   Playing any game
   Making a simple meal
   Making a sand castle
   Putting on shoes and socks

"Same" vs. "Different"

Materials. Paper, felt pen, blackboard, chalk, objects, pictures.

Criterion. Level IV
Twenty consecutively correct judgments of "same" vs. "different."

Purpose. To teach the concept of "same" and "different" through the adjectival form.

Demonstration Sequence

1. Draw a large zero. Draw another zero next to it. Say "same" loudly and clearly. Practice at Levels I, II, and III as needed.

2. Draw another circle.

   Draw an X.

   Practice at Levels I, II, and III as needed.

3. Remove the drawings. Begin a new drawing. Repeat steps 1 and 2 with the 0 representing "same" and X representing "different."

   Practice at Levels I, II, and III.

4. Repeat steps 1 and 2 with other simple forms, e.g., squares, triangles, wavy lines. Use either blackboard or felt pen and a large piece of paper.

5. When the student appears to have mastered simple forms go to objects, *or* begin with objects and go to simple forms.

   When using objects, use any which are familiar of which there are more than one, e.g., pencils, books, cups, etc.

   Repeat at Levels I, II, III, and IV.

6. Intermix "same" and "different" comparisons. Fade your cues until all that is required is the placement of two like objects to evoke the "same" response.

7. Increase the speed of the object selection so that many "same—different" combinations occur.

8. An alternative activity may be to go on a trip, naming a noun — e.g., WINDOW — and pointing to all the windows which can be located. *Another* object to which *you* point is "different" from a window.

9. Another alternative (higher level) activity may be to use items of same and different colors, shapes, and textures.

1. *Examples of drawings*

   THESE ARE THE *SAME*.

   THESE ARE THE SAME.

   THIS IS DIFFERENT.

   POINT TO THE ONE THAT IS DIFFERENT:

5. *Examples*
   THIS IS A *PENCIL*.
   THIS IS A PENCIL.
   THEY ARE THE *SAME*.
   THIS IS A *PENCIL*.
   THIS IS A *CUP*.
   THEY ARE *DIFFERENT*.

Identifying Pictures and/or Objects by Pointing Ba

Materials. Objects, pictures, colors, Refer to Commonly Occurring Words According to Topic in Word Finder (Appendix I).

Criterion. Level IV
Correct identification of 20 consecutive objects and/or pictures by pointing.

Purpose. To teach the recognition of objects and/or pictures through visual and auditory channels to establish a basic receptive vocabulary of nouns.

Demonstration Sequence

1. The decision to use objects alone or pictures alone or to intermix them depends upon the ability level of the participant. If in doubt, begin with less abstract objects, combining them with their counterparts in pictures.

2. Place one object before the person. Have on hand a second object.

   2. *Example*
   BALL. POINT TO BALL.

3. Allow the person to hold the object and look at it while it is in his hand.

   3. IT IS A BALL.

4. Bring the other object into closer proximity.

5. Take the first object from his hand and place it on the table top.

   5. BALL.

6. Place the other object adjacent to the first one.

   6. BALL. POINT TO BALL.
   CUP. THIS IS A CUP. POINT TO CUP.
   BALL. POINT TO BALL. CUP. POINT TO CUP.

7. Place the second object in the person's hand.

   7. CUP. IT IS A CUP.

8. Place the two objects together.

   Continue until the person points to either object on command.

   8. BALL. POINT TO BALL.
   CUP. POINT TO CUP.

9. Put both objects aside and introduce two new ones. Proceed with these as in steps 2—8.

   9. *Example*
   HAT
   SPOON

10. Return to the first two objects and repeat step 8. If the person completes this step at Level IV, continue with the two new objects. Repeat step 8 with these also.

11. Combine any three of the objects. Place them in front of the person. Repeat as in step 8.

    11. *Example*
    BALL. POINT TO BALL.
    HAT. POINT TO HAT.
    CUP. POINT TO CUP.

12. From this point on, teach more objects in combinations of two and three. Recombine and review objects previously learned.

    Although you may vary the means of presentation, it is still permissible to use pointing.

    Investigate to ascertain the number of consecutive objects and/or pictures the person can point to when you name them. Do this by gradually increasing the number of objects or pictures, teaching each one as in steps 2—11 but adding to the number. Thus, depending upon his abilities, you may call upon the student to point to one from groups of varying sizes (two, four, five, etc.).

    Although Criterion is met when the person is able to point correctly to 20 consecutive objects and/or pictures, you may wish to expand this set greatly.

    "Identification" games may be played in which the person is rewarded if he identifies a fairly large number of objects.

Associating Objects with Pictures

Materials. Pictures and matching objects.

Criterion. Level IV
Correctly match 20 consecutive objects with pictures which they represent.

Purpose. To teach the person to associate pictures and the objects they represent in order to establish a basic noun receptive vocabulary.

Demonstration Sequence

1. Place an object before the person. Say its name.

2. Place a picture of the object next to the object. Point to both in turn.

3. Put the object on the picture, identifying them as you do so. Remove the object.

4. As you name the object, take the participant's hand while you grip the object and place it upon the picture. Remove the object.

5. Place the object in the hand of the participant. Point to the picture of the airplane. Wait for the person to place the airplane object on the airplane picture. If he does not, do so. Repeat step 4.

6. Practice step 4 until the person performs correctly at Level IV with five consecutive repetitions.

7. Select another object—picture combination. Repeat steps 1–5.

8. Accumulate four separate object—picture correct identifications.

9. Combine two objects and two pictures. Have the participant choose the pairs that match.

10. After two object—picture combinations are achieved, increase the number of combinations to the limit of the person's ability to select the appropriate object from the group and place it upon the corresponding picture.

    This activity may eventuate in a competition in which the person attempts to beat the clock as he is timed while he puts objects on pictures OR pictures on objects, e.g., furniture, articles of clothing.

---

1. AIRPLANE. THIS IS AN AIRPLANE.

2. AIRPLANE. THIS IS AN AIRPLANE. THIS IS AN AIRPLANE.

3. AIRPLANE. THIS IS AN AIRPLANE. THIS IS AN AIRPLANE.

4. AIRPLANE.

5. AIRPLANE.
   PUT THE AIRPLANE ON THE AIRPLANE PICTURE.

9. *Example*
   BALL. PUT THE BALL ON THE BALL PICTURE.

   AIRPLANE. PUT THE AIRPLANE ON THE AIRPLANE PICTURE.

Materials. Pictures and matching objects.

Criterion. Level IV
Twenty consecutively correct identifications of nouns by pointing.

Purpose. To teach a basic noun vocabulary through aurally presented objects and/or pictures presented separately, then combined with visual stimuli.

Demonstration Sequence

1. Decide first if you intend to show the objects or pictures *before* putting them out of sight. Blindfold the person or have him turn his back on the table on which you intend to place the items.

   Out of visual range, select two or more objects or pictures, depending upon the person's ability level. Place them in clear view. Name one of them loudly. The person is to turn around and point to the named object, excluding the other.

2. Select two more noun objects or pictures. Repeat step 1. Repeat with as many noun objects and pictures as the person can deal with to Criterion.

3. Increase the selection group from two to three to more if the person is able to perform at least at Level III.

1. AIRPLANE. FIND THE AIRPLANE. POINT TO THE AIRPLANE.
   TURN AROUND. FIND THE AIRPLANE.

2. BALL. FIND THE BALL. POINT TO IT.
   TURN AROUND. BALL. FIND THE BALL. POINT TO IT.

3. BABY. FIND BABY. WHICH IS BABY? POINT TO BABY.
   TURN AROUND. BABY. FIND THE BABY.

Identifying Verbs by Pointing

Materials. Demonstrable verb list. Two persons (to demonstrate verbs in turn). See verbs in Word Finder action words.

Criterion. Level IV
Ten consecutively correct identifications of verbs by pointing.

Purpose. To teach the person to identify an action as being the performance of a particular verb.

Demonstration Sequence

1. Demonstrate two verbs by performing any action that will illustrate them. Use any object that logically accompanies the word.

1. *Examples of verb action words*

blow	drive	lift	run
bow	drop	listen	sit
brush	eat	look	skip
build	fall	march	sleep
call	fight	open	smile
catch	fly	paint	sneeze
chop	frown	pay	stand
climb	give	pick up	stop
close	go	point	swim
color	hide	pour	swing
cough	hop	pull	talk
crawl	jump	push	throw
cry	kick	put down	till
dance	knock	read	walk
dig	laugh	ride	wave
drink	leave	ring	work

2. Perform one verb. Say the verb clearly.

Perform the other verb. Say the verb clearly.

At Level I, take the participant's hand and point to and name the first verb. Repeat with the second verb.

2. THIS IS_____.
   (verb)

THIS IS_____.
   (verb)

3. Name one of the two verbs as they are acted out, one after the other (not spontaneously). The person is to point to the person who is performing the verb you name.

3. LOOK AT THIS ONE.
LOOK AT THIS OTHER ONE.
WHICH IS_____?

4. Repeat with as many verbs as the participant can handle to Criterion.

5. A higher level activity may be to model three verbs. (Three "actors" will be necessary.) Instruct the child to point to the person modeling the verb named. Include any objects which would naturally accompany the action of the word, e.g., "hitting" with a real hammer, "throwing" a real ball, "digging" with a real shovel.

5. WHICH IS "THROW"?
POINT TO "THROW."

Materials. Objects, pictures.

Criterion. Level IV
Twenty consecutively correct productions of Yes—No judgments by nodding, gesturing, or saying "yes" or "no."

Purpose. To teach the concept of yes and no judgment choices at the concrete object—picture noun identification level.

Demonstration Sequence

1. Establish nonverbal picture—object identification. If the person can say "yes," have him do so as he nods his head. Otherwise, omit this.

2. Place the object or picture in front of the person. As you say "Yes, it is a ball," nod your head up and down. As you do so, gently take the person's head and guide it through the affirmative up-and-down movement (Level I).

3. Repeat step 2 with other objects and pictures, beginning at Level II if necessary.

4. Place a picture or object other than a spoon before the person. As you say "NO, it is not a _____," gently take the person's head in your hands and guide it through the negative (side-to-side) movement (Level I).

   Repeat steps 2 and 4 variably. Intermix yes and no responses.

5. Various objects and pictures may be placed before the student. Point to pictures and/or pick up objects. As you do so, name the object with a questioning vocal inflection. The person is to say either "yes" or "no" and/or nod his head affirmatively or negatively. Vary yes and no responses. In other words, misidentify the object or picture in order to evoke the no response.

2. *Example*
   BALL. THIS IS A BALL.
   YES, IT IS A BALL.
   SAY "YES."_____
   (Person completes with nod or word)

4. *Example*
   SPOON.
   NO, IT IS NOT A SPOON. SAY "NO."

5. *Examples*
   BALL?   AIRPLANE?
   BALLOON?   BABY?
   SPOON?   HOUSE?   etc.

Discriminating Nouns and Verbs by Pointing: Negation

Materials. Objects and pictures, demonstrable verb list, persons to model verbs.

Criterion. Level IV
Twenty consecutively correct discriminations of nouns and verbs by pointing.

Purpose. To teach a basic noun and verb vocabulary by utilizing the visual and auditory discrimination modalities.

Demonstration Sequence

1. Present two pictures or objects simultaneously. Name one correctly and the other incorrectly. For example, present two pictures, one of a dog and another of a house. Identify the "house" picture correctly. Identify the "dog" picture incorrectly (as "spoon").

2. Wait for the person to respond. Then provide the correct answer.

3. Present three pictures, identifying one correctly and two incorrectly.

4. Wait for the response. Then provide the correct answer.

5. An alternative discrimination activity is to present one picture or object, name it either correctly or incorrectly, and have the person indicate whether you named the item correctly or not.

   Accept any gesture of negation, such as a head movement from side to side, or any affirmation, such as an up and down movement of the head.

6. Repeat steps 1 through 5 with verbs. Use any objects which accompany the action words. Begin with two persons, each modeling a different verb. Name one correctly and the other incorrectly.

1. THIS IS HOUSE.
   THIS IS SPOON.
   HOUSE — SPOON
   POINT TO HOUSE (Wait)

2. THIS IS WRONG. (Point to the dog picture.)
   IT IS NOT "SPOON."
   IT IS "DOG."

3. BALL.
   TREE.
   CHAIR.
   POINT TO CHAIR.

4. THESE ARE WRONG.
   THIS IS "FLOWER."
   THIS IS "DOOR."

5. LET'S DO IT ANOTHER WAY.

   Example
   CLOCK. CORRECT?
   IS THIS A CLOCK?

6. RUN.
   SIT.
   POINT TO SIT.
   ("drink" has been identified incorrectly as "run.")

Naming Objects and Pictures: Nouns

Materials. Objects, pictures.

Criterion. Level IV
Twenty consecutively correct verbal
identifications of objects or pictures.

Purpose. To teach verbal identification
of noun aspects of the environment.

Demonstration Sequence

1. The term "objects" refers to any noun aspect of the child's
environment.

   Refer to Appendix I, Word Finder, Commonly Occurring
   Words According to Topic. Select words from any group.
   Omit action words.

2. Place an object or picture before the participant, or touch
   the article of clothing, room part, body part, etc., which is
   the "target."

   At Level IV, you may indicate the item you wish to have
   identified by pointing to it or touching it. Accept any
   utterance which in any way resembles the target noun.

2. *Examples*

   Level II
   HAND. SAY "HAND" WITH ME.
   Level III
   SAY "HAND."
   (Pointing) IT IS A (pause)__HAND__.
   　　　　　　　　　　　　　(person says)
   Level IV
   HOLD UP YOUR HAND.
   THIS IS A_____(wait for the person to fill in the
   proper word).
   Or point to a noun in a picture.

3. Once an item is learned, fade cues to Level IV and provide
   minimal cue support. Give the person time to think about
   his target.

4. Depending on the picture, more than one noun may be
   identified. Select pictures that are not too abstract or
   confusing but which do contain a number of nouns.

Producing Common Expressions

Materials. A list of two-word expressions.

Criterion. Level III
Correct consecutive production of 10 common two-word expressions.

Purpose. To begin the establishment of two-word commonly occurring stereotyped or fragmented phrases.

Demonstration Sequence

1. Accompany any verbal modeling with the related gesture. Omit gestures if they are obviously too difficult.

1. *Examples of two-word expressions*

THANK YOU	I'M FINE
GOOD MORNING	HOW'RE YOU?
GOOD NIGHT	I DUNNO
MAY I?	LET'S GO
I'M SORRY	COME HERE (com mere)
NO THANKS	SHAKE HANDS
LATER ON	DON'T CRY
AFTER AWHILE	BE CAREFUL
COME ON	HELP ME
I'M HOT	WITH ME
I'M COLD	GOOD NIGHT
YOU'RE NICE	LET'S GO
HI (person's name)	I'M HUNGRY

2. Add other expressions which seem to be natural to the child or occur normally in his environment.

Naming Pictures and Objects: Vocabulary Expansion

Materials. Pictures, objects.

Criterion. Level IV
Thirty consecutively correct picture identifications.

Purpose. To expand vocabulary by teaching identification of pictures and objects representing mixed parts of speech.

Demonstration Sequence

1. Select pictures with easily recognizable noun and verb themes. Work with one at a time or spread them out on a table top as they are identified one after the other. If the picture has a number of items, use as many per picture as is practical.

1. THIS IS_____ .
           (name of picture/object)

   SAY_____ .
         (name of picture/object)

   TELL ME THE NAME OF THESE PICTURES.
   (OR THINGS.)

   or

   SAY THE NAME OF THE PICTURE WITH ME.

   THIS IS_____ .
          person completes

   or

   (as you point to various items in the picture)

   THIS IS_____ .
         (name of item)

   SAY_____ .
      (name of item)

   NAME THESE_____ .
         (person completes)

Identifying Actions: Verbs

Materials. Action words. See Verbs section in Word Finder, Appendix I.

Criterion. Level IV
Twenty consecutively correct verbal identifications of actions being performed.

Purpose. To teach verbal identification of an action being performed in order to establish an expressive vocabulary of basic verbs.

Demonstration Sequence

1. A higher level activity than simple imitative gestures is a form of guessing game or charades in which you or another person act out a "part." You may also use a picture which corresponds to the "part," and act out the picture. This game may be played once certain action words are learned.

2. Select the "part." Say the name of the part loudly. Repeat it over and over as you practice the action related to the word.

   At Level IV, when you say the action word, the participant is to perform the action; or, as you produce the action, the person is to name it.

   Either the verb or the participial form is acceptable: "eat" or "eating," "laugh" or "laughing."

2. *Examples*

blow	eat	open	skip
bow	fall	paint	sleep
brush	feel	pay	slide
call	fly	pick	slip
catch	frown	play	smile
chew	get	point	sneeze
chop	give	pour	stand
climb	go	pull	stop
cook	have	push	swim
cough	hide	put	take
crawl	hop	read	talk
cry	jump	ride	throw
cut	knock	rock	tie
dance	laugh	run	turn
dig	lift	saw	walks
draw	listen	show	want
drink	look	sing	wash
drive	make	sit	wave

3. The length of time devoted to any one level and the number of repetitions required to move to a higher level will depend upon response capabilities.

4. Prolong the time interval between your presentation or modeling of the action word and your cue to the student to either identify it verbally or imitate the action.

5. Go outside or into another location in order to better demonstrate a verb, e.g., "dig" with an actual shovel, "throw" with an actual ball, "pay" money in an actual store. A field trip may be planned to coincide with this set.

6. Visual-auditory memory may be combined with this activity. Demonstrate as in step 2, but wait for varying lengths of time between demonstration and asking for identification.

Auditory Decoding and Listening: Recognizing Sounds

Materials. Sound-producing objects.

Criterion. Level IV
Identify ten sound sources verbally or gesturally with eyes closed.

Purpose. To establish listening behaviors by activating the auditory decoding process, which results in the recognition of various sounds.

Demonstration Sequence

1. Begin at the visual level and proceed to a finer acoustic point at which sounds are identified with closed eyes.

2. Produce the sound or indicate the sound-producing source. If the person is not yet verbal, he may use an appropriate gesture to indicate the origin of the sound: e.g., for a plane passing overhead, he points upward. If he is verbal, have him tell what made the sound.

3. Take the person outside blindfolded and instruct him to tell what he hears. Go on a blindfolded tour with him and have him attempt to identify everything heard.

2. WHAT'S THIS?
   IT IS _____ .

3. Any recognizable sounds are appropriate.

   Examples

   Inside
   Voices in general
   Ball bouncing
   Water running
   Spoon in a cup
   Door opening and closing
   Desk drawer opening and closing
   Window opening
   Table being moved across the floor
   Running
   A percussion instrument

   Outside
   Trains
   Car going by
   Voices
   Airplane overhead
   Dog barking
   Birds chirping

4. Introduce a wider variety of ever more perceptually difficult sounds.

5. For a group activity, make a tape recording of many sounds and play it for the group. Each person raises his hand when he recognizes the sound. Be sure, when you make the recording, not to place the sounds too close together so you do not have time to turn the recorder off between sounds. Be careful also not to use too much bass. This mode tends to obscure the realism of the sounds being produced.

Auditory Closure: Word Completion

Materials. Cue words and sentences.

Criterion. Level IV
Twenty consecutively correct productions of words presented as partial cues.

Purpose. To exercise the auditory closure function by teaching the student to complete a word verbally after it is presented as a partial stimulus.

Demonstration Sequence

1. First model the word, then have the student complete it after you begin it. Refer to Appendix I, Word Finder, or any other list of words in common use. Use *no* picture cues.

2. A higher level of activity is to present word pairs at varying levels of abstraction. If the student does not know the second word of the pair, provide him with the answer and repeat the cue for the word. Give the student time to try to think of the answer, however.

   More word pairs may be found in Set A j.

1. *Examples*
   SAY BABY. BA_____
   (person completes)
   MOTHER MOTH_____
   (person completes)
   TABLE TA_____
   (person completes)
   GOING GO_____
   (person completes)
   WANT WA_____
   (person completes)

2. FINISH THE WORD. SALT AND PEP_____
   (person completes)

   THAT WAS SALT AND PEPPER.
   FINISH THE WORD. SALT AND PEP_____
   (person completes)

   Examples

TABLE	AND	CHAIR
BOY	AND	GIRL
YOU	AND	ME
SUN	AND	MOON
DOG	AND	CAT
KNIFE	AND	FORK
SMILE	AND	FROWN
HAIR	AND	HEAD
CUP	AND	SAUCER
DOOR	AND	WINDOW
MAN	AND	LADY
BAT	AND	BALL
BLUE	AND	GREEN
WARM	AND	DRY
BIG	AND	STRONG
LONG	AND	SHORT
ONE	AND	TWO
YOURS	AND	MINE
HAPPY	AND	SAD

3. Another form of word completion is to provide minimal cues. Say only a portion of the word without having previously modeled it. You may wish to separate the word into syllables, leaving various portions out. If this is too difficult, provide the answer only after the student has been given time to think of it himself. Model the word, leaving a pause where the missing sound should go. If you have used more than one pause, repeat it with only one if the student is drawing a blank. Refer to the Word Finder for readily available most commonly occurring words to practice.

3. *Examples*
   NAME THE WORD.

   PEN_____IL
      (C)

   PA_____ER
     (P)

   PO_____ICE_____AN
     (L)   (M)

   TEL_____SION
      (EVI)

   BA_____BA_____
     (SE)   (LL)

   G_____DEN
    (AR)

   PRE_____Y
     (TT)

F_____ER
(LOW)

WOR_____ING
(K)

MO_____CY_____
(TOR)   (CLE)

SW____MM_____
(I)   (ING)

GIV_____
(ING)

S_____ND_____ICH
(A)   (W)

BR_____CE_____T
(A)   (LE)

BA_____R_____M
(TH)   (OO)

Materials. Objects and pictures.

Criterion. Level IV
Twenty consecutively correct identifications of objects or pictures from memory after varying time delays.

Purpose. To utilize the sequential memory function as vocabulary is being taught.

Demonstration Sequence

1. Present a picture or object.

   1. *Example*
      THIS IS A CHAIR.
      IT IS A CHAIR.
      IT IS A CHAIR.

2. Remove the object or picture from view. Wait briefly, then ask

   2. WHAT WAS IT?
      IT WAS A _____ .
          (person completes)

3. Perform steps 1 and 2 with a number of single objects or pictures. Gradually increase the time interval between the removal of the item and the request for its identification (2—3—4—5—7) seconds.

   When the person can remember one item after a 5-second delay, substitute another item and begin again, starting with no delay.

4. Repeat steps 1 and 2 with two items. You may intermix objects with pictures.

5. Continue varying the objects and pictures until the person reaches the upper limits of his ability to retain them after a time delay between their visual and auditory presentation; or DO NOT vary time, but increase the number of items presented.

6. Another form of visual and auditory memory practice is to group objects and/or pictures by class. Use as many as the person can tolerate. Some will only be able to retain one or two items at any time.

   6. *Example:* The class is transportation.
      REMEMBER THE NAMES OF THESE.
      THEY ARE:
      CAR
      BUS
      AIRPLANE
      TRAIN
      BOAT
      BICYCLE
      MOTORCYCLE

7. Remove the group from sight.

   7. NAME THE TRANSPORTATION PICTURE
      (or things if objects were used).

      WAIT UNTIL I TAKE THEM AWAY.

      REMEMBER THEM. SAY THEIR NAMES OVER AND OVER TO YOURSELF.

      NAME THEM.

8. Identify as many objects and persons as possible from the therapy room.

   8. LOOK AROUND THE ROOM.

      THERE IS A (<u>door</u>).
      THERE IS A (<u>floor</u>).
      THERE IS A (<u>table</u>).
      THERE IS A (<u>window</u>).

   If the person will not keep his eyes closed, blindfold him and play a "naming" game.

      CLOSE YOUR EYES. WHAT DID YOU SEE?
      REMEMBER WHAT YOU SAW.

      YOU SAW A (<u>door</u>), a (<u>floor</u>), a (<u>table</u>), a (<u>window</u>), etc.

      TELL ME WHAT YOU SAW.

Arranging Words into Classes

Ch

Materials. Objects, pictures, Commonly Occurring Words According to Topic in the Word Finder, Appendix I.

Criterion. Level IV
Twenty consecutively correct verbal classifications of objects and/or pictures.

Purpose. To teach basic vocabulary through meaningful grouping of words ("context clusters").

Demonstration Sequence

1. Refer to Most Commonly Occurring Words According to Topic in the Word Finder.

   Inventory your pictures and objects and group them according to their context cluster. The task is both to name items and to identify the class to which they belong.

   Practice all clusters at Levels II and III, if necessary, before going to Level IV.

1. *Examples of context clusters*
   Body parts
   Things we eat
   Things we wear
   Eating utensils
   Rooms
   Furniture
   Animals
   Transportation
   People
   Things to use
   Things to see outside
   Things to play with

2. Show one object or picture at a time. Continue with all pictures and/or objects in the class. After each three items, identify the class category. Level II.

2. THIS IS A SHIRT.
   SAY "SHIRT" WITH ME.

   THIS IS A BELT.
   SAY "BELT" WITH ME.

   THESE ARE TROUSERS.
   SAY "TROUSERS" WITH ME.

   THEY ARE CLOTHES.
   SAY "CLOTHES" WITH ME.

   WHAT ARE THEY?
   THEY ARE CLOTHES.

   WHAT ARE THEY?_____
   (person completes)

3. Begin another class. Repeat step 2.

4. Repeat step 2 with as many classes as the person can tolerate.

5. Intermix the classes until all you have to do is name any item of any class and the person can identify that class.

6. One group game activity is to have each person say the class as quickly as he can after hearing the word.

7. Another group activity is to name the class and have the group name as many items in it as they can.

8. An alternative means of presentation may be to say the carrier phrase (together with the student) each time you place the object or picture into its group adjacent to the name of the cluster written on the large piece of paper. Repeat with another cluster if you feel the child has the ability to handle two categories at once.

   Go to more than two clusters if that seems possible.

8. *Examples*
   THIS IS AN ANIMAL.
   THE HORSE IS AN ANIMAL.
   THE LAMB IS AN ANIMAL.
   THE DOG IS AN ANIMAL.
   THE CAT IS AN ANIMAL.
   THE LION IS AN ANIMAL. etc.

   THIS IS FOOD.
   A BANANA IS FOOD.
   A POTATO IS FOOD.
   A SANDWICH IS FOOD.
   PIE IS FOOD.
   BREAD IS FOOD.

9. Remove the cluster grouping. Scramble the groups. Instruct the student to arrange the cluster items correctly.

   At first, present items that belong to one cluster only, to provide a high success ratio. Then present two cluster topics, to bring into play the sorting, selection, and classifying conceptualization activity.

10. The number of cluster topics that may be practiced simultaneously again depends upon the ability of the person to retain the basic vocabulary word and the concept of arranging the words appropriately.

11. Another group game is to see how fast each person can sort a group or class, e.g., have two or three classes with only two or three objects or pictures in each.

    An alternative to this is to have the group listen as you name an object or picture, then scan the group and place the object or picture into the appropriate classification.

Learning Noun Phrases: Article plus Noun

Materials. Objects, pictures, room parts, body parts, etc.

Criterion. Level IV
Twenty consecutively correct article + noun phrases.

Purpose. To teach two-word noun phrases which include the articles "a," "the," and "an" plus a noun.

Demonstration Sequence

1. Establish which picture or object nouns you will use. This set may serve to introduce articles.

1. *Example*

   Article plus Noun
A	Any appropriate object, picture,
THE	room part, body part, etc.
AN (indef.)	

2. Model the article + noun using a variety of nouns per article.

2. *Examples*

   Article plus Noun
A	BALL
A	TREE
A	CHAIR
A	LADDER
A	FOOTBALL
THE	ORANGE
THE	BOAT
THE	DOG
THE	CANDY
THE	LAMP
AN	ARM
AN	APPLE
AN	AIRPLANE
AN	OWL
AN	ELEPHANT

3. Once step 2 is established at Level III for "a," "the," and "an," go to Level IV.

3. *Examples*
   Person says:
A	BOY
THE	BARN
AN	ELEPHANT

4. Select pictures with a number of nouns contained within them. Those which were used in Set C a will also apply here.

Visual – Motor Organization: Learning Numbers, Conceptualizing, Counting

Materials. The same object in quantity; numerals, number pictures, fingers, felt pen, paper.

Criterion. Level IV
Twenty consecutively correct identifications of numbers from 1 to 10.

Purpose. To teach the concept of numbers through the establishment of simple counting ability, utilizing the visual–motor organizing process.

Demonstration Sequence

1. Assemble a number of different objects that can be counted, such as poker chips and pencils. Begin with the simplest number concept.

   If the person is nonverbal, he may use the objects to show you the numbers. He may also point to the numeral itself. For example, "4."

2. Level I. Take the hand of the student to make him put one object, e.g., one poker chip, on an uncluttered background. Emphasize "one."

   Level II. Place one poker chip on the background. As you do so, say "one."

   Level III.

   Level IV.

2. ONE.
   SAY *ONE* or POINT TO *ONE.*

   SAY *ONE* WITH ME. *ONE.*
   Or
   POINT TO *ONE. ONE.*

   SAY *ONE* AFTER ME. *ONE.*
   Person says ONE.
   Or
   POINT TO *ONE* AFTER I DO. Person says ONE.

   SAY *ONE.* Person says: *ONE.*
   SAY IT AGAIN. Person says: *ONE*
   Or
   POINT TO *ONE.* (Person points)

3. Once "one" is established at Level IV, go on to "two," etc. As the ability to say or point to various small numbers accumulates, intermix the numbers.

4. Once the recognition of numbers up to "five" is established, return to "one," write the numeral "1" on a large piece of paper, and place the poker chip adjacent to it. If the person can write, have him write the numbers also.

   Repeat through Levels I to IV.

4. THIS MEANS "ONE."
   WRITE "ONE" WITH ME.
   WRITE "ONE" AFTER ME. WRITE "ONE."
   SAY "ONE" WITH ME.
   SAY "ONE" AFTER ME.
   SAY "ONE."
   SAY AND WRITE "ONE" WITH ME.
   SAY AND WRITE "ONE" AFTER ME.
   SAY AND WRITE "ONE."

5. Add *other* object combinations. As the person is able to conceptualize "same" object accumulations, interject different objects, e.g., a pencil, toy car, and cup equals a numeral "3."

6. Use the felt pen and paper to make numbers. Remove all objects. Rely upon only the felt marker and paper to establish numbers.

Conceptualizing Categories: Plurals Ck

Materials. Objects, pictures. Items from contest clusters (see Word Finder, Appendix I).

Criterion. Level IV
Ten consecutively correct identifications of plurals.

Purpose. To teach the concept of "categories" into which words fall, i.e., one ball or three balls are still one category, "balls." Also to teach that the plural signifies "more than one."

Demonstration Sequence

1. Assemble items for categories. These may be objects and pictures. You may wish to work with objects first because they are less abstract than pictures.

   Proceed at a level of abstraction appropriate to the student's ability level.

   More than one item representative of a category should be obtained, e.g., five balls, each one different but each one a "ball." This concept also applies to picture topic groupings, e.g., a number of different pictures of airplanes.

2. Repeat step 1 with various object or picture categories. After five separate categories have been learned, go to other object categories found in everyday living, e.g., body parts, shirts, walls, windows, tables, shoes. Model the plural "s" ending clearly.

3. This may be a game. Make selections from a group of objects or pictures, the size of the group depending upon ability level: e.g., two balls and one car. Be sure to listen for "s" endings indicating plurals.

4. Mix many categories together. In this case the person sorts through the assembled items and separates them into their categories. Omit this step if it is obviously too difficult.

5. An alternative activity is to instruct the person to "make up your own." He then tells you all the items he would choose for any context cluster. These may be visually present as objects or pictures, or he may use recall and name them from memory. A competition may be arranged to see who can name the most "round-robin" or individually.

6. Verbal production of any complexity may accompany this activity. Thus, single word utterances may be acceptable for one child, but a small phrase or sentence may be more appropriate for another. The sentences should include the correct use of plurals with subject—verb agreement.

1. *Example*
Show an object or picture.

   Level I
   HERE IS A BALL. HERE IS ANOTHER BALL. POINT TO A BALL. I'LL HELP YOU.

   Level II
   LET'S POINT TO THE BALL TOGETHER.

   Level III
   I'LL POINT TO THE BALL. THEN YOU POINT RIGHT AFTER ME.

   Level IV
   POINT TO THE BALL WHEN I SIGNAL.

2. *Level III*
THESE ARE BALLS. SAY BALLS.

   Level IV
   SAY IT AGAIN.

3. *Example:* Plurals.
POINT TO WHAT I NAME.
CARS
BALLS
FEATHERS
AIRPLANES

4. PUT ALL THE CARS TOGETHER.
PUT ALL THE BALLS TOGETHER.
PUT ALL THE PENCILS TOGETHER.
NAME THEM.

5. *Examples*
Favorite food
Things for breakfast, lunch, etc.
Favorite outfits to wear
Favorite toys
Christmas things (any holiday)
Furniture around the house
Animals I like
People (family, postman, grocer, etc.)
What's in the kitchen? (and other rooms)
Name body parts as fast as you can
Things to see outside where I live

Identifying Colors: Conceptualizing Adjectives

Materials. Objects, pictures of the usual color.

Criterion. Level IV
Twenty consecutively correct identifications of five different colors.

Purpose. To teach the concept and identification of the basic colors singly and as adjectives.

Demonstration Sequence

1. Obtain all possible solid color pictures and objects. Decide which mode (verbal or nonverbal) is most appropriate.

2. Say the color. Point to the object or pick the object up. Or point to the color in a picture.

3. Practice *one* color through to Level IV, or establish various colors to the level of the capability limits of the student.

1. *Example*
   YOU HAVE A RED PEN, A RED BALL, A RED COLOR PLATE, AND A RED BLOCK.

2. RED (pen)
   RED (ball)
   RED (book)
   RED (color plate)
   RED (block)
   RED. SAY "RED" WITH ME. SAY "RED."
   THIS IS_____.
          (student completes)

Making Yes – No Judgments: Conceptualizing "Yes" and "No"

Materials. Yes–no sentences, pictures, objects.

Criterion. Level IV
Twenty consecutively correct yes or no judgments.

Purpose. To teach the concept of "yes" and negation by providing contrasts and activating the auditory decoding process.

Demonstration Sequence

1. Provide the statement, the question, and the answer at first. Begin at a simple level and proceed into more abstract sentences.

   Ask easy questions based upon pictures which you have selected for which there is a yes or no answer.

2. Indicate various objects. Mix up the yes and no questions. Answer the questions yourself only if you must. Begin fading your answering as soon as the person seems to be able to answer by himself.

1. *Examples*
   YOU ARE A GIRL.
   ARE YOU A GIRL? YES.
   YOU ARE NOT A BOY.
   ARE YOU A BOY? NO.
   YOU ARE NOT TALL.
   ARE YOU TALL? NO.

2. THIS IS A CHAIR.
   IS IT A TABLE? NO.
   IS IT A TABLE? (person completes)
   IS IT A CHAIR? (person completes)

Learning Noun Phrases: Noun plus Adjective, Adjective plus Noun

Materials. Objects, pictures, body parts, room parts, etc., adjective word list.

Criterion. Level IV
Twenty consecutively correct adjective noun phrases.

Purpose. To teach two-word noun phrases which include an adjective plus a noun.

Demonstration Sequence

1. Establish which object or picture nouns you intend to use. The adjectives studied may be new in this set.

1. *Examples*

Adjective	*plus*	*Noun*
any colors		any appropriate
any number		object, picture,
any shape		body part, room
any size		part, etc.
any quality		
any texture		
any weight		

2. Select object(s) which clearly possess identifiable characteristics. An alternative is to teach one characteristic at a time.

2. *Examples of characteristics*

RED	BALL	ROUGH	SANDPAPER
ONE	BALL	SMOOTH	SILK
ROUND	BALL	HEAVY	TABLE
SMALL	BALL	LIGHT	CHAIR
NICE	BALL		
SMOOTH	BALL		
LIGHT	BALL		

3. Once step 2 is established, repeat all adjectives at Level IV.

3. *Examples*

   Person says:

HEAVY	TABLE
SMALL	BALL
TWO	PENCIL(S)
NICE	GIRL
GREEN	PAPER

4. Reverse the position of the Adjective + Noun to Noun or Pronoun + Adjective. Practice as in steps 2 to 4.

4. *Example*

Pronoun or Noun	*plus*	*Adjective*
Any referent,		any color
object, picture,		any shape
etc.		any size
		any quality
		any texture
		any weight

5. Accept nongrammatical productions such as "two pencil" for "two pencils."

Understanding Relationships: Prepositions

Materials. Noun or pronoun referent object. Pictures.

Criterion. Level IV
Twenty consecutively correct identifications of prepositions.

Purpose. To teach the vocabulary and concept of prepositions.

Demonstration Sequence

1. Obtain any objects, pictures, etc., which may assist you in illustrating the relationship between the word (preposition) and its meaning.

   Accompany any verbal illustration with appropriate movements. One object may be used to illustrate a number of prepositions. An alternative is to use *many* objects to illustrate *one* preposition.

1. *Examples of prepositions*

ABOUT	NEAR
ABOVE	NEXT
ACROSS	OF
AFTER	OFF
AGAINST	ON
ALONG	OPPOSITE
AMONG	OUT
AROUND	OUTSIDE
AT	OVER
AS	PAST
BEFORE	THAN
BEHIND	THROUGH
BELOW	THROUGHOUT
BENEATH	TILL
BESIDE	TO
BETWEEN	TOWARD
BEYOND	UNDER
BY	UNDERNEATH
DOWN	UP
DURING	UPON
FOR	UNTIL
FROM	WITH
IN	WITHIN
INSIDE	WITHOUT

2. This set may be practiced at a nonverbal or verbal level. For instance, present two examples which may be illustrated by performing an action or showing pictures. Model two sentences. Ask the person to point to the preposition you name (which is shown in the picture).

2. *Example*
(Present a picture of a person wearing a hat.)

THE HAT IS *ON* THE HEAD.

(Present a picture of a person standing up.)

THE MAN IS STANDING *UP*.

Emphasize "on."
POINT TO THE HAT *ON* THE HEAD.

Emphasize "up."
POINT TO THE MAN STANDING *UP*.

3. Use, for example, a chair and toy car.

   Hold the toy car above the chair.

   Hold the car below the chair.

   Hold the car under the chair.

   Lean the car against the chair.

   Place the car near the chair.

3. *Example*

CAR *ABOVE* CHAIR.

CAR *BELOW* CHAIR.

CAR *UNDER* CHAIR.

CAR *AGAINST* CHAIR.

CAR *NEAR* CHAIR.

4. Using selected pictures, practice many prepositions at Level III only, before proceeding on to Level IV.

Learning Verb Phrases: Subject plus Verb

Materials. Objects, pictures, action word list, "Most Commonly Occurring Words" list.

Criterion. Level IV Twenty consecutively correct subject + verb phrases.

Purpose. To teach two-word verb phrases which include a subject plus a verb.

Demonstration Sequence

1. Establish which nouns and which verbs you intend to use. Select first those nouns and verbs with which some motion may be associated.

   Practice each two-word expression with the accompanying movement (if possible).

   When a number of subject + verb phrases have been produced at Level III, go to Level IV.

   Repeat Level III followed immediately by IV for each subject + verb combination.

   Accept verbs with "s" endings absent, e.g., "dog run, girl sleep, mommy walk, boy fall."

1. *Examples*

Subject	*plus*	*Verb*
Any appropriate object or picture.		Any appropriate action word
CAR		RUNS
BALL		BOUNCES
BEE		STINGS
BUNNY		HOPS
CLOCK		TICKS
CANDLE		BURNS
BROOM		SWEEPS
CHILD		SMILES
COWBOY		RIDES
CAT		CLIMBS
DOG		BARKS
FINGER		POINTS
FISH		SWIMS

2. An alternative activity is to present one noun and to combine many verbs with it.

Learning Adverb Phrases: Verb plus Adverb

Materials. Adverb phrase list, pictures.

Criterion. Level IV
Twenty consecutively correct adverb phrases.

Purpose. To teach the use of adverbs to modify verbs. Adverbs may be used to add information to verbs in terms of "when, where, how (or to what extent), how much (or how little)."

Demonstration Sequence

1. Establish which verbs and adverbs you intend to use. Make up a list using the examples as a guide. Accompany any verb and adverb with movements and objects which are logical.

   Select each two-word expression and practice separately through Levels II, III, and IV. Accept non-"ly" ending adverbs if that is the person's capability level at this point.

2. Select pictures that may be used to provide a reference for verb—adverb models.

1. *Examples of adverbs*

Verb	plus	Adverb
POUR		QUICKLY
HEAD		NORTH
GO		NOW
RUN		THERE
LEAVE		TOGETHER
LOOK		CAREFULLY
RUN		SLOWLY
BUY		LESS
READ		CAREFULLY
DO		SOMETHING
LEFT		YESTERDAY (adv. of time)
PAINT		WELL
SMILE		ALWAYS
COME		HERE
BE		STILL
SIT		THERE

Identifying Characteristics by Sight and Touch: Adjectives Cr

Materials. Objects and/or pictures.

Criterion. Level IV
Twenty consecutively correct verbal identifications of adjective characteristics.

Purpose. To teach common adjectives by associating them with aspects of objects and/or pictures by sight or touch.

Demonstration Sequence

1. A basic noun vocabulary should have been established prior to this set. The adjective is here combined with the noun either singly or as contrasts when comparing characteristics.

   With the presentation of the object(s) or picture(s), include any gesture or motion which may further illustrate the concept.

   Decide whether you are going to teach via a single characteristic or by contrasts.

2. Place the object(s) or picture(s) before the person.

3. Point to or pick up the big object. Point to or pick up the small object.

4. Obtain any other big or small objects. Repeat step 2 with them. A more abstract form of practice is to combine two dissimilar objects which still may be contrasted as big and little.

1. *Examples of contrasts and characteristics*

WET — DRY	THIN — FAT
BIG — LITTLE	WIDE — NARROW
TALL — SHORT	LIGHT — DARK
HOT — COLD	DIRTY — CLEAN
MANY — FEW	FULL — EMPTY
HEAVY — LIGHT	HARD — SOFT
ROUGH — SMOOTH	SMALL — LARGE
FAST — SLOW	SHINY — DULL

2. *Example:* A basketball combined with a golf ball to demonstrate BIG — LITTLE.

3. BIG BALL.
   LITTLE BALL.
   SAY "BIG BALL" WITH ME.
   SAY "LITTLE BALL" WITH ME.
   SAY "BIG BALL."
   SAY "LITTLE BALL."
   THIS BALL IS_____.
   (person completes)

4. *Example:* A pencil combined with a chair to demonstrate
   BIG — LITTLE.
   BIG CHAIR
   LITTLE PENCIL
   SAY "BIG CHAIR" WITH ME.
   SAY "LITTLE PENCIL" WITH ME.
   SAY "BIG CHAIR."
   SAY "LITTLE PENCIL."
   THIS CHAIR IS_____.
   (person completes)

Materials. Objects, pictures, plural duplicates.

Criterion. Level IV
Twenty consecutively correct quantifier + noun phrases.

Purpose. To teach two-word noun phrases which include quantifiers plus nouns, and to use them as plural transformational practice items. Quantifiers may be adjectives and pronouns.

Demonstration Sequence

1. Establish which objects or pictures you intend to use as nouns.

   Quantifiers (plurals) may be studied for the first time with this set. Numbers will have been studied previously. Review them here as an initial activity.

2. Plural transformations are now being taught. The complexity and extent of the use of plurals as quantifiers will depend upon the person's ability to grasp the concept of "more than one."

3. Hold up, point to, and/or isolate the noun items. Practice *each phrase* through Levels II and III. Continue in III with many illustrations before proceeding on to Level IV. Move from the least to more abstract items.

   Point to one item.
   Point to another item.
   Point to another item.

   Proceed until "one" is established to Level III with a number of nouns.

   Point to two items.
   Point to two other items.
   Point to two other items.

   Proceed until "two" is established at Level III.

   Practice number concepts to whatever number is optimal for the student. Then go to another quantifier.

   Point to an assembled group of objects.

   Remove most of the objects from the group.

   Put two of the objects together. Remove the rest.

   Replace almost all the objects.

   Remove all objects. Replace each, one at a time.

   Add to the objects.

4. Repeat step 2 with a variety of items keeping the item constant and varying the quantifier.

5. Practice each quantifier at Level IV, waiting for the student to complete his portion of the phrase.

   Point to one item.

   Point to another item.

   Point to another item.

   Point to two items.

   Point to two other items.

   Point to two other items.

1. *Examples:* Practice numbers — 1, 2, 3, etc. — *first.*

Quantifier	*plus*	*Noun*
Any numbers		Any appropriate objects and pictures
ALL		
MORE		"s" endings are not
FEW		mandatory here,
BOTH		but may occur
MOST		naturally.
EACH		
ANY		
EVERY		

3.

   ONE BALL
   ONE CHAIR
   ONE NOSE

   TWO BALLS
   TWO CHAIRS
   TWO NOSES

   Examples

   ALL TOYS

   FEW TOYS

   BOTH TOYS

   MOST TOYS

   EACH TOY

   MORE TOYS

5. *Example:* Repeat at Level III, then go immediately to Level IV.

   ONE BALL

   ONE CHAIR

   ONE NOSE

   TWO BALLS

   TWO CHAIRS

   TWO NOSES

6. Practice number concepts to whatever number is optimal at Level IV. Then go to other quantifiers and practice them at Level IV immediately after a repetition of Level III.

6.

Point to an assembled group of objects.

ALL BALLS

Remove most of the objects from the group.

FEW BALLS

Remove all the objects. Replace two objects.

BOTH BALLS

Replace almost all the objects.

MOST BALLS

Identifying Persons: Pronouns "I" and "You"

Ct

Materials. Persons.

Criterion. Level IV
Twenty consecutively correct identifications of persons by their names.

Purpose. To teach the concept that persons may be identified by their names and that they may be differentiated by the pronouns "I" and "you."

Demonstration Sequence

1. Begin by identifying only two persons, you and the student. Point to the student and yourself as you do so.

Repeat your name.

Repeat the student's name.

If the student is nonverbal, he may point to whomever you identify by name.

Take the person's hand and point to him and you selectively. (Level I)

Point to yourself. Point to the person. (Level II)

Point to yourself. Point to the person. (Level III)

(Level IV)

2. After the person has learned your and his name, emphasize "I." Point to the person. Proceed through Levels II to IV with "I" and "you."

3. Add one other person to the group. Teach the name of that person as in step 1. Continue to add new persons and intermix their names with "I" and "you."

1. *Examples*

MY NAME IS _____.
(your name)

YOUR NAME IS _____.
(person's name)

_____
(your name)

_____
(person's name)

_____
(person's name)

_____
(your name)

I AM _____.
(your name)

YOU ARE _____.
(person's name)

SAY _____ WITH ME.
(your name)

_____
(your name)

SAY _____ WITH ME.
(person's name)

YOU ARE _____.
(person's name)

SAY _____ AFTER ME.
(your name)

_____
(your name)

SAY _____ AFTER ME.
(person's name)

_____
(person's name)

SAY _____ AGAIN.
(your name)

SAY _____ AGAIN.
(person's name)

2. *I* AM _____.
(your name)

SAY *I* AM _____.
(person's name)

C. Expressive Syntax — Words and Phrases **75**

Learning Verb Phrases: Verb plus Object

Materials. Verb, noun, and pronoun word lists. Pictures.

Criterion. Level IV
Twenty consecutively correct verb + object phrases.

Purpose. To teach two-word verb phrases which include a verb plus object.

Demonstration Sequence

1. Establish which verbs and objects of verbs you intend to use. Pronoun objects are more abstract and may be studied for the first time with this set. Accompany any verb with the movement or gesture appropriate to it.

   Select two-word expressions and practice separately.

1. *Examples*

Verb	*plus*	*Object*
Any appropriate verb.		Any appropriate noun or pronoun (as the direct object or receiver of the action.)
DROP		BALL
CLIMB		LADDER
DRINK		MILK
PAY		MONEY
LIFT		IT
FIND		THEM
GET		SOME
SEE		HER
POUR		WATER
WATCH		CLOCK
READ		PAPER

2. Show a picture and provide a model beginning at Level II.

Using Nouns and Possessive Pronouns: Conceptualizing Possession

Cv

Materials. Objects, pictures, body parts, etc.

Criterion. Level IV
Twenty consecutively correct possessive pronouns in phrases.

Purpose. To teach two-word noun phrases which include a possessive pronoun, a noun, and the concept of possession.

Demonstration Sequence

1. Establish which noun objects or pictures you intend to use. The pronoun and concept of possession may be studied for the first time with this set.

   "S" endings may be too difficult for some students but not for others. While some phrases will not be grammatically correct at this point, they will be directed toward the objectives of this set.

   Plural possessives should be studied with groups. The concept of collective possession will thus be demonstrable.

1. *Examples*

Noun	*plus*	*Pronoun*
Any appropriate object, picture, body part, etc.		MINE
		YOURS
		HIS
		HERS
		OURS
		THEIRS

   or

Possessive	*plus*	*Noun*
Person's name (s) ending		Any appropriate object, picture,
MY		body part, etc.
YOUR		
HIS		
HER		

2. Hold up an object or point to a body part, etc.

2. *Example:* Possessive + noun.
   YOUR ARM.

3. Point to a part of your own body.

   Practice through Levels I, II, and III.

3. MY ARM. POINT TO MY ARM. POINT TO YOUR ARM.

4. Continue to intermix "my" and "your" examples with other body parts at first, then go to other objects and pronouns.

   Practice through Levels I, II, and III.

4. POINT TO YOUR (person's) ARM. SAY *"MY* ARM."

   POINT TO MY (clinician's) ARM. SAY *"YOUR* ARM."

5. Expand step 4 to include other persons in the room and groups of objects in singular or collective possession.

   Practice through Levels I, II, and III.

5. *Examples*

Noun	*plus*	*Pronoun*
PENCILS		THEIRS
BALLS		OURS
DRESSES		THEIRS
HANDS		OURS

6. Practice steps 2—5 at Level IV, waiting for the child to complete the phrase. For example:

   Point to the person's arm.

   Point to your arm.

   Point to a group of toys, then to the entire group of students in general.

   Point to everyone's shoes.

   Point to your shoe.

   Point to person's shoe.

   Point to another person's shoe.

   Point to another person's shirt or dress.

(Person says italicized word.)
MY ARM

YOUR ARM

OUR TOYS

SHOE *OURS*

SHOE *MINE*

SHOE *YOURS*

HER SHOE

SHIRT *HIS*.
DRESS *HERS*.

Learning Verb Phrases: Verb plus Particle, Preposition, Pronoun

Materials. Lists of verbs, particles, prepositions, pronouns. Pictures.

Criterion. Level IV
Twenty consecutively correct verb + particle or preposition or pronoun phrases.

Purpose. To teach two-word verb phrases which include a verb plus particle or preposition or pronoun.

Demonstration Sequence

1. Establish which verbs you intend to use. Particles, prepositions, or pronouns may be studied for the first time with this set. Some of the verbs presented here will also be new. Thus, this is a higher level activity than the two-word phrases in the other sets in this section.

   Practice first any expression that has a gesture which accompanies it. Any objects that fit into the activities should also be used.

1. *Examples*

Verb	*plus*	*Particle, Preposition, or Pronoun*
ASK		HIM
BEGIN		THERE
BURN		ONE
CLEAN		IT
DRESS		UP
GO		ALONG
COLOR		IT
EAT		THOSE
WALK		AROUND
LEAVE		US
REST		THERE
START		NOW
HOLD		THESE
LIE		DOWN
DRIVE		THERE
LOVE		THIS
PULL		UP
TELL		ME

2. Demonstrate with movement and object through Levels II and III. When a number of two-word expressions are established at Level III, repeat Level III and go immediately to Level IV.

3. Go now to the more abstract expressions and begin to fade the motion and visible noun referent. Continue through Levels to IV.

4. Obtain any pictures that illustrate the form of phrases which this set teaches. Use these as visual cues for the phrases which will be taught.

Learning Predicative Phrases: Demonstrative plus Possessive Pronouns and Full- to Substitute-Form Transformations   Cx

Materials. Objects.

Criterion. Level IV
Twenty consecutively correct phrases that include demonstrative and/or possessive pronouns.

Purpose. To teach the concept of possession and the use of demonstrative and possessive pronouns.

Demonstration Sequence

1. Establish which noun objects you intend to use. The concept of the demonstrative and possessive pronoun need not be known prior to this set.

   The phrases are not grammatically correct at this point, but they do imitate the use of pronouns in possession and demonstration.

2. Hold up or touch an object and/or point to one or more items. Practice each two-pronoun phrase through Levels III and IV.

   Touch, for example, the person's shirt.

   Touch your dress or shirt.

   Point to a group of toys.

   Repeat with person naming.

   Point to another person's shoe.

   Point to a number of articles of clothing.

   Point to a number of articles of clothing belonging to a number of persons.

3. Practice step 2 at Levels III and IV, waiting for the person to complete the phrase.

   Touch your own dress or shirt.

   Point to a group of toys.

   Point to another person's shoe.

   Have the person point to and touch articles of clothing which he is wearing.

   Point to and touch the shoulder, arm, and hand of another person.

   A higher level activity is presented below.

4. The third person plural (nominative case) pronoun "they" should be included here. Select a group of objects, pictures, etc. Present them.

1. *Example*

Demonstrative Pronoun	plus	Possessive Pronoun
THIS		YOURS
THESE		MINE
THOSE		OURS
IT		HERS
THAT		HIS
THEY		THEIRS

2. *Examples*
   SAY AFTER ME.

   THIS YOURS.

   THIS MINE.

   THOSE OURS.

   SAY_____
   (person completes, repeats sequence)

   IT HIS.

   THESE YOURS.

   THOSE THEIRS.

   SAY_____
   (person completes, repeats sequence)

3. *Examples:* (After Level III.)

   THAT YOURS.

   THOSE OURS.

   IT HIS.

   THESE MINE.

   THOSE HERS or HIS.

   SAY_____
   (person completes, repeats sequence)

4. *Examples*
   THIS IS A BALL.
   THIS IS A PLANE.
   THIS IS A DOLL.

   THEY ARE TOYS.

   THIS IS MARY.
   THIS IS JOHN.
   THIS IS BILL.

   THEY ARE CHILDREN.

   SAY_____
   (person completes, repeats sequence)

Learning Designative Phrases: Locator, Demonstrator, Identifier plus Noun, and Plurals and Interrogatives

Cy

Materials. Objects, pictures.

Criterion. Level IV
Twenty consecutively correct locator, demonstrator, identifier + noun phrases.

Purpose. To teach two-word designative phrases which include locators, demonstrators, and identifiers plus a noun along with plurals and interrogatives.

Demonstration Sequence

1. Establish which picture or object nouns you will use.

   The locators, demonstrators, and identifiers may be studied for the first time with this set. Establish which locator, identifier, or demonstrator you will study. Accompany each two-word expression with any logical movement.

2. Hold up an object. Put it behind your back.

   Practice at Levels I, II, III, and IV until the person can ask the question and/or produce the movement.

   Point to any picture or object.

   Assemble two groups of objects. Use pointing to, taking away, or adding to movements along with the two-word expression.

1. *Examples*

Locator, Identifier, or Demonstrator		*plus*	*Noun*
THERE	THIS		Any appro-
HAVE	THAT		priate object,
THESE	THOSE		picture, etc.
OTHER	ANOTHER		
WHERE	WHICH		
WHOSE	WANT		
HERE	IT (ITSA)		
	('SA)		
	('S)		

2. *Example*

   WHERE BALL? SAY "WHERE BALL?"

   IT'S A CHAIR.
   IT'S AN ARM.
   IT'S AN AIRPLANE.

   THAT HAT
   THOSE TOYS
   HERE BALL
   THESE TOYS
   THIS CAR

Materials. Pictures, sentences.

Criterion. Level IV
Twenty consecutively correct sentences.

Purpose. To provide sentence production practice by utilizing the auditory sequential memory channel and increasingly larger sentence formats.

Demonstration Sequence

1. Preestablish a number of sentences from pictures or produce sentences spontaneously as they occur to you. Room parts, body parts, and other visual stimuli may also provide ideas. Decide which part of speech or which specific word you wish to use as a beginning point around which the sentence will be built.

   Model the entire sentence first.

   Require the student say only *one* word of the sentence.

   Repeat the sentence. Require two words.

   Repeat the sentence. Require three words.

   Repeat the sentence. Require the entire sentence.

   Remember that you may practice this arrangement at Levels II and III and then go to IV. Use as many repetitions at each point as you deem necessary.

2. An alternative form of this activity is to choose which part of speech you wish to teach and retain that *one* word as a constant. Construct sentences from pictures which illustrate "on" visually. Also, choose one object and place it "on" any other surface in your immediate environment.

   When the student achieves 90 percent accuracy with "on," return to step 1 and proceed to add words to "on" until each entire sentence is repeated back at Level IV.

   Refer to subsequent sets in this section. You may teach any sentence form in the manner suggested here. The examples here can serve as models and the format of this set may serve as your teaching vehicle.

1.

Example
THE TABLE IS BIG.
SAY "BIG." _____
                 (person completes)
THE TABLE IS BIG. SAY "IS BIG."

_____
(person completes)
THE TABLE IS BIG. SAY "TABLE IS BIG."

_____
(person completes)
THE TABLE IS BIG. SAY "THE TABLE IS BIG."

_____
(person completes)

2. *Example:* Using pictures to teach the preposition "on" along with its usage in sentences.
THE HAT IS ON THE HEAD. SAY "ON . . . ."

_____
(person completes with ON THE HEAD)
THE CAR IS ON THE GROUND.
SAY "ON . . . ."

_____
(person completes with "on")
THE SHIRT IS ON THE MAN.
SAY "ON . . . ."

_____
(person completes with "on")
(from object)
THE BLOCK IS ON THE TABLE.
SAY "ON . . . ."

_____
(person completes with "on")
THE BLOCK IS ON THE FLOOR.
SAY "ON . . . ."

_____
(person completes with "on")
THE BLOCK IS ON THE BOY.
SAY "ON . . . ."

_____
(person completes with "on")

Auditory Sequential Memory: Remembering Word Sequences

Materials. Words, numbers.

Criterion. Level IV
Twenty consecutively correct sequenced word identifications.

Purpose. To bring the sequential association function into use by practicing the retention of a preestablished *order* of items presented auditorily.

Demonstration Sequence

1. Begin with one word. Practice at Levels II, III, and IV.

2. Repeat step 1 with more single words. Gradually increase the time interval between the word presentation and your signal; i.e., 2—4—3—5 seconds.

   When one word can be remembered after a 5-second delay, add another word and begin with no delay.

   Repeat steps 1 and 2 with two words. The words chosen should not "go together," e.g., "BALL" and "HOUSE."

3. Continue adding words to be remembered in sequence. Vary either time *or* the number of words presented. Practice until you achieve the upper limits of the student's ability to remember a sequence of words presented orally. No time delay need be used if you present larger groups of words.

4. Step 2 may be repeated with easy numbers presented in random sequence, e.g., 1—4—2—5.

5. An alternative activity may be to give sentences to repeat, beginning with two words and gradually adding more and more.

6. An alternative means of exercising the recall function is to have the person turn his back while you say the names of two pictures. Wait for a brief interval, then have the person turn around, look at the pictures, and tell you or point to the one whose name he heard first.

   Increase the pictures to three after two are mastered at high correct frequency.

7. Present the names of the pictures about one second apart.

   The complexity of the activity may be increased by naming three pictures, but presenting *more* than three pictures from which to choose.

1. LISTEN CAREFULLY. I'LL SAY A WORD. REMEMBER IT. SAY IT BACK TO ME WHEN I SIGNAL. I'LL HELP YOU AT FIRST.
   "BOY"
   LET'S SAY IT TOGETHER.
   "BOY." SAY IT AFTER ME. "BOY."
   SAY "BOY" WHEN I SIGNAL.

2. I'LL SAY A WORD. WAIT FOR THE SIGNAL BEFORE YOU SAY IT BACK.

   LET'S DO IT WITH TWO WORDS. LISTEN CAREFULLY. I'LL SAY THE WORDS. REMEMBER THEM. SAY THEM BACK TO ME WHEN I SIGNAL. I'LL HELP YOU AT FIRST.
   "BALL"   "HOUSE"
   LET'S SAY IT TOGETHER. "BALL"   "HOUSE."
   SAY IT AFTER ME. "BALL" "HOUSE."
   SAY "BALL" "HOUSE" WHEN I SIGNAL.

3. LET'S REMEMBER MORE WORDS.
   I'LL SAY THEM FIRST, YOU REMEMBER THEM.
   (Continue as in step 2.)

4. I'LL SAY SOME NUMBERS.
   REMEMBER THEM. SAY THEM BACK TO ME WHEN I SIGNAL. I'LL HELP YOU AT FIRST.
   "THREE" "ONE." LET'S SAY THEM TOGETHER.
   "THREE" "ONE." SAY THEM AFTER ME.
   "THREE" "ONE." SAY THEM WHEN I SIGNAL.
   "THREE" "ONE."

5. *Example*
   Let's go
   Let's go to the
   Let's go to the store
   Let's go to the store and buy
   Let's go to the store and buy a squirt
   Let's go to the store and buy a squirt gun.

6. I'LL SAY TWO WORDS. POINT TO THE PICTURE OF THE WORD YOU HEARD FIRST.
   "HOUSE"
   "BALL"
   TURN AROUND. TELL ME WHICH NAME YOU HEARD FIRST.

7. NOW TELL ME WHICH PICTURE I NAMED FIRST, SECOND, AND LAST.
   "BALL"
   "BOY"
   "TREE"

8. Another activity may be to play a memory game in which each person verbally adds to the list of things which were "seen" or "done" on an imaginary trip. As his turn occurs, the person attempts to name the entire list in order (or as close to the order as possible). The game may be played at varying complexity levels, e.g., *easy:* name only three nouns, name only three verbs. *more difficult:* name an adjective and a noun (noun phrase); name a noun and verb object (e.g., "boy running"). *most difficult:* add to noun and verb phrase groups as the round robin continues to the limit of the student's ability to remember.

Give the person time to think. Wait for his responses.

8. *Example of memory game*
I WENT TO THE PARK, AND AT THE PARK
I SAW_____.

Other examples of topics
DISNEYLAND
BASEBALL GAME
SCHOOL
THE BEACH
HOME
FARM
GRANDPA'S HOUSE
OUTSIDE
THE FAIR
THE SHOW
PLAYGROUND
GROCERY STORE
RESTAURANT
DIME STORE
SHOE STORE
FIREHOUSE
UNDER WATER
TO THE NORTH POLE
COUNTRY
MOUNTAINS
BOATING
ATTIC/BASEMENT
IN AN AIRPLANE
IN A CAR
TO A CHRISTMAS SHOP

Grammatical Closure and Sequential Memory: Sentence Completion

Materials. Sentences, phrases, pictures.

Criterion. Level IV
Twenty consecutively correct sentences produced with varying words omitted from the cue.

Purpose. To use auditory closure and sequential memory in verbal productions.

Demonstration Sequence

1. Prepare a number of easy two-word sentences from pictures or lists.

2. Level II.

3. Wait for the person to say the word "smile." If he does not, supply the word.

4. Level II.

5. Wait for the person to say the word "barn." If he does not, supply the word.

6. Proceed on through two-word phrases until the sentence can be completed with only minimal repetitions of the sentence.

7. As the ability to complete two-word combinations develops, proceed with three-word combinations, leaving out various words.

   After the idea has been established in three-word sentences, model subsequent three-word sentences as little as possible, pausing at the appropriate place where the word is to be supplied.

   Do not provide words unless you must. Make up sentences of varying length.

8. An added activity may be to produce a sentence with various words missing. Model each sentence form with the words missing. Wait for the person to fill in the words.

1. *Examples*
BIG SMILE	ROUND BALL
RED BARN	LONG WALK
MY HAT	SUNNY DAY

2. BIG SMILE. SAY "BIG SMILE" WITH ME.

3. FINISH THE SENTENCE.
   SAY "BIG_____."

4. RED BARN.
   FINISH THE SENTENCE WITH ME. RED BARN.

5. FINISH THE SENTENCE. SAY "RED_____."

6. MY HAT. FINISH THE SENTENCE.
   "MY_____."

7. IT IS MINE. IT IS_____ .
   IT_____ MINE.
   IT IS MINE._____ IS_____ .
   _____ _____ MINE.

8. *Example*
   I'LL SAY A SENTENCE. LISTEN CAREFULLY AND REMEMBER IT.

   FILL IN THE MISSING WORDS.

   THE BOY RAN UP THE STREET.
   THE_____ RAN UP THE STREET.
   THE BOY_____ UP THE STREET.
   THE BOY RAN UP THE_____ .
   THE_____ RAN_____ THE STREET.
   THE_____ _____ _____THE_____ .

Grammatical Closure: Sentence Completion Dd

Materials. Sentences, pictures.

Criterion. Level IV
Twenty consecutively correct sentence productions made from skeletal sentences.

Purpose. To utilize the grammatical verbal sequential closure function by completing sentences presented in skeletal form.

Demonstration Sequence

1. Model a skeletal sentence. Do not provide the missing word(s). The missing words are to be provided by the person. If the person is unable to supply, suggest them yourself.

   Begin with very easy sentences, gradually increasing the number of words in the sentence along with grammatical complexity. Be sure the phrases and sentences make sense.

2. Any one of a number of words may serve to complete the sentence. Provide cues only if absolutely necessary.

3. Once the person has the idea of sentence completion by fitting in the missing last word, provide a sentence with a word *other* than the last missing.

   Again, more than one word may be chosen to complete the sentence.

   Model the sentence first. Then request that it be finished.

4. Gradually increase the number of words which are left out of the sentence. By this time the idea of what is required should be clearly established.

5. From this point on, provide any skeletal sentence format around which a sentence can be built. Intermix these.

6. An alternative activity may be to provide skeletal sentences with the auxiliary verbs present. The person is then asked to fill in as many completions as he is able for each skeletal sentence. Use auxiliary verbs "is" and "can." The noun subject may also be changed. This activity may also serve as a written exercise in which the person *writes* the answers for as many sentences as you provide. If necessary, place answers somewhere on the page and instruct the client to select the correct ones and write them where they belong.

1. I'LL START A SENTENCE. YOU FINISH IT WITH YOUR OWN WORD(S).
   SHARP *(knife)*
   FALL *(down)*
   FILL *(up)*
   GO TO THE *(store)*
   PICK UP THE *(package)*
   SWIM IN THE *(pool)*

3. THE *(sky)* IS BLUE.
   MY *(foot)* HURTS.
   THE *(knife)* IS SHARP.
   THOSE *(flowers)* ARE PRETTY.

4. THOSE *(boys)* ARE *(big)*.
   THOSE *(girls)* ARE *(pretty)*.
   THE *(sun)* IS *(hot)*.
   MY *(stomach)* IS *(full)*.
   I *(like)* *(to)* *(swim)*.
   WILL YOU *(go)* *(today)*?
   WE *(would)* *(like)* SOME HELP.
   CAN YOU *(jump)* *(rope)*?

6. *Examples*
   A MOUNTAIN IS _____.
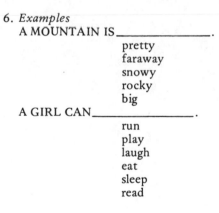

   A GIRL CAN_____.

Materials. Noun pictures, objects, verb referent pictures. Persons to model verbs.

Criterion. Level IV
Twenty consecutively produced subject + verb + object sentences.

Purpose. To assist the person in learning basic sentence production by practicing simplified (nongrammatical) constructions.

Demonstration Sequence

1. Subject, verb, and object names should be known before beginning this set. Return to Section C activities if this is necessary.

   Show picture, object, and act out the accompanying verb if that is possible. Combine pictures and objects.

   Attempt as much as possible to relate the subject + verb + object sentences to the world of the person. Make up a list of your own which is more relevant.

   This may be a set at which you wish to remain for a long period of time while vocabulary usage in the three-word combinations presented here is developing.

1. *Examples*

Subject	+ Verb	+ Noun Object
BOY	FALL	FLOOR
BABY	SLEEP	CRIB
GIRL	RUN	HOME
JOHNNY	THROW	BALL
MARY	TIE	SHOELACE
TEACHER	GIVE	SMILE
I	GET	DRINK
I	HAVE	DIME
I	HAVE	SHIRT
I	OPEN	WINDOW
SUE	BUY	PRESENT
TEACHER	STAND	FLOOR
BILLY	CLOSE	DOOR
TODD	GO	SCHOOL
I	GO	BATHROOM
MARY	CUT	PAPER
BOY	SKATE	ICE
BILLY	READ	BOOK
SALLY	CUT	FINGER
MOMMY	COOK	SUPPER
I	HELP	TEACHER
I	PAINT	PICTURE
I	DRAW	PICTURE
I	CALL	BILLY
TEACHER	POUR	MILK
I	WAVE	TEACHER
JOHN	CLIMB	FENCE
TIM	BLOW	BALLOON
I	LIFT	BOX
GIRL	PULL	STRING
I	LISTEN	MUSIC
I	TURN	FAUCET
I	TURN	DOORKNOB
I	MOVE	CHAIR
TIM	PICK	JOHN
BILLY	CATCH	BALL

Materials. Negative sentences.

Criterion. Level IV
Twenty consecutively correct negatives used in sentences.

Purpose. To teach the use of negatives by providing transformational practice in sentence form.

Demonstration Sequence

1. Practice the nontransformed version first. Immediately after the first sentence, provide the sentence containing the negative.

2. Practice each through Levels II, III, and IV.

3. When a number of sentences with negatives have been established, model a sentence, but do *not* provide the negative.

   Allow the person to produce the negative spontaneously.

Examples

THANK YOU.
NO THANK YOU.

SOME FOR ME.
NONE FOR ME.

SOMETHING ELSE.
NOTHING ELSE.

SOME MORE NOW.
NO MORE NOW.

MORE COOKIES.
NO MORE COOKIES.

SOMETHING NOW.
NOTHING NOW.

ENOUGH WATER.
NOT ENOUGH WATER.

LET'S DO IT.
DON'T DO IT.

LET'S GO.
LET'S NOT GO.

WE'LL GO.
WE'LL NOT GO.

COME!
DO NOT COME.

DO THIS.
DON'T DO THAT.

I WANT SOME.
I DON'T WANT ANY.

THEY WANT SOME.
THEY DON'T WANT ANY.

THERE IS SOME LEFT.
THERE IS NO MORE.

SHE WANTS IT.
SHE DOES NOT WANT IT.

THE LAMP IS BROKEN.
THE LAMP IS NOT BROKEN.

THEY CAME.
THEY DID NOT COME.

SOMETHING IS IN THE BOX.
NOTHING IS IN THE BOX.

THE WINDOW OPENS.
THE WINDOW DOES NOT OPEN.

THE CAR WILL START.
THE CAR WILL NOT START.

THE BASKET IS HEAVY.
THE BASKET IS NOT HEAVY.

THE GLASS WAS FULL.
THE GLASS WAS NOT FULL.

Learning "Is" in Present Indicative

Materials. Objects, pictures.

Criterion. Level IV
Twenty consecutively correct productions of "This is a + noun" sentences.

Purpose. To teach the use of "is" as the present indicative form of the verb "to be" (infinitive) or "be."

Demonstration Sequence

1. Study the example. The carrier phrase should accompany each naming. Proceed through Levels II, III, and IV with a variety of selected objects and pictures which are known to the student. Utilize as many "nouns + is" from each picture as possible.

2. Present the picture or object. Level II.

3. Level III.

4. Level IV.

   Accept contracted versions such as "This's a ball."
   Continue to model "is" clearly, however.

1. *Example*

   Carrier Phrase   *plus*   *Noun*
   THIS IS A or AN   Any object, picture, room part, etc.

2. SAY THIS WITH ME.
   THIS IS A BALL.

3. I'LL SAY IT, THEN YOU SAY IT BACK.
   FINISH THE SENTENCE FOR ME.

4. THIS _____ A BALL.
         (person completes)

Learning "Is" with an Adjective

Materials. Objects, pictures, word list of adjectives.

Criterion. Level IV
Twenty consecutively correct "is" sentences with a complement.

Purpose. To teach the use of "is" in conjunction with an adjective functioning as a predicate complement.

Demonstration Sequence

1. Select which nouns and adjectives you will use in each carrier phrase. Use as many pictures as possible to provide visual referents. Practice each new phrase through Levels II, III, and IV.

   Accept contracted productions such as "he's big, she's pretty, it's heavy, the stove's hot." Present the object or picture. Level II.

3. Level III.

4. Level IV.

1. *Examples* from pictures or object referents.

   Carrier Phrase   *plus*   *Complement*
   THE _____ IS _____ .
       (noun)   (adjective)

   THE STOVE IS HOT.
   HE IS BIG.
   SHE IS PRETTY.
   IT IS HEAVY.

   Example
   SAY THIS WITH ME. THE STOVE IS HOT.

3. I'LL SAY IT, THEN YOU SAY IT BACK. THE STOVE IS HOT.

4. FINISH THE SENTENCE FOR ME.
   THE STOVE _____ HOT.
             (person completes)

Materials. Action words in Most Commonly Occurring Words, Appendix I, pictures.

Criterion. Level IV Twenty consecutively correct productions of "is" with an "ing" verb in a sentence.

Purpose. To teach "is" in conjunction with the present participle "ing" of of another verb to express continuation. These "ing" words are active participles which are verb forms used as adjectives.

Demonstration Sequence

1. Ready the group of pictures and/or action sentences which you will use.

2. Provide the carrier phrase and supply the "ing" verb. As you do so, provide any movement or gestures.

3. Practice through Levels II, III, and IV.

   Accept contracted productions such as "He's smiling, she's smiling, it's going, the tree's growing."

4. Present the pictures and/or model the action. Level II.

5. Level III.

6. Level IV.

1. *Examples*

Carrier Phrase	*plus*	*Pres. Part.* *"ing" Verb*
HE IS		SMILING.
SHE IS		SMILING.
IT IS		GOING.

or

Person's name	
JOHNNY IS	RUNNING.
THE TREE IS	GROWING.
THE GIRL IS	GROWING.
THE BOY IS	GROWING.

4. SAY THIS WITH ME. HE IS SMILING.

5. I'LL SAY IT, THEN YOU SAY IT BACK. HE IS SMILING.

6. FINISH THE SENTENCE FOR ME.
   HE _____SMILING.
   (person completes)

   WHAT IS HE DOING?
   HE _____SMILING.
   (person completes)

   SAY THE SENTENCE. Person completes:
   HE IS SMILING.

   Example
   HE'S SMILING.
   IT'S GOING.
   THE TREE'S GROWING, ETC.

Learning to Use Pronouns with "Is"

Materials. Pictures, objects, persons.

Criterion. Level IV
Twenty consecutively correct pronouns produced in simple sentences.

Purpose. To establish the use of pronouns in basic sentence patterns.

Demonstration Sequence

1. Action words, nouns, person's and picture-object names should be known prior to this set.

   Begin at the most suitable level. Use any gesture or motion which helps to illustrate the pronoun.

1. *Examples of pronouns*

ALL	IT	THEIR
ANOTHER	IT'S	THEM
BOTH	ME	THESE
EACH	MINE	THIS
FEW	MY	THEY
HE	MYSELF	THOSE
HER	ONE	US
HERSELF	OTHER	WE
HIM	OUR	WHAT
HIMSELF	SHE	WHICH
HIS	SOME	WHO
I	THAT	YOU (YOUR)

2. Establish the noun referent(s) first. A male and female are needed. Have each person produce some easily recognizable action word.

   Point to Johnny. Emphasize "he." Accept contractions, e.g., "He's" or simply "He Johnny."

   Level II.

   Level III.

   Level IV.

2. *Examples:* Pronouns are "he, she."
   MARY IS POINTING.
   JOHNNY IS POINTING.

   WE CAN TALK ABOUT MARY AND JOHNNY ANOTHER WAY. WE CAN SAY:
   HE IS POINTING.
   HE IS JOHNNY.
   SAY "*HE* IS POINTING" WITH ME.
   HE IS POINTING.
   HE IS JOHNNY.
   SAY IT AFTER ME. *HE* IS JOHNNY.
   Person says: *HE* IS JOHNNY.
   HE IS POINTING.
   Person says: *HE* IS POINTING.
   SAY IT AGAIN. *HE* IS POINTING.
   Person says: *HE* IS POINTING.
   Person says: *HE* IS POINTING.

3. Point to Mary. Emphasize "she." Accept "she's" or simply "she pointing." Level II.

   Level III. Therapist models sentence first.

   Level IV. Sentence is not repeated by therapist.

3. *SHE* IS POINTING.
   SHE IS MARY.
   SAY "*SHE* IS POINTING" WITH ME.
   SHE IS MARY.
   SHE IS POINTING.
   SAY IT AFTER ME. *SHE* IS POINTING.
   Person says: *SHE* IS POINTING.
   SAY IT AGAIN. *SHE* IS POINTING.
   Person says: *SHE* IS POINTING.

4. Intermix "he" and "she" with the verb "pointing." Select other action words which are known by the students.

   Repeat "he" and "she" with these.

   Accept contractions (he's, she's).

4. HE IS SITTING.
   HE IS STANDING.
   HE IS HOPPING.
   HE IS SMILING.

   SHE IS SKIPPING.
   SHE IS FOLLOWING.
   SHE IS CATCHING.
   SHE IS BRUSHING.

5. Assemble a number of like objects. Point to one ball at a time.

   Point to a ball. Emphasize "it." Accept "it's a ball" or simply "it a ball."

5. *Examples:* Pronouns are "it" and "another."
   A BALL (object 1)
   A BALL (object 2)
   A BALL (object 3)
   A BALL (object 4)

Level II.

Level III.

Level IV.

WE CAN TALK ABOUT THE BALLS ANOTHER WAY.
WE CAN SAY:
IT IS A BALL.
SAY IT WITH ME.
IT IS A BALL.
SAY IT AFTER ME.
IT IS A BALL.
Person says:
IT IS A BALL.
SAY *IT* IS A BALL.
Person says:
IT IS A BALL.
SAY IT AGAIN.
Person says:
IT IS A BALL.

6. Point to a second ball. Pick it up and hand it to the person. Emphasize "another."

   Level II.

   Accept "Here's another ball" or simply "another ball."

6.

   HERE IS *ANOTHER* BALL.
   SAY IT WITH ME. HERE IS *ANOTHER* BALL.
   OR HERE'S *ANOTHER* BALL.
   OR *ANOTHER* BALL.

7. Pick up a ball. Emphasize "my." Hand the ball to the person. Level III.

   Level IV.

7. HERE IS *MY* BALL.
   SAY "HERE IS *MY* BALL."
   Person says: HERE IS *MY* BALL.

   SAY IT AGAIN.
   Person says: HERE IS *MY* BALL.

8. Point to the ball which the person is holding.

   Hand the child another ball.

8. THERE IS *YOUR* BALL.

   HERE IS *YOUR* BALL.

9. Repeat the action of step 8 with the participant performing the pointing and handing of the ball to the therapist.

   Level III.

9. SAY "THERE IS *YOUR* BALL."
   SAY "HERE IS *YOUR* BALL."

   SAY IT WITH ME. THERE IS *YOUR* BALL.
   HERE IS *YOUR* BALL.

10. Repeat various levels and steps often. Go on to new pronouns providing help with illustrative gestures as needed. On occasion, more than two persons will be needed to teach such pronouns as "their," "them," etc.

Learning "Is" and "Are" with Pronouns and Nouns

Materials. Pictures, objects.

Criterion. Level IV
Twenty consecutively correct four-word
"are" and "is" sentences.

Purpose. To teach the use of "is" and
"are" utilizing practice with various
pronouns and nouns in four-word
sentences.

Demonstration Sequence

1. Establish which four-word sentence you will teach the person from selected pictures.

2. Repeat each sentence at Levels II through IV. Accompany any sentence with appropriate gestures.

3. Accept such contracted verb forms with pronouns as "it's, this's, that's, he's, she's."

1. *Examples*

Pronoun +	is +	Poss. Pronoun or Person's Name +	Noun or Pronoun
IT	IS	HIS	BALL.
THIS	IS	MARY'S	DRESS.
THAT	IS	JOHNNY'S	HAND.
THIS	IS	MY	SHOE.
THIS	IS	YOUR	EYE.
HE	IS	MY	FRIEND.
SHE	IS	MY	FRIEND.
THESE	ARE	MY	THINGS.
THOSE	ARE	SALLY'S	TOYS.
THEY	ARE	OUR	PENCILS.
WE	ARE	ALL	PEOPLE.
YOU	ARE	HER	FRIEND.
SOME	ARE	BOBBY'S	THINGS.
THESE	ARE	OUR	NOSES.

4. An alternative activity is to focus on one form of pronoun, "be" verb, and noun. Place a picture or object referent or group of noun pictures in view of the client. Point to it. Provide the stimulus sentences.

4. *Example*

THAT	IS	A	CAR.
THAT	IS	A	BARN.
THAT	IS	A	BALL.
THAT	IS	A	BOY.
THAT	IS	A	GIRL.

Using Adjectives as Predicate Complements

Materials. Predicate complement sentences, pictures.

Criterion. Level IV
Twenty consecutively correct adjectives used as predicate complements.

Purpose. To teach the use of adjectives which describe or explain the subject of the sentence. These adjectives, appearing as they do in the predicate part of the sentence, are called *predicate complements.*

Demonstration Sequence

1. Using the examples as models, generate other sentences from your pictures.

2. Cover many sentences. Proceed through them at the highest level of which the person is capable.

   An added "make up your own" component at Level V may also be included.

3. Accept contracted productions of the "be" verb copula as a linking verb in the predicate part of the sentence, e.g., "girl's happy, grass's green."

1. *Examples*

Pronoun or Article +	*Noun* +	*Verb* +	*Adjective Complement*
THE	GIRL	IS	PRETTY.
THE	CHILDREN	ARE	SMALL.
HIS	MOTHER	IS	KIND.
THE	BABY	IS	HAPPY.
HIS	CLOTHES	ARE	DIRTY.
THE	GLOVES	ARE	HIS.
HIS	JACKET	IS	GREEN.
THEIR	COATS	ARE	WARM.
THE	DRESS	IS	LONG.
THE	BELT	IS	BIG.
THE	CLOTHES	ARE	CLEAN.
THE	TOMATO	IS	RED.
THE	PEAS	ARE	GREEN.
THE	TOAST	IS	WARM.
THE	COOKIES	ARE	HARD.
THE	NAPKINS	ARE	WHITE.
THE	GLASS	IS	FULL.
THE	BREAD	IS	FRESH.
THE	CAKE	IS	BEST.
THE	CLOUDS	WERE	DARK.
THE	GRASS	IS	GREEN.
THE	TREES	ARE	TALL.
THE	BOY	IS	TALL.
HER	FRIENDS	ARE	YOUNG.

4. An alternative expansion of the sentence form would be to add a conjunction and adjective to the sentence already formed to include the predicate complement.

4. *Example*
THE TREES ARE TALL *AND GREEN.*

Expanding the Use of "Is"

Materials. "Is" expansion list (attached), pictures.

Criterion. Level IV Thirty consecutively correct productions of "is" in varying syntactic constructions.

Purpose. To teach the usage of "is" in an increasing variety of syntactic environments.

Demonstration Sequence

1. Select which pictures you will use. Study the "is" model sentences on succeeding pages. Select the model(s) which is most suitable and begin there. If in doubt, begin with the NP + is + Adv., Adj., Prep., or NP and work your way through the sentences.

   Present pictures or model the sentence without a picture stimulus. Level III.

   Level IV.

   Accept contracted copula productions with all sentences if that is more natural for the student: "Her room's next to mine, That car's red, The blanket's warm."

1. I'LL SAY THE SENTENCE, THEN YOU SAY IT. LITTLE DAVID IS A GOOD BOY.

   FINISH THE SENTENCE. LITTLE DAVID___ __ _____ ___.

   WHAT IS LITTLE DAVID? HE___ __ _____ ___.

"Is" Expansion List

Noun Phrase	"Be" Verb	Adverb Phrase, Adjective Phrase, Prepositional Phrase, or Noun Phrase
Little David	is	a good boy.
The car	is	there.
My car	is	there.
That car	is	red.
Our house	is	in the country.
Her school	is	far away.
Her sister	is	a pretty girl.
His coat	is	bright green.
The blanket	is	very warm.
The match	is	over there.
The brown horse	is	back there.
The football player	is	very big.
The old man	is	across the street.

Noun Phrase	"Be" Verb	Adverb Phrase, Adjective Phrase, Prepositional Phrase, or Noun Phrase
Her new suit	is	in the closet.
Their father	is	out of work.
The orange juice	is	ice cold.
The old turtle	is	moving slowly.
Her mother	is	a good cook.
Her father	is	a good mechanic.
The little girl	is	all alone.
The red rose	is	most beautiful.
The broom	is	behind the door.
Her room	is	next to mine.
His room	is	down the hall.
The gray mouse	is	under the carpet.

Person's Name He She It	is	"ing" Verb	Prepositional Phrase
Joan	is	going	to the store.
She	is	riding	on a horse.
He	is	playing	across the street.
Mary	is	laughing	at a joke.
She	is	looking	for her bracelet.
He	is	fighting	with his brother.
It	is	snowing	in the mountains.
She	is	sitting	between her parents.
He	is	leaning	against the fence.
Henry	is	picking	up the papers.
Susan	is	running	down the street.
He	is	watering	with a hose.

Person's Name He She It	is	"ing" Verb	Prepositional Phrase
Bobby	is	skiing	down the mountain.
She	is	staying	at the hotel.
He	is	smiling	at the children.
Billy	is	walking	next to his father.
Jerry	is	crawling	across the floor.
She	is	skipping	around the yard.
He	is	growing	out of his clothes.
She	is	sailing	across the lake.
He	is	moving	from the city.
She	is	beginning	to like them.

Article	Noun Object	is	Prepositional Phrase
The	boy	is	on the grass.
The	girl	is	under the table.
The	dog	is	in the car.
An	apple	is	on the table.
The	coffee	is	in the pot.
The	carpet	is	on the floor.
The	dog	is	across the street.
The	cat	is	under the couch.
The	store	is	around the corner.
A	tree	is	next to the house.
The	school	is	near the park.
A	blanket	is	on the bed.
A	cloth	is	over the table.

Article	Noun Object	is	Prepositional Phrase
The	boy	is	with his friends.
The	present	is	for your birthday.
The	television	is	in the living room.
The	lamp	is	between the chairs.
The	boy	is	at the circus.
The	teacher	is	behind the desk.
The	girl	is	without her coat.
The	fence	is	around the house.
The	stove	is	in the kitchen.
The	chair	is	by the lamp.
The	farm	is	along the way.
The	sun	is	beyond the earth.
The	nest	is	in the tree.

Pronoun or Adverb	+ is +	Possessive Article	+ Adjective	+ Noun		Pronoun or Adverb	+ is +	Possessive Article	+ Adjective	+ Noun
There	is	my	big	hat.		It	is	a	good	hamburger.
It	is	a	nice	day.		She	is	my	best	friend.
It	is	a	green	ball.		He	is	a	good	worker.
Here	is	the	lost	dog.		This	is	my	favorite	game.
Mine	is	the	blue	coat.		It	is	a	sweet	pie.
There	is	her	pretty	picture.		There	is	our	beautiful	mother.
This	is	his	pet	pig.		Here	is	her	red	coat.
It	is	a	clear	day.		It	is	a	heavy	blanket
Hers	is	the	other	one.		He	is	a	kind	person.
His	is	a	big	horse.		He	is	an	airline	pilot.
There	is	our	summer	home.		Hers	is	the	little	doll.
Here	is	my	last	dollar.		There	is	the	football	player.
It	is	a	hot	day.		Mine	is	a	bright	color.

Coordinate Transformations: Making Two Sentences One Sentence or Making One Sentence Two Sentences

Materials. Objects, pictures, Key Sentences.

Criterion. Level IV
Twenty consecutively correct sentences which demonstrate the coordinate function.

Purpose. To teach the usage of coordinate or binary transformational patterns by deriving one sentence from two sentences and/or two sentences from one longer sentence.

Demonstration Sequence

1. The parts of speech that are utilized in this set should have been practiced previously. The examples provide only a reference point from which to work. Examine your pictures and objects and generate the sentences from those.

   Place the object or picture in clear view. Model each sentence as needed. As soon as possible, require that the person produce the desired sentence transformation at Level IV. Prior to this, however, he may require rehearsal at Levels II and III.

   An activity may be to array many clearly recognizable pictures on a table and go through the entire group quickly, generating derived sentences continually. The child may produce all three sentences in each practice group if he is able.

   Reverse the order and present one longer sentence from which two shorter sentences are produced which contain the elements of the first sentence.

1. *Examples*

Pronoun	+	*Verb*	+	*Article*	+	*Noun*
		"be"				
THIS		IS		A		BALL.

   and

Article	+	*Noun*	+	*Verb*	+	*Adjective*
				"be"		
THE		BALL		IS		RED.

   Derivation

Pronoun	+	*Verb*	+	*Article*	+	*Adjective*	+	*Noun*
THIS		IS		A		RED		BALL.

   Other examples
   THIS IS A BOOK.
   THE BOOK IS BLUE.
   THIS IS A BLUE BOOK.

Producing Expanded Sentences Using "Is" and Other Subjects, Verbs, Prepositions, and Objects of the Preposition

Do

Materials. Key Sentences lists, objects, pictures.

Criterion. Level IV
Twenty consecutively correct sentences with "is" and various subjects, verbs, prepositions, and objects of prepositions.

Purpose. To provide expanded sentence practice using the "be" verb "is" as a control element and using certain key formats as basic sentence patterns.

Demonstration Sequence

1. Refer to the Key Sentences provided on succeeding pages and/or use your set of pictures to generate visual cues.

   Select the format you will practice first. Proceed through other Key Sentence patterns as needed.

   Provide any visual picture or demonstration cues which apply to the sentence group.

   Originate your own Key Sentence patterns using those presented here and your pictures as guides.

1. THE BOY IS SITTING ON THE FLOOR.
   SAY IT AFTER ME.
   THE BOY IS SITTING ON THE FLOOR.
   SAY IT.
   Person says:
   THE BOY IS SITTING ON THE FLOOR.

Key Sentence: Subjects

Article	Subject	Verb	Preposition	Article	Object of Preposition
The	boy	is sitting	on	the	floor.
	girl				
	child				
	farmer				
	dog				
	cat				
	man				
	woman				
	teacher				
	family				
	father				
	mother				
	player				
	gardner				
	squirrel				
	racoon				
	bear				
	fireman				
	milkman				
	lady				
	baby				
	brother				
	sister				
	policeman				

Article	Subject	Verb	Preposition	Article	Object of Preposition
The	animal	is sitting	on	the	floor.
	youngster				
	infant				
	grand-mother				
	grand-father				
	student				
	artist				
	neighbor				
	visitor				
	guest				
	friend				
	mommy				
	daddy				
	worker				
	uncle				
	aunt				
	group				
	class				
	rabbit				
	chipmunk				
	skier				
	skater				

Key Sentence: Verbs

Article	Subject	Verb	Preposition	Article	Object of Preposition
The	girl	is sitting	in	the	room.
		is playing			
		is sewing			
		is studying			
		is working			
		is singing			
		is dancing			
		is jumping			
		is cooking			
		is fighting			
		is painting			
		is eating			
		is hopping			
		is skipping			
		is crawling			

Article	Subject	Verb	Preposition	Article	Object of Preposition
The	girl	is looking	in	the	room.
		is sleeping			
		is crying			
		is exercising			
		is dressing			
		is cleaning			
		is frowning			
		is drinking			
		is moving			
		is living			
		is lying			
		is reading			
		is remaining			
		is speaking			
		is staying			

Article	Subject	Verb	Preposition	Article	Object of Preposition
The	girl	is laughing	in	the	room.
		is hiding			
		is running			
		is standing			
		is talking			
		is writing			

Article	Subject	Verb	Preposition	Article	Object of Preposition
The	girl	is rolling	in	the	room.
		is sneezing			
		is turning			
		is vacuuming			
		is ironing			
		is screeming			

Key Sentence: Prepositions

Article	Subject	Verb	Preposition	Article	Object of Preposition
A	dog	is sleeping	in	the	box.
			under		
			by		
			near		
			inside		
			beneath		
			above		
			below		
			against		
			on		
			behind		
			across		
The	girl	is running	in	the	street.
			near		
			toward		
			around		
			across		
			by		

Article	Subject	Verb	Preposition	Article	Object of Preposition
The	girl	is running	into	the	street.
			down		
			from		
			past		
			to		
			beside		
			up		
			along		
			through		
			over		
The	boy	is walking	with	the	girl.
			toward		
			without		
			beside		
			next to		
			from		
			behind		
			beyond		

Key Sentence: Object of Preposition

Article	Subject	Verb	Preposition	Article	Object of Preposition
A	boy	is sitting	in	the	box.
					tree
					chair
					room
					library
					closet
					bathtub
					garden
					car
					house
					pool
					river
					street
					playroom
					puddle
					bus
					truck
					swing
					sandbox
					field
					corner
					hall

Article	Subject	Verb	Preposition	Article	Object of Preposition
A	boy	is sitting	in	the	barn.
					bank
					buggy
					driveway
					forest
					gutter
					circle
					sink
					taxi
					train
					church
					classroom
					park
					hole
					ditch
					creek
					kitchen
					bedroom
					restaurant
					canoe
					boat

Building Sentences: "Wh" Questions and Other Interrogatives   Dp

Materials. "Wh" questions lists, objects, pictures.

Criterion. Level IV
Twenty consecutively correct "wh" questions and answers.

Purpose. To provide sentence building practice by teaching emerging transformations in the form of interrogative pronouns and adverbs along with other demonstrative pronouns.

Demonstration Sequence

1. Using the examples, establish a group of "wh" questions which you will develop into sentences. These will form the basic working format for this set. Select these from your group of pictures and/or objects.

2. Identify a series of objects, pictures, parts of a room, etc. The person is to ask the question prior to each new item. He may then answer it himself.

   Do not elaborate on each question. State it and go on.

   Practice at Levels III and IV.

3. Once the person has the question-asking concept established, proceed with the other pronouns or adverbs noted in the example. Use concrete referents which have visual answers at first.

   Model as in Level III only enough to initiate the procedure. Continue only at Level IV after that.

4. Proceed with the more abstract "wh" questions. Model as in Level III only when necessary. Otherwise remain at Level IV.

   Accept contractions such as "what's that?"

   Photographs of individual children, parents, friends, etc., will be helpful in establishing the "who?" pronoun. Pictures might be arranged and fastened to a large piece of cardboard.

1. *Examples*

WHAT	WHEN
WHO	WHERE
WHICH	WHY
WHOSE	HOW (Interrogative)

2. *Examples*
   WHAT IS THAT? THAT IS A _____ .
   ASK THE QUESTION YOURSELF.
   Person says:
   WHAT IS THAT? THAT IS A _____ .
   or THAT'S A _____ .

3. *Example (pointing to Mary's dress)*
   WHOSE DRESS IS THAT? IT IS MARY'S.
   ASK THE QUESTION YOURSELF.
   Person says:
   WHOSE DRESS IS THAT? IT IS MARY'S.
   or IT'S MARY'S.

4. *Example*
   WHEN WILL WE EAT LUNCH? AT TWELVE O'CLOCK.

   WHERE WILL WE EAT LUNCH? IN THE CAFETERIA.

   WHY WILL WE EAT LUNCH? WE WILL BE HUNGRY.

   WHAT IS THE DOG DOING? THE DOG IS RUNNING.

   WHERE IS THE TOY AIRPLANE?
   THE TOY AIRPLANE IS IN THE BOX.

   HOW MANY TOYS ARE THERE?
   THERE ARE THREE TOYS.

   WHO IS THAT?
   THAT IS MARY.

   WHAT DO YOU WANT?
   I WANT A PENCIL.

   WHAT DO YOU SEE?
   I SEE A BOOK.

   WHAT COLOR IS THE BALL?
   THE BALL IS RED.

   WHAT DO YOU HAVE?
   I HAVE A PENCIL.

   HOW DO YOU FEEL?
   I FEEL FINE.

Learning "Am, Are, Was, Were," Using Pronouns, Adjectives, and Verbs

Materials. "am, are, was, and were" sentences, pictures.

Criterion. Level IV Twenty consecutively correct "am, are, was, and were" productions in sentences.

Purpose. To teach the use of the present indicative "be" verb (I) *am* and (we, you, they) *are*. Past indicative conjugations include (I, he, she, it) *was* and (we, you, they) were.

Demonstration Sequence

1. Examine the examples of sentences. Select those which appear to be most appropriate.

   Practice through Levels III and IV.

   Accept such contractions as I'm, they're, we're, you're, it's, that's, he's, she's, etc.

   Select any pictures which provide visual referents from which the sentence model can be generated.

1. *Examples*

Pronoun +	Verb +	Adjective, Verb, Pronoun
WE	ARE	HERE.
THOSE	ARE	YOURS.
WHOSE	ARE	THEY?
THEY	ARE	MINE.
YOU	ARE	NICE.
THESE	ARE	OURS.
OURS	WERE	THERE.
MANY	WERE	CALLED.
THEIRS	WERE	GREEN.
FEW	WERE	LEFT.
SOME	WERE	GONE.
IT	WAS	RUNNING.
WHAT	WAS	HAPPENING?
WHICH	WAS	YOURS?
WHOSE	WAS	THAT?
HERS	WAS	BEST.
THAT	WAS	GOOD.
YOURS	WAS	BLUE.
I	AM	FINE.
I	WAS	TIRED.

2. Present picture or provide the verbal stimulus. Level II.

2. *Examples*
SAY THIS WITH ME. WE ARE HERE.

3. Level III.

3. I'LL SAY IT, THEN YOU SAY IT BACK.

4. Level IV.

4. FINISH THE SENTENCE.
WE _____ _____ .
WHERE ARE WE?
WE _____ _____ .

Learning to Use Pronouns with Verbs:
Want – See – Have – Has

Materials. Pictures, objects, sentences.

Criterion. Level IV
Twenty consecutively correct sentences with want, see, have, has verbs.

Purpose. To teach the functional use of "want, see, and have" with pronoun preceding the verb and a noun phrase following the verb.

Demonstration Sequence

1. Select which noun referents you will use. Accompany any sentence with the appropriate action which accompanies the verb, e.g., if *you* "have" the airplane, actually pick up the airplane and hold it, so the person sees that you "have" the airplane.

   You may wish to precede each sentence with "What do you want (have or see)?"

1. *Examples*

Pronoun or Person's Name +	Want See Have	+ Noun Phrase
I	WANT	A BALL.
I	HAVE	A BALL.
I	SEE	A BALL.
I	WANT	THE BOAT.
I	HAVE	A BOAT.
I	HAVE	THE AIRPLANE.
I	SEE	THE AIRPLANE.

Continue with:

WE	WANT	A COOKIE.
YOU	SEE	A TREE.
THEY	HAVE	A PENCIL.

2. Once the "I, we, you," and "they" pronouns are established, go on to include "have" and "has." Be sure to emphasize the "s" ending on each verb when applicable.

2. *Examples*

MARY	WANTS	A PENCIL.
SHE	WANTS	A PENCIL.
BILLY	SEES	A BANANA.
HE	WANTS	A BANANA.
HE	HAS	A BANANA.
SALLY	HAS	A SORE.
SHE	WANTS	A BANDAGE.
SHE	SEES	THE SORE.

3. An alternative activity is to combine "want-wants, have-has," and "see-sees" in dual presentations.

3. *Examples*

I	WANT	A COOKIE.
MARY	WANTS	A COOKIE.
I	HAVE	A COOKIE.
MARY	HAS	A COOKIE.
I	SEE	A COOKIE.
MARY	SEES	A COOKIE.

4. An expanded form for practice may include combining completed sentence forms along with incomplete forms. The person then is to supply the missing pronoun. In this case we might add "they" and "it" to the list.

4. *Examples*

SUE WANTS A DRINK.
(SHE) WANTS A DRINK.

THE BOY HAS A BIKE.
(HE) HAS A BIKE.

THE ROCK IS BIG.
(IT) IS BIG.

MARY AND DON HAVE BOOKS.
(THEY) HAVE BOOKS.

JOHN AND TOM ARE BOYS.
(THEY) ARE BOYS.

THE SKY IS BLUE.
(IT) IS BLUE.

THE FROGS ARE HOPPING.
(THEY) ARE HOPPING.

Learning to Use Verbs: Past, Present, Future Tense

Ds

Materials. Verb tense sentences, pictures.

Criterion. Level IV
Twenty consecutively correct verb tenses in sentences.

Purpose. To teach the verb tense form that is appropriate to the thought.

Demonstration Sequence

1. Using the model sentence as a guide, formulate a list of your own which logically pertains to the student's needs. Select pictures that may provide visual cues.

   Model the present tense first.

   Then go to past. Be sure to specify the "ed" verb ending when applicable.

   Then go to the future.

   Practice each sentence through Levels III and IV or V. If the person can make up his own sentence at Level V, let him do so.

   Accept contracted "be" verb productions.

1. *Model*

		Adjective Phrase	*Adverb Phrase*
Noun + Verb +		or Adjective +	or Adverb

   Present: John is going home now.
   Past: John went home yesterday.

   Future: John will go home tomorrow.
   Present: Mary is reading the paper carefully.
   Past: Mary read the paper carefully yesterday.
   Future: Mary will read the paper carefully tomorrow.
   Present: Bill is combing his hair quickly.
   Past: Bill combed his hair quickly yesterday.
   Future: Bill will comb his hair quickly tomorrow.
   Present: Sam is running fast.
   Past: Sam ran fast.
   Future: Sam will run fast tomorrow.

Learning to Use Verbs: Actor – Action Sentences Dt

Materials. Actor—action sentences, pictures.

Criterion. Level IV
Twenty consecutively correct actor—action sentences.

Purpose. To teach actor—action sentences in mixed syntactic constructions.

Demonstration Sequence

1. The sentences presented on the succeeding page may be used as a guide which demonstrates the extent of sentence complexity at this level. From them you may generate more sentences of a similar form. Use your pictures as logical models from which to derive sentences. Practice each new sentence through Levels II, III, and IV.

Level II.

Level III.

Level IV.

Example

SAY THIS WITH ME. HE CLOSED THE WINDOW.

I'LL SAY IT, THEN YOU SAY IT BACK. HE CLOSED THE WINDOW.

SAY "HE CLOSED THE WINDOW." SAY IT AGAIN.

Examples of Actor—Action Sentences

Mommy put the car there.
Daddy drives the tractor.
He pours the milk.
She makes the beds.
I fly an airplane.
The farmer planted the corn.
He ran home.
The old man sat down.
The small child fell down.
His brother broke the truck.
The policeman stopped the cars.
The family went to church.
She swam in the river.
Mom and Dad danced to the music.

I washed the clothes.
The little boy blew up the balloon.
She is listening to the radio.
My brother fought with his friend.
Dad is watering the garden.
The dog is hiding under the table.
They worked hard this morning.
Mom made me a dress.
The frog hopped across the rocks.

I carried a basket.
Mom cooks the dinner.
He helps with painting.
She opened the door.
They ride horses.
She peeled the potatoes.
The chicken laid an egg.
The dog jumped the fence.
The other man got up.
She sang a happy song.
Her sister rode her bicycle.
The fireman put out the fire.
He fell and hurt his knee.
The boys climbed the mountain.

The children played in the park.
The football player threw the ball.
They are eating their dinner.
I got dressed in a hurry.
My mother brushed my hair.
He is eating a hamburger.
The bird built a nest in the tree.
The children visited their grandparents.
Dad paid for the bread and fruit.

Learning "ed" Verb Endings plus Past Tense Du

Materials. Verb pictures, verb list, objects, noun pictures, and a person to model verbs.

Criterion. Level IV
Twenty consecutively correct "ed" verb endings.

Purpose. To teach the past tense verb inflection by using "ed" endings as the primary vehicle.

Demonstration Sequence

1. Select the pronoun referents and verbs which most logically would form a part of the life of the person.

   Study the examples provided for ideas related to sentence forms.

   Practice with any accompanying pictures and persons who are to model the actions of the sentences. When this is not possible, model the sentence after first establishing noun and verb. Allow the student to participate. Wait a brief interval after modeling to illustrate the passage of time. Add the words "yesterday," "a minute ago," etc., if you think it is necessary to establish the "time past" concept more clearly.

   Omit the predicate part of the sentence if that appears to be redundant or too complicated.

1. *Examples:* "ed" verbs.

Mary	brushed	her hair.
They	rocked	the boat.
Jenny	opened	the window.
He	kicked	the tire.
They	tied	the knot.
John	worked	hard.
Sally	waved	goodby.
Todd	played	hard.
Bill	painted	the fence.
Daddy	paid	the bills.
We	opened	the presents.
Judy	closed	the door.
Shirley	pulled	the string.
They	danced	all night.
Mary	jumped	high.
She	burned	her arm.
Mary	skipped	home.
Billy	poured	a drink.
Cheryl	stopped	quickly.
Carlos	looked	at the floor.
We	brushed	our teeth.
The car	stopped	nearby.
She	pointed	her finger.
Sammy	turned	the page.
She	called	to us.
Bill	frowned	at us.
She	added	the numbers.
Mommy	asked	us.
We	learned	quickly.
They	crossed	the street.
Mommy	carried	me to bed.
I	loved	that song.
We	lifted	the table.
I	liked	her.
He	fielded	the ball.
We	knocked	quietly.
Diana	marked	the paper.

Learning to Use Verbs: Past Tense

Materials. Verb referents. Pronoun to model verbs. Objects.

Criterion. Level IV
Twenty consecutively correct verbs in sentence in past tense form.

Purpose. To teach the use of the past tense verb form.

Demonstration Sequence

1. Prearrange production practice so that as many visual referents as possible are present to provide a basis for sentence production.

2. In the absence of visual referents, model the sentence at Level III.

1. *Examples*

She	wrote	a letter.
The baby	slept	a long time.
We	stood	up.
They	sat	down.
They	drove	to the store.
He	felt	fine yesterday.
Mom	gave	me a present.
He	hid	the keys.
They	ate	their supper.
They	swam	across the pool.
We	blew	up the balloon.
They	left	yesterday.
The bird	flew	by.
She	caught	a cold.
Mom	gave	me a kiss.
She	got	it for me.
He	grew	tall.
I	lost	my voice.
We	dug	the hole.
Mommy	wound	her watch.
Sally	thought	carefully.

Materials. Verb phrases model, pictures.

Criterion. Level IV
Twenty consecutively correct verb phrase productions.

Purpose. To teach verbal sentences which include a verb plus or minus a particle, noun phrase, or prepositional phrase, and locator or demonstrator.

Demonstration Sequence

1. Select which sentences you will use from the Examples of Verb Phrase Constructions attached. These present logical verb phrase constructions that may form the basis for sentences you prepare from pictures or lists.

   Practice each new phrase through Levels II, III, and IV as needed.

2. Present pictures. Level II.

   Accompany any verb with logical movements or gestures. Level III.

   Level IV.

3. The following examples illustrate the sentence forms that you might generate from your set of pictures.

2. *Example*
   SAY THIS WITH ME. FLY A RED KITE.

   I'LL SAY IT, THEN YOU SAY IT BACK. FLY A RED KITE.

   SAY "FLY A RED KITE." SAY IT AGAIN. Person says: FLY A RED KITE.

Examples of Verb Phrase Constructions

Verb	+ Particle	+ Noun Phrase	and/or	*Prepositional Phrase*
Drive	in	the country		
Play	a	funny game		
Fly	a	red kite		
Dig	a	big hole		
Sleep	until	early morning		
Drink	the	warm milk		
See	the	baby chicks		
Start	the	new car		
Wash	the	dirty clothes		
Clean	up	the floor		
Pour	the	cold milk		
Eat	the	good dinner		

Verb	+ Particle	+ Noun Phrase	and/or	*Prepositional Phrase*
Wash	the	blue shirt		
Give	the	round ball		to John
Carry	it			in a box
Visit	them			during the day
Put	it			over there
Do	it			before you go
Ride				on a horse
Run				over there
Fly				above the clouds
Walk				along the ledge
Run				down the track
Go				with the others

Materials. Sentence transformations.

Criterion. Level IV
Twenty consecutively correct transformed sentence forms.

Purpose. To add to basic sentence
patterns by deriving transformed versions
of these same sentences according to
word order.

Demonstration Sequence

1. The sentences provided as examples constitute a basis
from which you may work in generating order sentence
transformations.

   Practice sentences through Levels III and IV.

   Use any pictures that may generate visual cues for the
sentence forms to be practiced here.

1. *Examples*

   My grandfather built this house.
   This house was built by my grandfather.

   My father drove the truck.
   The truck was driven by my father.

   My sister painted the picture.
   The picture was painted by my sister.

   Mom cleaned our laundry.
   Our laundry was cleaned by Mom.

   The barber cut his hair.
   His hair was cut by the barber.

   The boy and girl took the dog for a walk.
   The dog was taken for a walk by the boy and girl.

   All the students in the class took the test.
   The test was taken by all the students in the class.

   The pilot flew the airplane through the clouds.
   The airplane was flown through the clouds by the pilot.

   The girl sang a song for her friends.
   A song was sung by the girl for her friends.

Materials. Pictures, objects, storybooks.

Criterion. Level V
Fifty correct verbal sentences.

Purpose. To expand the use of connected sentences into natural, nonrote contexts.

Demonstration Sequence

1. Select, from the second column, one of the Selected Activities that is suitable for the person or group. Provide any sequence of cues which may be necessary.

   Practice at Level V if possible. However, you may have to demonstrate or repeat an activity or story a number of times before the person produces spontaneously.

   Use any storybooks, objects, or pictures that may assist conceptualization. Prepare a set of simple drawings that represent the important events of each story. These may be particularized to each student and may even bear the student's name.

   Some manufacturers provide sequenced cards which contain story pictures. Obtain these if possible.

   Have the person describe an object, picture, or person; e.g., the object is small, light, red. It is a ball. The person is young, a lady, pretty, etc.

   Describe the happenings of the day.

   Consider using any of the foregoing activities for use with your "nonstructured play" time (see Chapter 5).

2. You might also begin a "story" and have your student complete it. Provide as much stimulus as necessary, but no more than the minimum.

   Tell or read well-known stories, e.g., *The Three Bears, The Wizard of Oz.* Use accompanying pictures as cues. Have the students relate the sequence of events from the story.

3. Have one person teach an easy concept to others in the group; e.g., the activity of cutting out and coloring various forms may be performed while at the same time the person is "explaining" how to do it.

   Begin a story with each person contributing small bits until the last person in the group completes it. This can be a well-known story such as *The Three Little Pigs,* or it can occur creatively and spontaneously.

4. Have a word-defining contest in which each person in turn tells the meaning of a word. The words should be quite simple.

1. *Examples of selected activities*
   MAKE UP A STORY ABOUT_____.
   TELL US ABOUT_____.
   Fishing
   Being a hero
   What kids like to do most
   What scares me the most
   What to do at a birthday party
   What to do at the beach
   What to do in the snow
   Being a professional football player
   An insect war
   A great feat of strength
   What exercises I have done
   What grows in a garden
   What are my favorite outfits to wear
   What I like to eat most
   Going on a safari
   A ghost
   My biggest argument
   My favorite sport
   A dog or any animal
   A vacation

2. I'LL START A STORY. YOU FINISH IT.

3. making a paper airplane
   decorating a Christmas tree
   making cookies, popcorn, etc.
   making a sand castle
   making a fort from blocks
   how to swim
   how to add (easy numbers, 1 + 2, etc.)
   dusting objects
   sweeping the floor
   mopping the floor
   making toast
   frying an egg
   building anything
   potting a plant
   calisthenics
   setting the table
   doing the dishes
   playing a playground game
   getting ready for school

4. What does "run" mean?
   What is a window?
   What is a flower?
   What are vegetables?
   What is exercising?

What is a hi-fi set?
What is a baseball game?
What is a football game?
What does this do? (hold up any movable object)

5. Conduct a competition against time in which one person after another attempts to say as many words as he can as he looks around and names everything he sees. A further refinement might consist of confining the naming to words of certain categories: "Name all the animals you can think of in two minutes."

6. Conduct "dramatic play" which includes various life situations.

Conduct a "telephone" conversation with the student screened off from you. If toy telephones are available, use them. If it is possible to employ a real telephone, that would greatly enhance the effectiveness of this activity. Separate persons from the group and instruct them to have a make-believe telephone talk. You might model a typical conversation with an assistant or cooperative student to get the others started.

6. Asking directions — giving directions
Ordering food in a restaurant
Welcoming a friend
Talking about the weather
Meeting people; making and responding to introductions
Answering the telephone — telephone conversation
Being a radio or TV announcer
Being a disc jockey
Being a sports announcer
Giving instructions on folding paper
Going to a grocery store, asking prices, making purchases
Being a great track star
Being able to fly
Being an airline pilot
Being invisible
Being shipwrecked on a desert island
Something rough, soft, spooky, happy, sad, etc.
Hunting for buried treasure
Going on a bicycle trip
Building a dog house
Cooking a meal
Going shopping for food, clothes, a car, etc.
What I do at Christmas (and other holidays)

Monologue or Conversation Topics
"Make Up a Story About"
"Tell Us About"

Where do you ride your bike?
What are your jobs at home?
What do you do in girl or boy scouts?
What did you get for Christmas?
Tell us about your grandparents.
Tell us about your pet(s).
Tell us about your favorite animal.
Tell us about your favorite game.
How do you play monopoly (or any other game)?
How do you play baseball, football, basketball, etc.?
Tell us about a vacation you took.
What would you like to be when you grow up?
Tell us about your friends.
Do you have any hobbies? Tell us about them.
What do you like to do most?
What is your favorite meal?
What do you usually do after school?
If you could be anything, what would it be?
Tell us about a TV program you watched recently.
What are you studying in school these days?
Tell us about any place you ever visited.
Tell us about Disneyland.
What do you like doing most?
What do you do that sometimes gets you in trouble?
Hunting for buried treasure.
Something spooky.
Something rough.
Being shipwrecked on a deserted island.
Being invisible.
Being an airline pilot.
Being able to fly.
Being a famous author.

Being a great track star.
A vacation.
A dog or any animal.
A swimmer.
A lost child.
How a man got rich.
My favorite sport.
My biggest argument.
What I like most about people.
What I dislike most about people.
A ghost.
Fishing.
Going on a safari.
Making something with hammer and nails.
What kids like to do most.
What scares me the most.
What I like to eat most.
What did you do that was fun lately?
What are your favorite outfits to wear?
Books read lately?
What grows in a garden?
What exercises you have done.
A great feat of strength.
An insect war.
A great rain storm.
Being a hero.
Saving someone from destruction.
Being a professional musician, football player, etc.
What you would do with a pile of rocks.
What kind of sand sculpture you would make.
What you like to do in the snow.
What you like to do at the beach.

Being a famous cook or chef.
Having the greatest collection of jewelry in the world.
Being a champion automobile racer.
Being a famous explorer.
Being a famous mountain climber.
Being an Olympic skier.

Being lost in the woods.
Being lost in a big city.
Tearing down an old building.
Being a movie actor.
How you would plan a birthday party.
How you would plan a slumber party.

Materials. Word topics.

Criterion. Level V
Twenty consecutively correct word associations.

Purpose. To assist in the development of the cognitive—conceptualizing function by associating words with other words.

Demonstration Sequence

1. Select topic words and have the student tell you whatever words come to his mind which have anything to do with the topic word. Assist him at first, but go quickly to Level IV, then to Level V.

Model the word.

1. *Examples of word topics*

WATER	CLOTHES	SUMMER
BIRTHDAYS	WINTER	PAPER
SPRING	ANIMALS	FALL
ART	CHRISTMAS	MUSIC
WOOD	NAMES	GLASS
GIRLS	SPORTS	BOYS
PRETTY	TOYS	FUN
METALS	RACING	TV
BOOKS	FOOD	THE JUNGLE

Example: The word is "water."
TELL ME WHAT OTHER WORDS YOU THINK OF: "WATER." I'LL HELP YOU.
GLASS OF, RIVER, SEA, OCEAN, LAKE, STREAM, POND, PUDDLE, FISHING, SAILING, BOAT, RAIN, WATERFALL, SWIMMING, WADING, WET, COOL, THIRSTY, DRINKING, WASHING, POP, MILK, ICED TEA.

Materials. Topic words, pictures.

Criterion. Level V
Twenty consecutively correct word—sentence associations.

Purpose. To encourage the development of the associational process by combining words with relational comparisons.

Demonstration Sequence

1. Present the stimulus word along with the instruction. You want the student to search his mind for any and all relational aspects. This will generate associational thinking along with verbal production. Cue the student if he is not responding appropriately, but keep this to a minimum.

   Practice at Levels III, IV, and V.

2. An alternative activity might be to request that the student tell you all he can about a specific nonvisual or visual topic.

3. Another instruction might be "Tell me what you saw" or "Tell me about this." At this point you might choose to utilize visual memory by showing an object or picture sequence and then removing it from sight.

1. *Examples of associations:* Topic word is "apple."
   TELL ME ALL YOU CAN ABOUT AN APPLE.
   I'LL HELP YOU AT FIRST.
   IT IS RED
   ROUND, SMOOTH
   GOOD TO EAT
   GROWS ON TREES
   YOU CAN CUT IT INTO SECTIONS
   YOU CAN PUT IT IN FRUIT SALADS
   YOU CAN MAKE A PIE WITH IT
   YOU CAN PEEL IT
   SOMETIMES IT IS GREEN
   IT IS SOLID
   IT HAS SEEDS INSIDE
   YOU CAN MAKE JUICE FROM IT
   YOU CAN BAKE IT

2. TELL ME ABOUT A CAR.
   IT HAS WHEELS
   IT CARRIES PEOPLE
   IT RUNS
   IT COMES IN COLORS
   IT TAKES US ON TRIPS
   IT COSTS A LOT OF MONEY
   WE KEEP IT IN A GARAGE

3. I'LL HOLD THIS UP. TELL ME ALL YOU CAN ABOUT IT.
   SEE THESE. I'LL TAKE THEM AWAY.
   TELL ME WHAT YOU SAW. TELL ME ALL ABOUT THEM.

Associating Words

Materials. Multiple choice problems.

Criterion. Level V
18 of 20 consecutively correct choices
of matching words.

Purpose. To exercise the organizing
(association) process by showing that
certain words go together under one
classifying word, as items of a similar
class (animals, food, etc.).

Demonstration Sequence
1. Begin with only two-choice questions. Once these are
   established, go to three or as many as can be handled.

   Suit the level of abstraction to the ability of the person.

   Do not practice at too easy a level. However, answers
   may be given as the student is learning what is required
   of him. In this event, practice at Levels III and IV
   before attempting V.

   Practice at Level IV, then go to V as soon as possible.

1. *Examples of choice questions*

Topic	*Choices*
bacon, eggs	1. flowers
toast, milk	2. breakfast
zebra, tiger	1. cars
	2. colors
	3. animals
ducks, chickens	1. bicycles
	2. birds
	3. trees
	4. clothes

Example:
I'LL SAY SOME WORDS. LISTEN CAREFULLY.
I'LL SAY SOME OTHER WORDS. TELL ME WHICH
OF THE *OTHER* WORDS GO WITH THE FIRST ONES.

FIRST WORDS:
BACON, EGGS, TOAST, MILK

SECOND WORDS:
FLOWERS, BREAKFAST

WHICH SECOND WORD GOES WITH THE FIRST
WORDS?

BREAKFAST.

Associating Ideas Presented Orally: "What Is It?" "What Is Happening?"

Materials. "What is it?" and "What is happening?" sentences (attached).

Criterion. Level V
Twenty consecutively correct answers to "What is it?" and/or "What is happening?" sentences.

Purpose. To exercise the organizing (association) process by presenting words (nouns and participles) in association with meaningful concepts.

Demonstration Sequence

1. Model the cue sentences. The person is to tell you the answer as soon as he knows it.

2. A competition might be arranged in which the group members attempt to guess what it is ahead of each other.

3. Provide answers only if necessary.

   Practice at Levels III, IV, and V.

4. Examine the "Verbs — What is Happening?" list attached to this set. Another form of activity might be to ask *Why* is it happening? Model possible answers. Think of and utilize as many possible answers for each topic word group as possible. Expand from the word groups to any verb form activity.

1. *Example of "What is it?" sentence*
   I'M GOING TO SAY A NUMBER OF SENTENCES. TELL ME WHAT THEY ARE TALKING ABOUT. TELL ME AS SOON AS YOU CAN.

   Scissors
   They are sharp.
   They have two blades.
   They have handles.
   They are used for cutting.

   Balloon
   It is rubber.
   It can be blown up.
   It will pop if it is punctured.
   It is very light.

   Football player
   He wears a uniform.
   He wears a helmet.
   He plays on a big field.
   He plays with a ball.

   Blanket
   It is soft.
   It keeps you warm.
   It goes on a bed.
   It goes over the sheets.
   It goes under the bedspread.

   Kitchen
   It is in the house.
   It has a stove in it.
   It has a refrigerator in it.
   It is a room for cooking.

Nouns: "What Is It?"

Airplane
It is a means of transportation.
It has wings.
It has propellor or jet engines.
It flies at great speeds.

Clock/Watch
It has two or three hands.
It may be worn on your wrist.
It may hang on a wall.
It tells time.

Glasses
You wear them.
They are usually clear.
They have two lenses.
They help you see better.

Billfold
It is usually made of leather.
You carry it with you.
It is small.
You keep your money in it.

Shoe
You wear it.
You walk on it.
It covers your foot.
You wear two of them.

Plate
It is round.
It may be large or small.
It goes on a table.
You eat off it.
It is made of china.

Knife
It is thin.
It is sharp.
You use it for cutting food.
It is an eating utensil.

Cup
It is round.
You drink from it.
It is made of china.
It goes with a saucer.

Broom
It has a long handle.
It has brushes on the end.
It is found in the home.
It is used for sweeping.

Candle
It is tall and thin.
It comes in many colors.
You may light it.
It is made of wax.

Train
It is a means of transportation.
It has many cars.
The first car is the engine.
It runs on tracks.

Hair
It's on the top of your head.
It can be curly or straight.
It needs brushing often.
It can be long or short.

Tomato
It is a vegetable.
It is red.
It is juicy and has seeds.
It is used in green salads.

Gum
It is like rubber.
It comes in many flavors.
You chew it.
You can blow bubbles with it.

Television
It is found in the home.
It has a screen.
It may be colored.
You watch it.

Telephone
It is often black.
You talk to others with it.
It has a dial.
It rings.

Pillow
It is found in the bedroom
It is soft.
It is for your head.
It goes on the bed.

Piano
It is an instrument.
You can play it.
It has a bench with it.
It has black and white keys.

Fireman
He wears black clothes.
He drives a red truck.
He fights fires.

Turtle
It is a small animal.
It has a hard shell covering it.
It is green.
It moves very slowly.

Santa Claus
He is an old man.
He has a long white beard.
He wears a red suit.
He gives gifts to children.
He visits us at Christmas.

Ankle
It is part of your body.
It is part of your leg.
It is above your foot.
It connects your foot to your leg.

Knee
It is part of your body.
It is part of your leg.
It lets you bend your leg.
You kneel on it.

Fingers
They are part of your body.
You use them when you pick up something.
They are part of your hands.
You can wear rings on them.

Milk
It is liquid.
It is white.
It comes from cows.

Giraffe
It is a tall thin animal.
It comes from Africa.
It has very long legs.
It has a very long neck.
It has many spots or markings.

Grass
It is green.
It is soft.
It grows in front of houses.
It has to be mowed often.

Snow
It is cold.
It is white.
It falls from clouds.
It usually falls in the mountains.
It is good for skiing.

Nest
It is made of twigs and dirt.
It is found in a tree.
It is a bird's home.
Birds lay eggs in it.

Barn
It is a big building.
It is seen on a farm.
It is a house for animals.

Tricycle
It is a child's toy.
It has two handles.
It has two pedals.
It has three wheels.

Bat
It is made of wood.
It is long and round.
It is used to hit a ball.
Baseball players use it.

Kite
It is made of paper.
It has a long string attached to it.
You have to run with it.
It flies.
It has to be windy.

Verbs: "What Is Happening?"

Eating
You are sitting at a table.
You have a knife and fork in your hands.
You put food in your mouth.

Writing
You are sitting at a desk.
You have paper in front of you.
You have a pen in your hand.

Drinking
You have a glass in your hand.
You put the glass to your mouth.
You swallow.

Jumping (Rope)
This happens using a rope.
You hold the ends of the rope in your hands.
You throw the rope over your head.
The rope goes under your feet.
You bend your knees, your feet come off the ground.

Brushing (Hair)
This happens in the morning.
You use an object with a handle.
You reach to the top of your head.
You stroke your hair with a brush.

Swimming
This happens in water.
You use your arms and legs.
You pull with your arms.
You kick your legs.

Falling
This happens if you trip over something.
This happens if you lose your balance.
This can happen off a chair, down stairs, etc.

Dressing
You do this in the morning.
You put on underwear.
You put on a dress/shirt and pants.
You put on shoes.

Planting
This happens in the garden.
You dig holes in the ground.
You put flowers in the holes.

Watering
This is done in the garden.
You use water.
You use a hose.
You sprinkle the plants with water.

Washing
You do this to clothes.
You use soap and water.
You swish your clothes around.
You rinse out the soap.

Bowling
This is a game.
You use a ball.
There are ten pins.
You roll the ball down an alley.
You try to knock down the pins.

Reading
This is done with a book.
You use your eyes.
Your eyes move across the pages.
You think about what your eyes see.

Breathing
This happens every minute of your life.
You take in air.
You let out air.

Running
You do this if someone is chasing you.
You do this when you play tag.
You do this when you play baseball.
Your legs are moving very fast.

Laughing
You do this if you are happy.
You do this if something is funny.
You do this when you hear a joke.

Cooking
Mothers do this quite often.
It happens in the kitchen.
It happens at meal time.
It happens when preparing food.
You use a stove or oven.

Sleeping
It happens at nighttime.
It happens in bed.
You often dream while doing this.

Crawling
Most babies do this.
They use their hands and knees.
It happens when they can't walk.

Hopping
This is like small jumping steps.
Frogs do this.
Rabbits do this.
When people do this their feet are together.

Raining
This happens in winter.
It happens when it's cloudy.
You can get wet.
You wear boots.
You use an umbrella.

Chewing
This happens when you eat.
You are breaking up your food.
You move your jaw up and down.
Your teeth come together.

Pouring
You have a pitcher in your hand.
It is full of milk.
You are tipping the pitcher.
The milk runs into a glass.

Digging
This happens with a shovel.
You push the shovel in some dirt.
You lift the shovel full of dirt out of the ground.
You push the shovel back in the ground.
You lift out more dirt.

Singing
You usually do this when you are happy.
You use words and music.
You use your voice.
You are making musical tones.

Crying
This happens when you are sad or upset.
Your eyes get red.
Your eyes get watery.
Tears roll down your cheeks.

Throwing
This can be done with a ball.
The ball is in your hand.
You pull your arm back.
You extend your arm.
The ball leaves your hand.

Sitting down
This happens if you are tired of standing.
You bend your knees.
You lower your hips.
There is a chair behind.

Standing up
You are not lying down.
You put your feet on the floor.
You extend your legs.
Your weight is on your feet.

Walking
You do this to get from one place to another.
You do this with your feet and legs.
One foot moves forward at a time.
Your heels touch the ground first, then toes.
Left foot, then right foot, left, right, etc.

Climbing
You can do this on a ladder.
You go up one step at a time.
You can also do this in a tree.
You pull yourself up and step on the branches.
You go higher and higher.

Using Auditory Memory: Answering Questions

Materials. Short story expansions (attached).

Criterion. Level V
Twenty consecutively correct answers to questions presented from short story expansions.

Purpose. To teach the use of the auditory memory function in answering questions from a "story" presented in three sentences.

Demonstration Sequence

1. Select which short story expansions you will use (see attached list).

2. Tell the story.

3. Ask a question. Answer it. Ask another question. Answer it. Ask the same question. Wait for the child to answer it.

4. Repeat Step 3, giving only the questions and requiring the child to answer. From then on, do *not* answer the questions yourself but wait for the child to supply the answer. Ask as many questions as possible from each story.

1. *Examples*
LISTEN CAREFULLY TO THE STORY. AS SOON AS I TELL YOU THE STORY I'M GOING TO ASK YOU QUESTIONS ABOUT IT.

2. BELL RINGS.
THE BELL RINGS EVERY HOUR.
THE BELL RINGS EVERY HOUR ON THE HOUR.

3. WHAT RINGS?
THE BELL.
WHEN DOES IT RING?
EVERY HOUR.
WHEN DOES IT RING?
_____ .
(person completes)

Short Story Expansions

Birds fly.
The birds fly south in the winter time.
The birds fly south in the winter and north again in spring.

Blue eyes.
The baby has blue eyes.
The baby has blue eyes and blonde hair.

Blue skies.
Blue skies mean clear weather.
Blue skies mean clear weather and no rain today.

Boat sails.
The boat sails at dawn.
The boat sails at dawn and returns at sunset.

Check it.
Check it when you finish.
Check it when you finish to see if it is correct.

Earache.
An earache is painful.
An earache is as painful as a toothache.

Fence post.
The fence post is dirty.
The fence post is dirty and needs a coat of paint.

Fish swim.
Fish swim in water.
Fish swim in water and breathe through their gills.

Grass seed.
Grass seed is sown in the spring.
Grass seed is sown in the spring so that the lawn will be green all summer.

Green leaves.
Green leaves are pretty.
Green leaves are pretty in a vase of flowers.

Bookcase.
Put the book back in the bookcase.
Put the book back in the bookcase on the top shelf.

Box top.
Send a box top with the coupon.
Send a box top with the coupon, which is inside the box.

Brown hat.
Where is my old brown hat?
Where is my old brown hat that I left on the table?

Bus ride.
I took a long bus ride.
I took a long bus ride so I could see the city.

Car wash.
The car wash was busy.
The car wash was busy because so many people had dirty automobiles.

Door bell.
The door bell is ringing.
The door bell is ringing and I must answer it.

Farm house.
The farmhouse has new paint.
The farmhouse has new paint and a new roof.

Fire burns.
Fire burns the fields.
Fire burns the fields and clears the land of dead brush.

Foot hurts.
His foot hurts when he stands.
His foot hurts when he stands on it for a long time.

Gray suit.
The gray suit needed pressing.
The gray suit needed pressing before it could be worn.

Hairbrush.
The hairbrush has stiff bristles.
The hairbrush has stiff bristles which make my scalp hurt.

Headache.
I have a headache.
I have had a headache for three days.

Iced tea.
Iced tea tastes good in summer.
Iced tea tastes good in summer when the weather is hot.

Leaves fall.
Leaves fall when it rains.
Leaves fall when it rains in the late autumn.

Mailbox.
The mailbox is full.
The mailbox is full of advertisements but no letters.

New sled.
He bought a new sled.
He bought a new sled for his son.

Slide down.
Children slide down the hill.
Children slide down the hill on their sleds when it snows.

Soup bowl.
The soup bowl was cracked.
The soup bowl was cracked when it was dropped on the floor.

To school.
Children go to school.
Children go to school nine months out of the year.

Apple pie.
Apple pie and cheese are good.
Apple pie and cheese are good to eat after a bowl of soup.

Baby boy.
The baby boy looked like his father.
The baby boy looked like his father with his blonde hair and
    blue eyes.

Bat the ball.
He bats the ball over the fence.
He bats the ball over the fence and makes a home run.

Bathroom floor.
The bathroom floor is wet.
The bathroom floor is wet around the bathtub.

Black and blue.
His eye was black and blue.
His eye was black and blue after the fight.

Cake and pie.
Cake and pie are desserts.
Cake and pie are desserts which most people enjoy.

Candy bar.
The candy bar is sticky.
The candy bar is sticky when the weather is hot.

Cat and dog.
The cat and dog were fighting.
The cat and dog were fighting, and we were afraid one might
    be hurt.

Church music.
Listen to the church music.
Listen to the church music on the radio.

Closet door.
The closet door is open.
The closet door is open, so you can hang up your hat and coat.

Barbershop.
The barbershop was crowded.
The barbershop was crowded so I'll have my hair cut tomorrow.

Horn blows.
The horn blows too much.
The horn blows so much it disturbs the patients.

Key ring.
The key ring was in his pocket.
The key ring was in his pocket, but he thought it was lost.

Light bulb.
The light bulb burned out.
The light bulb burned out sometime during the night.

Match box.
The match box is on the shelf.
The match box is on the shelf over the stove.

Airplane flies.
The airplane flies through the air.
The airplane flies through the air high above the city.

Snowfall.
This is the first snowfall.
This is the first snowfall we have had in several years.

Sunshine.
The sunshine is bright.
The sunshine is so bright it hurts my eyes.

Watchband.
His watchband was broken.
His watchband was broken and the crystal was cracked.

Arm and leg.
Why are his arm and leg so dirty?
Why are his arm and leg so dirty when he has just had a bath?

Ball and bat.
The ball and bat are on the bench.
The ball and bat are on the bench down in the basement.

Dog collar.
The dog collar is made of leather.
The dog collar is made of leather and fits the dog well.

Down the steps.
I walked down the steps.
I walked down the steps to the first floor.

Belt buckle.
His belt buckle is broken.
His belt buckle is broken in the middle.

Boy and girl.
The little boy and girl sang together.
The little boy and girl sang together in the Christmas program.

Candlelight.
Candlelight is dim.
Candlelight is dim and not good for reading.

Cap and coat.
His cap and coat were on the chair.
His cap and coat were on the chair in the kitchen.

Chicken coop.
The chicken coop is too small.
The chicken coop is too small for all those baby chicks.

Clock or watch.
A clock or watch tells time.
A clock or watch tells time more accurately than a sundial.

Coat and hat.
He threw off his coat and hat.
He threw off his coat and hat and went right to work.

Coffee pot.
The coffee pot is on the stove.
The coffee pot is on the stove but may be empty.

Cow and calf.
The cow and calf were in the pasture.
The cow and calf were in the pasture when the storm came up.

Desk drawer.
The desk drawer is stuck.
The desk drawer is stuck and I can't get it open.

Dollar bill.
I put a dollar bill in your pocket.
I put a dollar bill in your pocket while you were out of the room.

Down the street.
Down the street is the store.
Down the street is the store where Joe works.

Ducks waddle.
Ducks waddle when they walk.
Ducks waddle when they walk, but they also can swim.

Engine house.
The engine house was painted.
The engine house was painted and had a new roof.

Feet and legs.
His feet and legs were cold.
His feet and legs were cold, but the rest of his body was warm.

Field of corn.
The field of corn needs plowing.
The field of corn needs plowing and the garden needs weeding.

Flowers bloom.
Flowers bloom all summer.
Flowers bloom all summer and make a garden look beautiful.

Fork and knife.
The fork and knife are on the table.
The fork and knife are on the table in the kitchen.

Fur collar.
She has a fur collar on her coat.
She has a fur collar on her coat and it keeps her neck warm in the winter.

In the tree.
The nest is in the tree.
The nest is in the tree on a high limb.

Iron my shirt.
Will you iron my shirt?
Will you iron my shirt before you leave?

Knife and fork.
A knife and fork are on the table.
A knife and fork are on the table along with a plate, cup, and saucer.

Leg of lamb.
We had leg of lamb for dinner.
We had leg of lamb for dinner, and it was very good.

Milk bottle.
The milk bottle is almost empty.
The milk bottle is almost empty and the coffee is almost gone.

Moon and stars.
Moon and stars shine at night.
Moon and stars shine at night, but the sun shines during the day.

On the roof.
The paper landed on the roof.
The paper landed on the roof near the chimney.

Comb and brush.
The comb and brush are on the dresser.
The comb and brush are on the dresser, but the mirror is broken.

Girl and boy.
The girl and boy were riding bicycles.
The girl and boy were riding bicycles to school every day.

Glasses case.
He lost his glasses case.
He lost his glasses case at the picture show last night.

Lamp gives light.
A lamp gives light to read.
A lamp gives light to read by when the room is dark.

Living room.
The living room has four windows.
The living room has four windows and two doors.

Goldfish bowl.
Change the water in the goldfish bowl.
Change the water in the goldfish bowl before you leave the house.

Grape jelly.
Put the grape jelly on the toast.
Put the grape jelly on the toast if you like something sweet for breakfast.

Ham sandwich.
I want a ham sandwich.
I want a ham sandwich and a glass of milk.

Hat and coat.
Bring my hat and coat.
Bring my hat and coat and I'll go with you to the store.

Hens lay eggs.
Hens lay eggs in the nest.
Hens lay eggs in the nest and then they sit on them to keep them warm.

House for sale.
On the next block is a house for sale.
On the next block is a house for sale which I would like to buy.

Picture show.
The picture show begins at 7:00.
The picture show begins at 7:00 every night.

Rainy day.
Yesterday was a rainy day.
Yesterday was a rainy day, but today is beautiful.

Rake the leaves.
We rake the leaves in the fall.
We rake the leaves in the fall and then burn them up.

Razor blades.
I need new razor blades.
I need new razor blades because mine are dull.

Red flannels.
In winter I wear red flannels.
In winter I wear red flannels to keep me warm.

Bacon and eggs.
Bacon and eggs are filling.
Bacon and eggs are filling and make a good breakfast.

The rope hangs.
The rope hangs from the roof.
The rope hangs from the roof of the barn.

Shirt and tie.
My shirt and tie are on the bed.
My shirt and tie are on the bed and my suit hangs in the closet.

On the stove.
The soup is on the stove.
The soup is on the stove ready to be heated.

On the tray.
His food is on the tray.
His food is on the tray and ready to be served to him.

Pen and ink.
The pen and ink are in the drawer.
The pen and ink are in the drawer of the desk.

Shoes and socks.
Give me my shoes and socks.
Give me my shoes and socks so that I can finish dressing.

Store window.
The store window was broken.
The store window was broken during a wind storm.

Auditory – Vocal Sequencing: Giving Directions and Instructions

Eg

Materials. Directions topics.

Criterion. Level V
Three successfully completed verbal
directions or instruction sequences.

Purpose. To encourage the auditory–
vocal sequencing function by teaching the
vocabulary and syntax characteristic of
directions and instructions.

Demonstration Sequence

1. Begin at a simple three-sentence level. Be sure that the
   directions are quite easy to follow. Gradually increase
   the complexity and length of the instruction sequence.

   Model as many sequences as necessary, but fade them as
   soon as possible.

2. A higher level activity is to require as many sentences as
   might be necessary to complete the sequence.

1. I WANT TO OPEN THE WINDOW. TELL ME WHAT
   TO DO.
   STAND UP, GO TO THE WINDOW. OPEN IT.

   I WANT TO PUT THIS HAT ON. TELL ME WHAT
   TO DO.
   PICK THE HAT UP. HOLD IT IN ONE HAND. PUT IT
   ON YOUR HEAD.

2. HOW DO WE GET TO THE WASHROOM?
   WALK ACROSS THE ROOM.
   OPEN THE DOOR.
   WALK DOWN THE HALL.
   TURN RIGHT, GO TO THE DOOR OF THE WASHROOM.
   OPEN IT AND WALK IN.

Materials. Problems list (attached).

Criterion. Level V
Twenty consecutively correct "problem" solutions.

Purpose. To exercise the organizing (association) process by presenting a means whereby the person must associate words with meaningful concepts.

Demonstration Sequence

1. A problem-solving group "forum" may be held in which possible solutions to various problems are offered.

   Provide solutions only if necessary. You will not be encouraging the idea associational function if you give the answers.

   Any one question may have different answers. Each person should be encouraged to provide as many answers as he can.

1. *Example*
   I'M GOING TO SAY A SENTENCE WHICH HAS A PROBLEM IN IT. THINK OF AS MANY ANSWERS AS YOU CAN.
   What would you do if you forgot to do your homework assignments?
   Suppose your best friend moved far away from you. What would you do?
   What would you do if you were flying a kite and the string broke?
   What would you do if you thought you saw a ghost?
   What would you talk about if you had to give a speech to the class?
   What would you do if you couldn't find your way home?
   What would you take with you on a camping trip?
   What would you take with you if you were going to a beach?
   What would you do if you saw a child fall off his tricycle?
   What would you do if you were in a burning building?
   What would you do if you dropped your ring down the drain in the sink?
   What would you do if you were hungry?
   What would you do if you were tired?
   If you had to paint your bedroom, what color would you use and why?
   If you could go to one of two schools, how would you decide to which one to go?

Solve These Problems

If you were on the roof of a house and the ladder fell down, what would you do?
What would you take with you on a hiking trip and why?
What would you take on a butterfly hunting trip and why?
What would you do if a bear chased you?
If you were in a boat and it started to sink, what would you do?
If a bee stung you, what would you do?
What would you take with you on a trip to a deserted island?
If you were climbing a tree and the branch that you were standing on started to crack, what would you do?
If you were lost in a city, what would you do?
If you couldn't find a toy in your toy box, how would you find it?
How do you get to school?
How does a person earn money?
How can you get from here to (anywhere else: home, the playground, lunchroom, etc.)?
How do you make a friend?
How do you make an enemy?
How is (anything: glass, a car, etc.) made?
If you were flying over a jungle and had to parachute out, what sort of things would you plan in order to get out?
How do you save money?
What would you do if you were fixing coffee for your father and you put salt in it instead of sugar?
Suppose you were walking on a frozen lake and the ice started to crack, what would you do?
What would you do if you fell in a pool with your clothes on?
If you went fishing and you dropped your pole into the water, what would you do?

Suppose you locked your bicycle in a bicycle rack and then
    you lost the key to the lock. What would you do?

Suppose you were a rancher and your cattle got through your
    fence. What would you do?

What would you do if a bee kept flying around your head?

What would happen if a cat and dog were put in the same
    room?

What would you do if you saw an accident?

What would you do if you saw a fire starting?

What would you do if you saw a kitten up in a tree and it
    couldn't get down?

Suppose you were walking down a street and you saw some-
    one breaking into a car. What would you do?

What would you do if you were at a circus and one of the
    tigers got out of its cage?

What would you take if you were going on a bike hike?

What would you do if you were riding your bike and you got
    a flat tire?

What would you do if you were cooking dinner and you
    burned the meat?

What would you do if you locked yourself out of your house?

What would happen if a cat got near a fish bowl?

Suppose it was raining and your bedroom window wouldn't
    close. What would you do?

Suppose you were driving down a road and there were some
    cows standing in the road. How would you get by?

Suppose you reached in a jar to get a penny out of the bottom
    and your hand got stuck. What would you do?

What would you do if it was night time and the electricity in
    your home went off and you didn't have any candles?

What would you do if you had offered to make your guests
    ice cream cones and then found your ice cream had melted?

What would you do if you were by yourself and your car got
    a flat tire?

What would you do if you were driving down a road and the
    road was washed out by a flooded river?

How would you raise enough money to buy your parents a
    special gift?

Suppose it snowed heavily during the night and you couldn't
    get your car out of the garage. What would you do?

Making Mental Judgments: "Alike – Different"

Materials. Two-word "alike–different" combinations list.

Criterion. Level IV
Twenty consecutively correct judgments of alike–different concepts presented orally.

Purpose. To practice the auditory associative process through "alike" and "different" concepts presented orally.

Demonstration Sequence

1. Present all examples orally. Do not use objects or pictures. The person is to try to judge as to whether or not the items are alike or different himself.

2. Ascertain the optimal level at which you should be working. For example, it may be necessary to present many answers to the word pair comparisons (at Level III) before the person is able to function at Level IV.

3. Go to the two-word alike and different list that follows. Expand upon the list with two-word combinations of your own.

1. *Examples*
CAR–AUTO
THEY ARE THE SAME.

PLANE–AIRCRAFT
THEY ARE THE SAME.

COUCH–CAR
THEY ARE DIFFERENT.

TELEPHONE–TELEVISION
THEY ARE DIFFERENT.

Two-Word Alike and Different Combinations*

car–auto (s)	market–store (s)	rough–smooth (d)	speak–talk (s)
plane–aircraft (s)	ship–boat (s)	glad–sad (d)	today–yesterday (d)
sunshine–sunlight (s)	story–tale (s)	shirt–blouse (s)	somebody–someone (s)
me–you (d)	sunrise–sunset (d)	book–encyclopedia (s)	blunt–dull (d)
me–(person's name) (d)	rock–stone (s)	thought–idea (s)	suitcase–suit (d)
you–(person's name) (s)	door–window (d)	plant–tree (s)	sunrise–dawn (s)
street–roadway (s)	sport–baseball (s)	drink–swallow (s)	single–unmarried (s)
house–home (s)	friend–enemy (d)	name–title (s)	cruise–voyage (s)
love–hate (d)	lawn–grass (s)	floor–ceiling (d)	sailor–saleswoman (d)
rabbit–bunny (s)	crib–cradle (s)	country–United States (s)	game–baseball (s)
pony–Shetland (s)	shop–store (s)	number–eleven (s)	king–ruler (s)
newspaper–magazine (d)	horse–colt (s)	fuel–gasoline (s)	hotel–inn (s)
apple–orange (d)	land–sea (d)	square–circle (d)	hand–fist (s)
happy–glad (s)	fruit–banana (s)	error–mistake (s)	game–contest (s)
dog–cat (d)	wagon–bicycle (d)	church–cathedral (s)	church–school (d)
beach–shore (s)	pretty–ugly (d)	ocean–sea (s)	crowd–mob (s)
ship–boat (s)	instrument–piano (s)	chicken-fowl (s)	ghost–spirit (s)
laugh–cry (d)	big–little (d)	cool–warm (d)	arm–limb (s)
plump–chubby (s)	bicycle–bike (s)	city–town (s)	chip–splinter (s)
fat–thin (d)	easy–simple (s)	shoe–sock (d)	telephone–television (d)
man–male (s)	sick–ill (s)	rope–cord (s)	clerk–saleswoman (s)
morning–evening (d)	these–those (d)	flower–bloom (s)	world–earth (s)
paper–pen (d)	wet–moist (s)	box–carton (s)	car–stationwagon (s)
dog–puppy (s)	sunglasses–eyeglasses (s)	bed–cot (s)	girl–lass (s)
cat–kitten (s)	company–guest (s)	arm–limb (s)	sum–total (s)
them–us (d)	noisy–quiet (d)	week–day (d)	toothbrush–toothpaste (d)
money–penny (s)	pants–slacks (s)	chair–window (d)	limb–branch (s)
highway–road (s)	dishwasher–stove (d)	boy–lad (s)	
hat–shoe (d)	bathingsuit–swimsuit (s)	street–avenue (s)	
cup–mug (s)	person–somebody (s)	test–examination (s)	

*(s) = same
(d) = different

Materials. Alike–different topics.

Criterion. Level V
Twenty consecutively correct alike–different judgment answers.

Purpose. To exercise the organizing (associational) process by generating comparisons of objects through their characteristics.

Demonstration Sequence

1. Provide the answers for the question. Continue providing answers until the idea of what is expected is established.

   On the other hand, allow the student time to try to think of the answers. Help him only as much as he needs. Practice at Level IV.

   Refer to the Questions and Answers listed below. They illustrate the form and level of abstraction of this set. Establish more topics based upon this format.

1. *Example*
   TELL ME WHAT IS ALIKE AND DIFFERENT ABOUT AN AIRPLANE AND A CAR. LET'S DO "ALIKE" FIRST: BOTH AN AIRPLANE AND A CAR:
   ARE USED FOR TRANSPORTATION
   HAVE ENGINES
   HAVE WHEELS
   HAVE WINDSHIELDS
   HAVE WINDOWS
   ARE MADE OF METAL
   HAVE DOORS
   HAVE SEATS

   NOW LET'S DO "DIFFERENT":
   AIRPLANES HAVE WINGS
   AIRPLANES GO FASTER
   AIRPLANES FLY
   CARS ARE SMALLER

Questions

1. How are a train and car
   (a) alike
   (b) different?

2. How are a car and truck
   (a) alike
   (b) different?

3. How are a canoe and rowboat
   (a) alike
   (b) different?

4. How are a dog and cat
   (a) alike
   (b) different?

5. How are a tiger and lion
   (a) alike
   (b) different?

6. How are a horse and cow
   (a) alike
   (b) different?

7. How are a radish and carrot
   (a) alike
   (b) different?

8. How are a pea and bean
   (a) alike
   (b) different?

Answers

General Answers in reference to likeness to Questions 1–3
Are used for transportation, have engines, wheels, windshields, windows, metal construction, doors, seats, storage space.

Specifics
1. (a) See general answers.
   (b) Train runs on track, has metal wheels, transports animals and other heavy loads; car has only 4 wheels, rubber tires, engine under the hood, smaller.
2. (a) Have windshield wipers, engine under hood, wheels.
   (b) Truck carries heavy loads, is generally bigger; car has back seat.
3. (a) Are for transportation, float, use paddles.
   (b) Canoe is narrower, paddles shorter; rowboat wider, carries more people.

General Answers to Questions 4–6
Are animals, have four legs, have fur coats.

Specifics
4. (a) Domesticated, house pets.
   (b) Cats drink milk, clean selves, are quiet; dogs are bigger, growl, chase cats, some have long ears.
5. (a) Live in plains, are circus animals, roar.
   (b) Tiger has stripes, lion has mane.
6. (a) Have ears, live on a farm, work for man.
   (b) Cow gives milk; horse has mane, is used for transportation.

General Answers to Questions 7–10
Foods, plants, can grow in your garden, have skin, are vegetables.

Specifics
7. (a) Roots grow underground, have green tops.
   (b) Carrot is orange, can be cooked, peeled, is long, thin; radish is red, round, hot.
8. (a) Are green, have pods over seeds, are climbing plants.
   (b) Beans long, thin; peas small, round, often sweet.

Questions	Answers

9. How are a tomato and potato
    (a) alike
    (b) different?
	9. (a) See general answers.
	    (b) Tomato red, juicy, has seeds; potato grows underground, has dark skin, is solid, hard, cooked to eat.

10. How are a hamburger and hot dog
    (a) alike
    (b) different?
	10. (a) Served in a bun, with mustard, catsup, etc., can be barbecued.
	    (b) Hamburger round, flat; hot dog long, thin, can be eaten cold.

General Answers to Questions 11–13
Articles of clothing, keep body warm, worn in cool weather, worn over the other clothing.

Specifics

Questions	Answers

11. How are a coat and robe
    (a) alike
    (b) different?
	11. (a) Button or zipper up front, usually long sleeves.
	    (b) Coat worn outside, heavy material, worn over dress, pants, etc.; robe worn in house, usually light material, worn over nightgown or pajamas.

12. How are a jacket and coat
    (a) alike
    (b) different?
	12. (a) Worn over other clothes, usually have long sleeves.
	    (b) Jacket shorter in length, usually to waist; coat long to knees.

13. How are a shoe and boot
    (a) alike
    (b) different?
	13. (a) Wear on feet, protect feet, made of leather.
	    (b) Boot worn in rain, higher on leg, has zipper; shoe has laces or slips on foot.

14. How are a rain hat and umbrella
    (a) alike
    (b) different?
	14. (a) Used in rain, keep head dry, made of plastic or cloth.
	    (b) Hat goes on head; umbrella opens up, bigger than hat, is held in hand.

15. How are the sun and moon
    (a) alike
    (b) different?
	15. (a) Round, shine, in the sky, give light, rise, set.
	    (b) Sun is warm, yellow; moon changes shape, is white.

16. How are a house and barn
    (a) alike
    (b) different?
	16. (a) Have walls, roof, windows, doors made of wood, things inside.
	    (b) Houses are for people, have furniture, etc.; barns bigger, hay inside, for animals.

17. How are a toothbrush and broom
    (a) alike
    (b) different?
	17. (a) Have bristles, long, thin handle, for cleaning.
	    (b) Broom bigger, for cleaning floor; toothbrush is small, used for cleaning teeth, kept in bathroom.

18. How are a piano and table
    (a) alike
    (b) different?
	18. (a) Made of wood, have legs, sit at table and piano.
	    (b) Play piano, has keyboard; eat from table, write on table, table top is flat.

19. How are a waitress and stewardess
    (a) alike
    (b) different?
	19. (a) Serve people, wear uniforms.
	    (b) Stewardess works in airplane, prepares meals; waitress works in restaurant, usually wears white.

20. How are an oven and refrigerator
    (a) alike
    (b) different?
	20. (a) Metal construction, doors, belong in kitchen, light inside, shelves inside, food inside.
	    (b) Oven for cooking, has hot temperatures; refrigerator for storing food, has cool temperatures, is bigger.

21. How are a lawnmower and pair of scissors
    (a) alike
    (b) different?
	21. (a) Have blades, handles, are used for cutting.
	    (b) Lawnmower is bigger, has wheels, more than two blades, used for cutting grass; scissors are small, have two blades, used for cutting paper, material, hair.

22. How are a radio and television
    (a) alike
    (b) different?
	22. (a) Electric, on-off switch, have volume, voices, music, etc.
	    (b) Television bigger, has screen for viewing, has more dials.

23. How are a football and baseball game
    (a) alike
    (b) different?
	23. (a) Use a ball, are played on a field, have officials, players wear uniforms, spectators, each team tries to get the most points.
	    (b) Baseball — hit the ball and run, 9 innings, no time for length of play, 9 players; football — pass or run with ball, time limit to play, 11 players.

24. How are a triangle and square
    (a) alike
    (b) different?
	24. (a) Constructed with line segments, geometric figure, lines touch at points.
	    (b) Square — each side equal in length, four sides, four corners; triangle — three sides, all sides not necessarily equal in length.

Associating Words: "Which Doesn't Belong?"

Materials. Lists of word groups, each group containing one word which is inappropriate.

Criterion. Level IV
Twenty consecutively correct selections of the word which is inappropriate to others in its group.

Purpose. To utilize and activate the auditory—vocal association psycholinguistic function by requiring the selection of the word that is inappropriate to the group in which it appears.

Demonstration Sequence

1. Select word groups which are most appropriate to the ability level of the person. The examples present only a beginning reference point from which to work. You are expected to add to this.

   Other variables may be added to this activity to increase the difficulty level or include other psycholinguistic aspects. You may, for instance, add auditory memory to this function by increasing the word group size and/or the time delay between the word presentations and your request for the answer.

   Provide the answers if you must. Continue doing so until the person has the idea of what is expected of him. Pictures may be used to provide visual stimulation.

   An alternative activity may be to have the person "make up his own," once he has the idea of grouping words into clusters.

   Reminder: Keep your talking to a minimum. As soon as possible, present only the topic and word group and wait for the answer.

   Competition may be arranged whereby the students think of the word and raise their hands as quickly as they can once they have the answer. The person who gets the most words with the least accumulated time delay wins.

   Another activity may be to present a four-word group with two which go together.

   Arrange the group to accommodate *any* selection criteria which you establish, e.g., after naming the topic, have the person tell you the *one* word which goes with it. You in this case, present all words which do not relate except for one.

1. I'M GOING TO SAY THREE WORDS ABOUT THE BEACH. ONE WORD WILL NOT BELONG BECAUSE IT IS NOT ABOUT THE BEACH. TELL ME WHICH WORD IT IS.

   THE BEACH: SAND, *RULER,* WATER

   WHICH WORD DOESN'T BELONG? RULER. BECAUSE WE DO NOT USUALLY FIND A RULER AT THE BEACH.

   Examples:
   Firehouse: fire truck, hose, *Aunt Mary*
   Breakfast: milk, *pot roast,* cereal
   Bedroom: blanket, pillow, *snow*
   Summer: *snowball,* swimming, baseball
   Food: vegetables, hot dogs, *glass*
   Car: gasoline, seats, *roses*
   Flowers: tulips, carnations, *tablets*
   Colors: blue, *lamp,* green
   School: books, pencils, *grandmother*
   Round things: *box,* moon, baseball
   Big things: mountain, *peanut,* elephant
   Animals: *orchid,* dog, sheep
   Wood: *hat,* lumber, door
   Cold: ice, freezer, *shoes*
   Drinks: *margarine,* Pepsi, water
   People: grocer, *Oldsmobile,* teacher
   Hot: *table,* fire, burn
   Happy: smile, laugh, *sick*
   Run: fast, *sit,* quickly
   Swim: water, bathing suit, *bricks*
   Picnic: food, drinks, *diamonds*
   Television: *hot dogs,* shows, actors
   Work: *sleep,* do, hard
   Read: book, newspaper, *toes*
   Hair: long, *pink,* short
   Girl: Susan, *Joe,* Mary
   Boy: Bob, Bill, *Ellen*
   Party: cake, candles, *onions*
   Christmas: *Studebaker,* tree, ornaments

Auditory Decoding – Encoding: Associating Ideas Presented Aurally: "What's Wrong with It?"

Materials. "What's wrong with it?" sentences.

Criterion. Level V
Twenty consecutively correct answers to "What's wrong with it?" sentences.

Purpose. To exercise the auditory decoding organizing (association) process by associating words with meaningful concepts. In the case of this set, the concept is "What is wrong with this sentence?"

Demonstration Sequence

1. Establish which sentences you will use. Those presented here are intended only as examples.

   Accept any form of answer that is correct.

   Provide answers if you must, but try to refrain from this, because it will greatly lessen the idea discrimination aspect.

   Intermix "wrong" with "right" sentences once the concept is established.

1. *Examples of sentences*
   I'LL SAY A SENTENCE. LISTEN CAREFULLY. TELL ME WHAT IS THE MATTER WITH IT.

   WIND *NEVER* BLOWS.
   THE BOY WALKED OVER THE *CLOUD*.
   FISH CAN *TALK*.
   THE WATER WAS *DRY*.
   TELEPHONES *NEVER* RING.

   THE SKY IS *NEVER* BLUE.
   THE BOY *DRANK* HIS *HAMBURGER*.
   ALL MONEY IS SILVER.
   THE GIRL RAN *THROUGH* THE STREET.
   THE BALL IS *SQUARE*.

   THE SUN RISES IN THE *EVENING*.
   SHE BRUSHED HER TEETH WITH A *COMB*.
   MOTHER SWEPT THE FLOOR WITH A *BASKET*.
   CARROTS ARE *GREEN*.
   SHE PUT A FRAME AROUND THE *LIGHT*.

   BABY CHICKS ARE *BLUE*.
   HER MOTHER COOKED THE POTATOES IN THE *REFRIGERATOR*.
   SHE HAD PRETTY BLOND *EYES*.
   THE HORSE HAD HIS DINNER IN THE *HOUSE*.
   THE SHIP SANK INTO THE *DIRT*.

What's Wrong With It?

All plates are round.
The chicken laid a *cookie*.
He wore a *watch* around his waist.
The *tractor* landed at the airport.
Mittens keep your *feet* warm.

Water is *always orange*.
All fish can *talk*.
The sun is *cold*.
Grass is *red*.
The horse *flew* over the fence.

The *animals* went to school.
All animals can *fly*.
The children played in the *flower*.
The box is *round*.
The sun sets in the *morning*.

He ate his meat with a *napkin*.
They sat and *watched* the radio.
Stars shine during the *day*.
The *fireman* delivered the milk.
Horses can sing.

She put the bedspread on the *phone*.
He wore his jacket *under* his shirt.
Sheep live in *houses*.
He planted tomatoes in the *carpet*.
The girl skied *up* the hill.

The *football player* struck out.
She brushed her hair with a *toothbrush*.
The hat kept his *chin* warm.
She rode to school on a *chair*.
New Year's is in *June*.

Cherries grow on *rose* trees.
He tied his shoes with *hair ribbons*.
The *gardner* repaired the broken pipe.
Celery is *purple*.
Chairs are for sleeping.

The farmer *milked* the *giraffe*.
She washed the dishes with *toothpaste*.
He put his *socks* on *over* his *shoes*.
He cut his meat with a *cane*.
The *snowman* skated down the street.

The boy blew up the *doll*.
Turtles move *quickly*.
They prayed in a *store*.
Easter is in *November*.
New Year's is in *July*.

Their house is built *under* a hill.
Fish swim *on top of* the water.
February is the *fourth* month of the year.
The *frog galloped* across the field.

The boy walked *on* the water.
The *cowboy* put out the fire.
Her *gloves* were too big for her *feet*.
She kept the ice cream in the *oven*.
Slippers keep your *hands* warm.

She wore a *belt* on her head.
He wrote a letter using a *nail*.
She knelt on her *elbows*.
He rode the *kite*.
The *teddy bear* played ball.

Strawberries are *yellow*.
He was stung by a *duck*.
Santa Claus left the *Easter eggs*.
Christmas is in *October*.
He used his *ring* to open the door.

His hair is dark *purple*.
They swam in a *basin*.
She ran *through* a car.
Rocks are *soft*.
Bread is *always* white.

The boy climbed over the *rainbow*.
Leaves fall off of *chairs*.
All animals have four legs.
Clouds are *always white*.
Boats have *wheels*.

Barns are made of *hay*.
Coffee is *light green*.
The *plumber* came down the chimney.
They barbecued the steak on the *couch*.
Ten comes *before* nine.

They bought food at the *gas station*.
The king wears a *rooster* on his head.
Cars have *five* wheels.
The *doctor* checked his *tires*.
Grapes are *pink*.

Winter days are always *cold*.
The frog *ran* down the path.
The boy washed his feet with a *cane*.
The *radio* had a clear picture.
Tomatoes grow on trees.

She washed her face with a *blanket*.
The fire was *cold*.
The children swam in the *dirt*.
Bathtubs are in *kitchens*.
He took a shower in the *basin*.

They sat *in* the floor.
Onions smell *sweet*.
She wrote a letter with a *hammer*.
Boys wear *dresses*.
Boys *never* have curly hair.

Windows are made of *rubber*.
Balls are made of *paper*.
She wore her *dress over* her coat.
The football player wore a *curtain* on his head.
Cherries grow on *strawberries*.

The *car* sailed across the ocean.
Tires are square.
The *baseball player* dribbled the ball.
The ice cube felt *warm*.
Summer days are *always hot*.

The car had four flat *hands*.
The school year *starts* in June.
Summer vacation is in *February*.
The gardner watered his yard with *milk*.
Lettuce is *orange*.

Elephants jump rope.
Sandwiches *grow* on trees.
Three comes *after* four.
He drank his milk out of a *plate*.
Rings are worn on *feet*.

They ate dinner in the *chimney*.
The campfire was built in the *lake*.
All children are boys.
Stoves are in *bathrooms*.
He kicked the ball with his *hands*.

The *cat* chased the *dog*.
The engine runs on *coffee*.
The artist painted a *paper*.
The *dentist* examined his *feet*.
Bananas are *purple*.

Horses can *talk*.
The boy *sipped* his sandwich.
The *cat* brushed his teeth.
The girl washed her hands with a *basket*.
The farmer *planted* some *tractors*.

All balloons are *red*.
Roses are planted in *lakes*.
Her mother baked the cookies in the *cupboard*.
The horse trotted on *two hooves*.
Wheels are *square*.

The girl ate her fruit with a *pen*.
She carried her purse on her *ankle*.
The man lighted his cigarette with a *jar*.
The *baby* prepared the dinner.
She chewed her vegetables with her *elbow*.

People see with their *stomachs*.
The boy smelled the meat with his *throat*.
Vegetables are *never* green.
The boy ate his soup with a *fork*.
She spread the butter on the *table*.

The boy drank a cup of *crackers*.
The *policeman* repaired the stove.
The *elephant* climbed up the tree.
The *stars* covered the *ground*.
The *bee paddled* across the river.

The *boy* played with the *doll*.
The *train* melted in the hot sun.
She *cut up* the *milk*.
The teacher wrote the lesson on the *sidewalk*.
Apples are always *green*.

Verbal Association: Answering Questions

Materials. Questions list.

Criterion. Level V
Twenty consecutively correct answers
to questions.

Purpose. To exercise the verbal–
associational function by providing
cognitive practice in the use of descriptive
words through listening.

Demonstration Sequence

1. Produce the key sentence. Give the instruction to listen
   carefully to the sentence and to provide the correct answer.

   Work at a logical ability level. If the student is capable of
   selecting from two possible answers, use only two.

1. I'LL SAY A SENTENCE. LISTEN TO IT CAREFULLY.
   THEN I'LL GIVE YOU SOME ANSWERS. SOME WILL
   BE WRONG. ONLY ONE WILL BE RIGHT. TELL ME
   THE ONE WHICH IS RIGHT.

   Examples
   Q. AT THE BEACH YOU PLAY IN THE_____ .
   A. GRASS DIRT CEMENT *WATER*

   Q. A BALL IS_____ .
   A. SQUARE *ROUND* LONG SHORT

   Q. WE SLEEP_____ .
   A. STANDING SITTING *LYING* WALKING

   Q. HORSES EAT_____ .
   A. *FOOD* BOTTLES CANS PAPER

   Q. A BOOK IS USED FOR_____ .
   A. PAINTING *READING* EATING THROWING

   Q. RAIN COMES FROM_____ .
   A. A STORE YOUR HOUSE *THE SKY* A FACTORY

   Q. A FIRE IS_____ .
   A. COOL *HOT* COLD SOFT

2. An alternative means of presentation is to place questions
   in clusters of experience categories.

3. Another possibility might be to provide more than one
   correct answer and instruct the student to sort out and
   tell you which is which.

2. *Examples*

   Christmas
   AT CHRISTMAS WE PUT UP A
   LAWN, *TREE,* SISTER, SPOON

   SANTA CLAUS COMES
   AT NOON, EASTER, THANKSGIVING, *CHRISTMAS*

   AT CHRISTMAS WE GIVE
   CHAIRS, ROCKS, *PRESENTS,* SHOVELS

   Bedtime
   WE SLEEP IN A
   CAR, BARN, *BED,* WAGON

   WE CLEAN OUR TEETH WITH
   SOAP, POP, *BRUSH,* CLOTH

136 II. The Language Sets

Materials. Objects, pictures.

Criterion. Level IV
Twenty consecutively correct identifications of an object or picture which has been partially obscured by figure-to-ground complexity.

Purpose. To teach the person to voluntarily force visual focusing behavior by responding to increasing figure-to-ground complexity.

Demonstration Sequence

1. Establish first the verbal identification of the object or picture.

2. Begin showing the item fairly close to the person.

3. Move it farther away.

4. Exchange the item. Show it from the "farther away" position.

5. Move the item farther and farther away or move the person farther from it. Exchange items.

6. Name the picture or object. As many pictures as possible may be randomly arranged into a group with some obscuring others. Shuffle the group around. A table top or floor may serve as the "ground" for the items.

   Other nonvocabulary items may be used to further obscure the objects or pictures.

   The person should be allowed to approach the group and clearly point to the item.

   An alternative group activity may be to randomly arrange the objects and/or pictures on a table top or floor; have some obscuring others and also being obscured by nonvocabulary items such as pieces of cloth.

1. THIS IS A _____ .
   (clinician completes)

2. LOOK AT THE PICTURE.
   WHAT IS IT?_____ .
   (person completes)

   WHAT IS IT?_____ .
   (person completes)

   WHAT IS IT?_____ .
   (person completes)

5. WHAT IS IT?_____ .
   (person completes)

6. FIND THE PICTURE AS FAST AS YOU CAN. POINT TO IT AS SOON AS YOU SEE IT. I'LL HIDE IT WITH THESE.

Visual Association: Consonant Recognition Fb

Materials. Lists of simple letter consonants and/or 3″ × 5″ or 4″ × 8″ cards with single consonants printed in large format.

Criterion. Level IV
Two hundred consecutively correct recognitions and verbal productions of randomly presented consonants.

Purpose. To teach the recognition and verbal production of isolated consonants.

Demonstration Sequence

1. Type or print a large highly repetitive list of single-letter consonants. This list might consist of one thousand or more random single-letter consonants arranged in horizontal lists of two hundred per 8½″ × 11″ page.

2. Some consonants will ultimately have variant spellings, e.g., the initial [dʒ] sound occurring as it does in the word "joy" and finally in the word "fudge." But for your purposes of this early consonant practice the "j" letter will suffice.

1. *Examples of pronunciation of single-letter consonants*
   p — "puh"
   b — "buh"
   t — "tuh"
   d — "duh"
   k — "kuh" (both k and c are produced
   c — "kuh" the same)
   g — "guh"
   f — "f-f-f"
   v — "v-v-v"
   l — "l-l-l"
   s — "s-s-s"
   z — "z-z-z"
   j — "juh"
   m — "m-m-m"
   n — "n-n-n"
   r — "ruh"
   x — "ks"
   h — "huh"

3. Begin practice at Level III. Model each sound representing the letter separately.

3. *Example*
   Letter is "p"
   THIS IS "PUH," SAY "PUH." *(person says PUH)*

   Letter is "b"
   THIS IS "BUH." SAY "BUH." *(person says BUH)*

4. Stop the student as soon as he has performed incorrectly on any consonant. Produce the sound yourself.

4. *Example:* (Interrupting the student as soon as the incorrect production occurs.)
   THAT'S F-F-F.
   SAY F-F-F. *(person says F-F-F).*

5. Once you have modeled them, request that your student continue naming each in succession.

5. NOW GO ON WITH THE LIST.
   SAY EACH SOUND WHICH THE LETTER MAKES.

6. If repeated mistakes are made on certain consonants, you might produce a list with that "problem" letter present in great magnitude, to provide rehearsal where it is most needed.

   The Criterion test will consist of your student producing all sounds with no verbal cues from you whatsoever.

7. If the student has difficulty focusing on the smaller format consonant lists, produce a set of cards with each consonant presented in large format. Sort these continually as you would shuffle a deck of cards to create a random group. Make as many cards as funds and time will allow. Proceed as in step 3 above.

8. Some consonants occur as digraphs. These are letter pairs which represent a single speech sound. Other consonants may appear singly. Perceptually, these are more difficult to learn. Use your judgment as to whether or not it is appropriate to study them here.

8. *Examples of digraphs*
   th (voiced as in "*th*em")
   th (unvoiced as in "*th*umb")
   ng (as in "si*ng*")
   sh (as in "*sh*eep")
   su (as in "plea*su*re")
   ch (as in "*ch*ew")
   f (as in "tou*gh*")

Visual Association: Combining Consonants with Vowels and Diphthongs

Materials. Typewritten or manually produced consonant—vowel combination word lists.

Criterion. Level V
Two hundred consecutively correct recognitions and verbal productions of words produced by combining consonants and vowels.

Purpose. To teach the recognition and verbal production of certain words by combining selected consonants with selected vowels.

Demonstration Sequence

1. Establish the list of words which contain target vowels and consonants. Keep the words as short as possible. If no elementary typewriter is available, print the various consonant—vowel word combinations in large format on 8½″ × 11″ paper.

1. *Example:* The vowel [i] (ee) is combined with selected consonants and respective appropriate spellings.

Three letters	*Four letters*
e*at*	e*ach*
b*ee*	e*asy*
sh*e*	t*ree*
e*ar*	e*ven*

2. A more convenient form of list to generate is one that contains all vowels in random occurrence. Be careful of spelling complications that may occur when some combinations are produced.

   Keep presentations simple. Note that the same letter(s) may represent a different vowel or diphthong depending upon the word in which it appears.

2. *Examples of vowels and diphthongs to teach with selected consonants*

   Vowels
   e as in b*ee*t
   i as in h*i*t
   a as in *a*te
   e or *ea* as in b*e*d or h*ea*d
   a as in b*a*t
   u as in h*u*t
   u as in c*oo*l
   oo or *ou* as in c*oo*k or c*ou*ld
   o as in b*oa*t
   a or *aw* as in b*a*ll   OR
   a as in f*a*ther

   Diphthongs
   i as in f*i*ne
   ou as in ab*ou*t
   oi or *oy* as in *oi*l or b*oy*

3. Begin practice at Level III. Model each word separately.

3. *Examples:* Vowel is [ɛ] or ea as in r*e*d or b*e*d.

   three letters
   *e*gg l*e*g l*e*t f*e*d T*e*d

4. Stop the student as soon as he has performed incorrectly. Produce the sound yourself.

4. THAT'S LEG. SAY "LEG." *(person says "leg")*
NOW GO ON.

Materials. Sound Blending Groups list, typewritten or manually produced (attached).

Criterion. Level IV
One hundred consecutively correctly produced words as a sound blending activity.

Purpose. To incorporate separate sound productions into combinations of other sounds that become words.

Demonstration Sequence

1. Establish a list for your student, using selected word groups. Arrange according to difficulty.

2. Refer to the Sound Blending Groups. Select the target sound(s) to be emphasized.

   If a vowel precedes the concluding part of the word, practice the vowel and suffix first. Next go to the consonant or consonant blend in the prefix word part.

3. Model and produce simultaneously. Use large format manually lettered examples if necessary.

3. *Example*
   THE WORD IS "CAME."
   SAY "AY" WITH ME.
   SAY "K" WITH ME.
   SAY "M" WITH ME.
   SAY "CAME" WITH ME.
   SAY "CAME" BY YOURSELF.

4. An alternative means of combining sounds is to model them in any (nonmeaningful) combination, gradually rearranging the combination until it becomes a word.

5. Practice initially at Level III. Model each sound blending word group separately.

Sound-Blending Groups — Word-Making Patterns

ab:	c, d, g, j, n, t, bl, cr, dr, gr, sc, sl, st	ath:	b, h, l, p, wr
ack:	b, h, j, l, M, p, qu, r, s, t, bl, cl, cr, sl, sm, sn, st, sh, wh, kn	aw:	j, l, p, r, s, cl, dr, fl, str, th
ace:	f, l, p, r, br, gr, pl, sp, tr	ax:	l, t, w, fl
act:	f, p, t, tr	ay:	b, d, g, h, l, m, p, r, s, w, cl, gr, pl, pr, sl, spr, st, str, tr
ad:	b, c, d, f, h, l, m, p, s, t, br, cl, gl, sc, sh	aze:	d, g, h, m, bl, gr
ade:	b, f, m, w, bl, gl, gr, sp, tr, sh	each:	b, p, r, t, bl, pr
ag:	b, f, g, h, j, l, n, r, s, t, w, br, cr, dr, fl, sl, sn, st, sh	eal:	d, h, m, p, s, t, v, st
ail:	b, h, m, n, p, qu, r, s, t, w, fr, sn, tr	eam:	b, r, s, t, cr, dr, gl, scr, st, str
ain:	g, m, p, r, br, dr, gr, pl, sl, spr, st, str, tr, ch	ean:	b, l, m, w, cl
ake:	b, c, f, l, m, qu, r, s, t, w, br, fl, sn, st, sh	eat:	b, f, h, m, n, s, cl, pl, tr, ch, wh
all:	b, c, f, h, m, t, w, sm, st	eck:	b, d, n, p, fl, sp, ch, wr
am:	d, h, j, r, y, cl, cr, dr, gr, scr, sl, sw, tr, sh	ed:	b, f, l, r, T, w, bl, fl, sl, sp, sh, shr
ame:	c, f, g, l, n, s, t, bl, fl, fr, sh	eed:	d, f, n, s, w, bl, br, gr
amp:	c, d, l, r, t, v, cl, cr, sc, st, tr, ch	eek:	l, m, s, r, w, cr, Gr, ch
an:	b, c, f, m, p, r, t, v, br, cl, pl, sc, sp	eel:	f, h, p, r, st, kn
anch:	r, br, st	eep:	d, p, s, w, cr, sl, st, ch, sh
and:	b, h, l, s, bl, br, gl, gr, st, str	eet:	b, f, m, fl, sl, str, sh
ang:	b, f, g, h, p, r, s, cl, sl, spr	eg:	b, k, l, p
ank:	b, h, l, r, s, t, y, bl, cl, cr, dr, fl, fr, pl, pr, sp, st, sw, sh, th	ell:	b, c, d, f, h, qu, s, t, w, y, sm, sp, sw, sh, dw, kn
ant:	c, p, r, gr, pl, sc, sl, ch	elt:	b, C, f, m, p, sp, dw, kn
ap:	c, g, l, m, n, r, s, t, cl, fl, scr, sl, sn, str, tr, ch, wr	em:	g, h, st, th
ar:	b, c, f, j, m, p, t, sc, sp, st	en:	B, d, h, m, p, t, y, gl, th, wh, wr
are:	b, c, f, m, sc, sp, st, fl, r, bl	ench:	b, qu, cl, dr, Fr, st, tr, wr
ark:	b, d, h, l, m, p, sp, sh	end:	b, l, m, s, t, bl, sp
art:	c, d, p, t, sm, st, ch	ent:	b, c, d, l, p, r, s, t, v, w, bl, sc, sp
ash:	b, c, d, g, h, l, m, r, s, br, cl, cr, fl, spl, sl, sm, tr, thr	ept:	k, w, cr, sl, sw
ask:	b, c, m, t, fl	ess:	l, m, bl, dr, pr, str, tr, ch, gu
asp:	g, h, r, cl, gr	est:	b, j, l, n, p, qu, r, t, v, w, z, bl, cr, ch, gu, wr
ass:	l, m, p, br, cl, gl, gr	et:	b, g, j, l, m, n, p, s, w, y, fr
ast:	c, f, l, m, p, v, bl	ib:	b, f, r, cr, gl, squ
at:	b, c, f, h, m, n, p, r, s, br, fl, pl, sl, sp, ch, th, gn	ice:	d, l, m, n, r, v, pr, sl, sp, spl, tw
atch:	b, c, h, l, m, p, scr, sn, th	ick:	D, k, l, n, p, qu, s, t, w, br, cl, cr, fl, pr, st, tr, ch, th
ate:	d, f, g, h, l, m, r, pl, sk, sl, st	id:	b, d, h, k, l, m, r, gr, sk, sl
		ide:	h, r, s, t, w, br, gl, pr, sl

ift,	g, l, r, s, dr, sw, sh, thr
ig:	b, d, f, g, j, p, r, w, br, pr, spr, sw, tw, Wh
ight:	f, l, m, n, r, s, t, bl, br, fl, fr, pl, sl
ike:	b, h, l, p, sp, str, tr
ill:	B, d, f, g, h, k, m, n, p, qu, s, t, w, dr, fr, gr, sk, sp, st, tw, ch, shr, thr
im:	d, h, r, v, br, gl, gr, pr, sk, sl, sw, tr, wh
ime:	d, l, t, cr, gr, sl, ch
in:	b, d, f, g, k, p, s, t, w, gr, sk, sp, tw, ch, sh, th
ind:	b, f, h, k, m, w, bl, gr
ine:	d, f, l, m, n, p, v, w, br, sp, sh, wh
ing:	k, p, r, s, w, br, cl, fl, sl, spr, st, str, sw, th, wr
ink:	k, l, p, s, w, bl, br, cl, dr, shr, sl, st, ch, th
ip:	d, h, l, n, p, r, s, t, cl, dr, fl, gr, qu, sk, sl, sn, str, tr, ch, sh, wh
ipe:	p, r, w, gr, str, sw
ish:	d, f, w, sw
iss:	h, k, m, bl
ist:	f, g, l, m, gr, tw, wh, wr
it:	b, f, h, k, l, p, s, w, fl, gr, qu, sl, sm, sp, spl, kn
ite:	b, k, m, sp, tr, wh, wr
itch:	d, h, p, w, st, sw, tw
ive:	d, f, h, l, dr, str, thr
ix:	f, m, s
oat:	b, c, g, m, bl, fl, gl
ob:	B, c, f, h, j, l, m, r, s, bl, sn, thr, kn
ock:	c, d, h, l, m, p, r, s, t, bl, cl, cr, fl, fr, sm, st, sh, kn
od:	c, G, n, p, qu, r, s, cl, pl, pr, tr, sh
og:	c, h, f, j, n, cl, fl, fr, gr, sl
oil:	b, c, f, s, t, br
oke:	c, j, p, w, y, br, sm, sp, st, ch
old:	b, c, f, g, h, m, s, t
one:	b, c, l, t, sh, thr
ook:	b, c, h, l, n, t, br, cr, sh
ool:	c, f, p, t, sch, sp, st
oom:	b, d, l, r, z, bl, br, gl, gr
oon:	b, c, m, n, sp, sw
oop:	c, l, dr, sc, st, tr
oot:	b, h, l, r, t, sh
op:	c, h, l, m, p, s, t, cr, dr, fl, pr, sl, st, str, ch, sh
ope:	c, d, h, l, m, p, r, gr, sl
orn:	b, c, h, m, t, w, sc, th
ose:	h, n, r, cl, ch, th
oss:	b, l, m, t, cr, fl
ot:	c, d, g, h, j, l, n, p, r, t, bl, cl, pl, Sc, sl, sp, tr, sh, kn
otch:	n, bl, cr, sc, spl
ound:	b, f, h, m, p, r, s, w, gr
ow:	b, c, h, l, m, n, r, t, bl, br, fl, gl, gr, pl, sl, sn, sh, kn
own:	d, g, t, br, cl, cr, dr, fr
ub:	c, d, h, r, s, t, cl, fr, gr, scr, shr, sn, st, ch, th
uck:	b, d, l, m, p, s, t, cl, pl, st, str, tr, ch
ud:	b, c, m, sc, sp, st, th
uff:	b, c, h, m, p, R, bl, fl, gr, sc, scr, sn, st
ug:	b, d, h, j, l, m, p, r, t, dr, pl, shr, sl, sm, sn, th
ull:	c, d, g, h, l, m, n, sc, sk, tr
um:	b, g, h, m, r, s, dr, gl, gr, pl, sc, sl, st, str, sw, ch
ump:	b, d, h, j, l, cl, pl, sl, st, tr, ch, th
un:	b, d, f, g, H, n, p, r, s, sp, st, sh
unch:	b, h, l, m, p, cr, scr
ung:	h, l, r, s, cl, fl, sl, spr, st, str, sw, wr
unk:	b, h, j, p, s, dr, shr, sk, sl, sp, tr, ch
unt:	b, h, p, r, bl, br, gr, st, sh
up:	c, p, s
ush:	g, h, l, m, r, bl, br, cr, fl, pl, sl, thr
ust:	b, d, h, j, m, r, cr, thr, tr
ut:	b, c, h, j, m, n, r, str
utch:	D, h, cl, cr
y:	b, m, cr, dr, fl, fr, sk, sl, sp, spr, st, tr, wh

Materials. Typewritten or manually produced words with letters variously spaced, 8½″ × 11″ paper, felt pen.

Criterion. Level IV
One hundred consecutively correct identifications of words with varying letter spacing.

Purpose. To teach the visual recognition of words by forcing the visual closure function.

Demonstration Sequence

1. If you can obtain an elementary school typewriter, the lower case keys may be used to construct word lists with variable spacing. If no typewriter is available, carefully print the word lists in elementary script on 8½″ × 11″ paper.

   Obtain a graded word list from any source. The Word Finder in Appendix I will also assist you. Examine a set of graded readers and select appropriate vocabulary suitable to the ability level of your student.

   Make quite an extensive list. Once you have it completed, it may be used over and over again with other students. Arrange the words in terms of the number of letters in them. A minimum of ten pages of 100 words per page should be produced.

   Results will possibly be slow in coming. For this reason, a great deal of practice is necessary with many, many words.

   Attempt Level V first. You want to ascertain if your student can visually recognize the word after producing it with the designated pause with no prompting from you.

1. *Examples:* Words here are of varying levels.

m e	u s	ri ght
y es	w e	ov er
hi s	s he	o nly
u p	mi ne	n o
o ut	o ne	o ff
b u t	i t	n ow
bel ow	th em	no t
s ee	hi m	ne xt
o f	m e	mo st
o ff	a ll	mo re
b y	bo th	lat er
do wn	w hen	h ow
ab out	wh y	h ot
aft er	w ell	h ere
a t	to d ay	goo d
nea r	th e re	ev er
y ou	so on	ea ch
m y	so me	a s
a g ain	pu ll	a sk
a ll	pu sh	b e
w or k	p lay	bu y
wi n dow	na me	c a ll
wa t er	s ave	cli mb
a ll	ra n	c ut
ev ery	re a d	d ress
h a pp y	ste p	fo ll ow
p a y	te ll	g r ow
rou nd	ra n	woo d
wen t	p ut	ti me
w al k	o pen	tr ee
thi n k	mus t	s un
s t o p	m ay	p a per

SAY EACH WORD, BUT PAUSE FOR EACH SPACE. SAY THE SOUNDS OF THE WORD. THEN SAY THE WHOLE WORD.

Example: Interrupting the student when an incorrect production occurs.
THAT'S BU-OH-TH
BOTH
SAY BU-OH-TH
BOTH _____
       (person completes)

Stop the student as soon as he has not performed correctly on any word. Produce the word yourself with appropriate pauses. Then produce it normally. Have the student produce the mistaken word at Level III, then go on to a new word.

Gradually increase the difficulty of the word lists.

The Criterion test will consist of having the student produce all words-with-pauses with no verbal cues from you whatsoever.

Materials. Pictures, objects, 3" × 5" or 5" × 8" cards, felt pen.

Criterion. Level IV
Fifty consecutively correct word—picture associations.

Purpose. To teach the use of visual association preparatory to reading instruction by matching a written word with its visual counterpart, such as a picture or object.

Demonstration Sequence

1. Select which word picture you will employ. They should be known to the person.

   Decide how many pictures to present (two, three, four, etc.) as the group from which he is to select the picture which represents the word.

   In large, easy-to-see letters, print the name of the picture on a card. Make as many printed word cards as you desire.

   The complexity of this activity may occur in relation to ability level. You may wish to arrange only one or two choice situations, or you may array your entire collection of objects and pictures in various sized groups.

   An alternative activity is to array the same number of written name cards as pictures and objects; cards on one side and objects on the other. The person is to place the appropriate card next to its counterpart, such as an object or picture.

   You might number the card to correspond with the number of the picture. In this way, you may quickly assemble the group.

1. HERE ARE SOME PICTURES.
   HERE IS A CARD WITH A WORD ON IT.
   MATCH THE CARD WITH THE WORD ON IT WITH THE PICTURE.

Visual Association: Word Recognition Fg

Materials. Typewritten word lists and/or manually produced word lists.

Criterion. Level V
Two hundred consecutively correct recognitions and verbal productions of selected words.

Purpose. To establish a basic sight recognition vocabulary of most frequently occurring words.

Demonstration Sequence

1. Study any reference that provides you with a compilation of words characteristic of the reading-grade level at which you intend to work. You may need to go completely back to pre-primer vocabulary lists.

2. Produce your own list with repetitions of the same word occurring variously. Gradually lessen the frequency of repetitions until only one occurs in a subsequent list.

2. *Example*

TO	AND	HER
AND	HIM	AND
BUT	TO	BUT
SHE	AND	HER
TO	HIM	SHE
BUT	ME	ME
SHE	YOU	YOU
ME	YOU	AND
TO	TO	ME

3. Begin practice at Level III. Model each word once. Quickly go to Level IV, in which you provide no verbal cues. If a misrecognition does occur, correct and go to the next word.

   If no elementary typewriter is available, produce the lists on 8½″ × 11″ paper in careful printing.

3. *Example*
THAT'S BOY. SAY "BOY."_____
(person says BOY)

Visual Association: Reorganizing Written Phrases

Materials. 4″ × 5″ or 5″ × 8″ cards, felt pen, paper, pen.

Criterion. Level IV
Fifty consecutively correct phrase reorganizations.

Purpose. To learn phrase patterns by visually reorganizing them from a scrambled format presented visually.

Demonstration Sequence

1. Refer to any syntactic model that illustrates a phrase form. Work at the ability level of the student. Be sure to include varying parts of speech.

Prepare a set of cards which, when placed together, will form phrases. One word should appear on each card.

Practice phrase reorganization to any extent desired. In fact, this activity may be practiced to a great extent. It may serve as a review of all previous phrases or may be used in conjunction with each set.

Phrases may be rewritten in correct form by either filling in the missing word or unscrambling two phrases.

Practice phrases through Levels II, III, and IV. After Level IV attempt Level V, provided the person is able to understand what is required of him.

Combine the manual card reorganization and/or sentence completion with verbally reproducing the sentence at Level IV.

A list of scrambled phrases may be prepared which the person is to rewrite correctly.

1. *Example*
   A BALL
   BALL A
   SEE, THIS IS THE WAY IT SHOULD BE.

   NOW I'LL MIX IT UP.
   PUT IT BACK THE WAY IT SHOULD BE.

   SAY THE WORDS.
   Person reorganizes card and says:
   A BALL

   HERE IS A PIECE OF PAPER. WRITE THIS PHRASE CORRECTLY.

   BALLOON RED

   Person writes or says:
   RED BALLOON

Materials. 4″ × 5″ or 5″ × 8″ cards, felt pen, paper, pen.

Criterion. Level IV
Fifty consecutively correct sentence reorganizations.

Purpose. To generate the visual association modality by reorganizing sentence patterns presented in a scrambled written format.

Demonstration Sequence

1. Use any syntactic model which illustrates a phrase or sentence form. Work at the ability level of the person. Very brief sentences may be necessary.

   Prepare a set of cards which, when placed together, form sentences. One word should appear on each card.

   Practice sentences at Levels III and IV. At IV, attempt V, providing the person understands what is required of him.

   Combine the manual card reorganization with the verbal production of the sentence.

   Be sure to keep the vocabulary level of the sentences at the reading grade level of the person.

2. Level V productions may occur by providing random cards with basic parts of speech and requesting that sentences be made. If picture story sequences are available, arrange the cards, one sentence at a time to tell the story.

   This activity should be practiced intensively. It may serve as a review of selected previously verbally practiced sentences. Before practicing this set the student should have some knowledge of reading and writing. Omit this set if the student is incapable of either reading or writing.

1. *Examples*
   brown dog The is
   SEE. THIS IS THE WAY IT SHOULD BE.
   The dog is brown
   I'LL MIX IT UP. YOU PUT IT BACK THE WAY IT SHOULD BE. SAY THE SENTENCE.
   The person reorganizes the cards and says: THE DOG IS BROWN.

2. HERE ARE SOME CARDS.
   MAKE SOME SENTENCES FROM THEM.

Materials. Graded reading series.

Criterion. Level IV
Verbal recreation of a printed text at
100 percent accuracy for four consecutive
sessions.

Purpose. To teach reading in its usual
contextual form.

Obtain a set of graded readers that go as far back to beginning skills as possible. Some programmed materials are of a simpler level than pre-primers. None are particularly recommended here, because there are many that are of equal quality. The elementary education department of any college or university, or any catalog that illustrates grade-level reading materials, will provide you with necessary sources.

Begin this activity even while you are working with other sets in this section. Work at the lowest possible level initially. Your reference point of beginning should be at a point where the student reads at approximately 80 percent of accuracy. (Count each sentence as one response.) Correct as in other sets. If the student misidentifies a word, stop him immediately, say the word, have him repeat it and go on. Do not say "good" after the incorrect word is corrected as part of your instruction. Say "Good" only at the successful completion of *each* sentence.

Proceed through the reading material, increasing the level of difficulty only when your student has achieved Criterion at his present level.

Silent reading may be started when you feel (based upon an administered reading inventory) he is achieving near his grade level. Examine the material and formulate a set of questions based upon it which test comprehension. The depth with which you practice comprehension will depend upon the auditory memory skills of your student. You may request that the student read only one sentence and try to remember it. Ask him the question after a brief delay. You are *not* asking that the sentence be repeated. Rather, you wish to ask a question *about* the sentence. Increase the number of sentences until you have reached the paragraph level. Remain there until at least five questions can be answered correctly from each paragraph. Re-read paragraphs only if you have run out of your present supply of similarly graded materials.

Visual – Motor Sequencing: Manually Duplicating an Ordered Sequence

Materials. Geometric pictures, felt pen, paper, 3" X 5" or 5" X 8" cards.

Criterion. Level IV
Twenty consecutively correct manual duplications of a sequence of pictures or drawings.

Purpose. To teach the use of visual motor sequencing by manually duplicating a sequence of forms and symbols preparatory to writing.

Demonstration Sequence

1. Prepare a set of simple geometric drawings and symbols. Decide at which level of difficulty to work. The person may be required to manually arrange the previously presented set of symbols, or you may request that he *draw* the set of symbols from memory. He may draw the set while looking at it first, but his actual task is to draw the set after you *remove* it. Begin with only two symbols. Gradually increase the form and complexity of the activity.

1. LOOK VERY CAREFULLY AT THIS SET OF DRAWINGS. REMEMBER WHICH COMES AFTER WHICH.

Examples of symbols

I'LL TAKE IT AWAY. NOW PUT IT BACK THE WAY IT WAS.

or

NOW DRAW IT THE WAY IT WAS.

Materials. Form drawings, word pictures, tracing paper, felt pen, blackboard, chalk.

Criterion. Level IV
Ten consecutive correctly drawn forms and/or pictures.

Purpose. To teach the person to recognize that a form is incomplete and to complete the drawing himself preparatory to writing.

Demonstration Sequence

1. Prepare a number of single incompletely drawn forms and/or object pictures.

   These should at first be quite easy to complete. Either place the original (complete) illustration immediately adjacent (see examples) to or under the drawing which is to be completed.

   Make the drawings as large as possible — e.g., one drawing per 8½″ × 11″ piece of paper — or use a blackboard and make the drawings extremely large.

   An alternative means of presentation is to divide a page in half placing the completed design on one side and the incomplete design on the other. Only *one* design should appear at a time.

   Proceed from gross to more subtle differences in the drawings.

   Investigate to see if the person is able to complete *object picture* drawings which you have traced. This is a higher level activity than form completion but the person may be able to handle it.

1. LOOK CAREFULLY AT THIS PICTURE.
   (Point to original)

   LOOK AT THIS PICTURE. (Point to incomplete picture)

   IT IS NOT FINISHED. FINISH IT SO IT LOOKS JUST LIKE THIS ONE. (Point to original again)

   Original   *To be completed*

2. Another activity is to draw two identical shapes on the blackboard. After the participant has his eyes closed, add some detail to one of the circles. In carefully graded increments increase the complexity of the additional design feature.

2. CLOSE YOUR EYES WHILE I CHANGE ONE OF THESE SHAPES.

   NOW OPEN YOUR EYES. LOOK AND SEE WHAT I HAVE CHANGED.

   FIX THE OTHER TO LOOK JUST LIKE THE ONE THAT I HAVE CHANGED.

3. A means of detail accumulation is to use the same two shapes, continuing to add detail over and over again, as the person's eyes are closed.

   Each person of a group might have his designs in front of him as you circulate among them. This activity may become a contest in which a person attempts to "hold out the longest" as he attempts to locate and duplicate the change you have made in his design.

4. Line drawings of familiar objects — houses, cars, etc. — may be partially drawn. Drawings are then completed by the participant.

4. FINISH THESE DRAWINGS.

5. Another activity is to make a dot-to-dot game from a very simple picture, number, or letter. As soon as the person observes what it is, he verbally identifies it. Trace over any picture with dots. This may also be done with letters of the alphabet.

5. TELL ME WHAT THIS IS AS SOON AS YOU KNOW. CONNECT THE DOTS TOGETHER WITH A LINE.

Visual Memory: Making Simple Drawings Gc

Materials. Blackboard, chalk, felt pen, paper, simple form drawings.

Criterion. Level IV
Twenty consecutively correct simple drawings of forms from memory.

Purpose. To exercise the visual memory and motor expression function by reproducing simple forms from memory preparatory to writing.

Demonstration Sequence

1. Make simple pictures of shapes on an 8½" X 11" piece of paper or produce the drawings on the blackboard.

   Show only one illustration at a time at first. Gradually increase the complexity of the drawing as the ability of the person to remember the shape increases.

1. *Examples of forms*

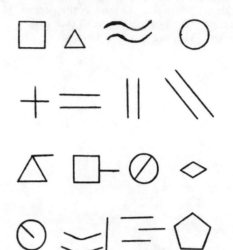

2. Present the form. Remove or erase the picture. At first the time delay between the removal of the picture and cue to reproduce it should be brief. Increase time delays to the limit of the person's ability to retain the mental picture and/or reproduce the shape.

2. LOOK AT THIS. REMEMBER WHAT IT LOOKS LIKE.

   CLOSE YOUR EYES. PICTURE WHAT IT LOOKS LIKE IN YOUR MIND.

   OPEN YOUR EYES. LOOK AT IT AGAIN. REMEMBER IT. WHEN I TAKE IT AWAY, I WANT YOU TO DRAW IT. GET READY. (Time delay)

   GO!

Materials. Paper, blackboard, pens, chalk, crayons, pencils, etc.

Criterion. Level IV
Ten "drawings" which provide a recognizable topic picture.

Purpose. To teach the motor encoding activity by providing simple line drawing practice.

Demonstration Sequence

1. Prepare simple drawings that have a recognizable topic. If a blackboard is available, the large format which is possible there may be a considerable assistance.

   Examine your collection of pictures for those which are most readily copied or traced.

   Before practicing this set, conduct a probe check which will establish the most realistic level. Decide which level you will employ first.

1. THIS IS A PICTURE OF A HOUSE.

LET'S DRAW IT TOGETHER. NOW YOU DRAW IT.

THIS IS A PICTURE OF THE SUN.

LET'S DRAW IT TOGETHER. NOW YOU DRAW IT.

THIS IS A PICTURE OF A CLOCK.

DRAW THE CLOCK.

Writing the Letters of the Alphabet

Materials. Blackboard, chalk, paper, felt pen.

Criterion. Level V
Twenty consecutively correct written productions of the letters of the alphabet.

Purpose. To teach the letters of the alphabet in written form.

Demonstration Sequence

1. Make an extremely large (but within reach) lower case letter "a" on the blackboard or piece of paper.

2. At Level I, trace over the letter, guiding the hand of the person.

3. Make another letter "a." At Level II, produce your letter immediately adjacent to the one which the person is making.

4. At Level III, write the letter "a." Pause and then request that the person do so.

5. At Level IV request that the person write the letter "a."

6. Once Level IV has been reached, begin decreasing the size of the letter "a" until the person is able to produce an "a" about one inch tall on paper and two to three inches tall at the blackboard. Do not attempt to move from very large to very small letters in one session. This may in fact take weeks.

7. Proceed through the alphabet at Levels I, II, III, and IV for each letter.

8. Review constantly. Intermix those letters already "learned" with the new one in random order.

9. Teach printing at first, guiding the hand of the student in the proper sequence of motions for each letter. Use any elementary school lettering motions guide. As soon as possible, move on to cursive writing.

1. THIS IS AN "a" (lower case).
   MAKE AN "a" WITH ME.

2. THIS IS HOW WE MAKE A LETTER "a."
   I'LL HELP YOU.

3. LET'S MAKE THE LETTER "a" TOGETHER.
   LOOK AT THE WAY I MAKE THE LETTER.

4. I'LL MAKE IT FIRST. THEN YOU MAKE IT.
   WATCH ME MAKING THE LETTER "a."
   NOW YOU WRITE THE LETTER "a."

5. WRITE THE LETTER "a."

6. NOW LET'S MAKE A SMALLER LETTER "a."

Visual – Auditory Sequential Memory: Spelling

Materials. Spelling words, felt pen, paper or 3" × 5" or 5" × 8" cards.

Criterion. Level IV
One hundred consecutive correctly spelled words presented verbally.

Purpose. To teach the use of auditory sequential memory and basic spelling by combining both in high magnitude of response practice.

Demonstration Sequence

1. Practice at Levels II and III first, then go to IV.

2. Prepare flash cards with the lower case alphabet lettered in large format. Select the words which are at or beneath the ability level of the person. Total nonreaders should begin at the easiest word level possible. Refer to any previously studied picture which might serve as a visual cue. It may be used along with the letter symbols.

3. You may or may not wish to teach the entire alphabet first. Simply begin with each word and its spelling as a separate entity.

4. Remove the visual cues of picture and lettered cards as soon as the child appears to be able to remember the sequence of aurally presented letters.

5. Practice each word singly or, if that appears boring, choose two or three words to practice simultaneously. The person's ability level will indicate which is more appropriate.

6. Fade picture and flash card presentations until the person can spell selected words presented as a word and/or repeat the spelling of words which have been spelled aloud to him. Time delays between stimulus and response may be included in this step.

1. LET'S LEARN THE ALPHABET.
LET'S SPELL THIS WORD.

Example
Show a picture of a boy, point to a boy. Put down the "b-o-y" lettered cards.
"B" "O" "Y" SPELLS "BOY."
SAY IT WITH ME. LOOK AT THE LETTERS "BEE-OH-WHY," THEN SAY "BOY."
SAY "BOY" — SAY "BEE-OH-WHY" WITH ME.
(Point to the letters) BEE-OH-WHY.
THEY SPELL "BOY." SAY "BEE-OH-WHY."
POINT TO BEE.
POINT TO OH.
POINT TO WHY.
(Remove the letters. Allow the picture to remain.)
HOW DO YOU SPELL "BOY"? (Remove the picture.)
SPELL "BOY."

Materials. Paper, felt pen, tracing paper.

Criterion. Level IV
Twenty consecutively correctly spelled written words.

Purpose. To teach the student to write simple words, using sequential and visual memory.

Demonstration Sequence

1. Refer to the Word Finder (Appendix I) or other word list. Select the easiest words. Print them in large format on 8½″ × 11″ paper. Place the tracing paper over one word and have the person trace over the word while saying the word.

   Practice at Level I.

2. Practice at Level II.

3. Practice at Level IV.

4. Remove the original word. Repeat steps 1 to 3 without the word underlay.

5. Repeat steps 1 to 3 with a new word, including the visual help of the underlay.

6. Repeat steps 1 to 3 with simple words. As these accumulate, a "flash card" game may be played: Hold up the card. The student is to look at it, copy it, and tell you the name of the word. From these flash card words, word lists for writing practice may be generated which include all those previously studied. See sets in Section E. Add to the list as words accumulate. Constant repetition of each written word will be necessary if they are to be successfully learned.

7. An alternative activity is to present a new word. Model it and have the student say it. Then obscure the word and have the student reproduce it in writing. This form of practice will use sequential visual memory if you present words of increasing length.

---

1. *Example:* The word is "CAT."
   LOOK AT THE WORD.
   THE WORD IS "CAT."
   WRITE THE WORD "CAT" THIS WAY.

2. LET'S WRITE "CAT" TOGETHER.
   SAY "CAT" AS YOU WRITE IT.

3. WRITE "CAT."
   SAY "CAT" AS YOU WRITE IT.

4. LET'S WRITE "CAT" AGAIN.
   SAY "CAT" AS YOU WRITE IT.

5. LET'S DO ANOTHER WORD.

7. THIS IS "FLOWER."
   SAY "FLOWER."
   NOW WRITE IT.
   SAY THE WORD AS YOU WRITE IT.

Writing Sentences

Materials. Blackboard, chalk, paper, felt pen, tracing paper, pictures.

Criterion. Level V
Twenty consecutive correctly spelled simple sentences from dictation.

Purpose. To teach the written production of sentences.

Demonstration Sequence

1. Print commonly occurring words clearly on cards. Use articles, nouns, verbs, and adjectives at the simplest level you can establish. Select a two-word combination.

    Either use the cards or write the words on the blackboard.

    Place tracing paper over the cards or write over those that were written on the blackboard.

    Practice at Levels II, III, and IV.

2. Remove the underlay or erase the board.

    Practice step 1 without the original through Levels II, III, and IV.

3. Practice giving words via dictation through Levels II, III, and IV. At Levels II and III, write the words yourself after you say them.

    Face your written cue support as you enter Level IV.

4. An alternative activity might be to cover or erase one word at a time from a two-word sentence, leaving the other word visually present. Request that the student write the missing word in its appropriate place.

5. When incorrect words occur, return to a level that is more likely to produce a correct response.

6. Review all two-word sentences often, to the point where you say the words and the person writes them.

7. When the criterion is met, go to three-word written sentences and continue to four-word sentences, etc.

8. Refer to all sets in Sections B, C, and D. Refer to your pictures. Place the noun or verb picture next to the sentence that characterizes it. Any of the sentences that previously were practiced orally may now be included in written practice.

9. Continue to expand this activity until you have achieved some sentences at three conceptual writing levels: description, narration, exposition. Use any sentences previously taught verbally. Use any picture cues. Include varying transformational levels, verb tenses, and abstraction levels. Intermix levels in sentences.

    Description
    Size:
    Shape:
    Age:
    Color:
    Texture:
    Value:
    Quality:
    Quantity:

    Combine all descriptive aspects into longer sentences.
    Size, age, quality:

    Size, quality, color:

    Quality, color:

1. *Example*
    THIS IS THE WORD "RED."
    THIS IS THE WORD "BALL."
    WRITE "RED BALL" WITH ME.
    SAY "RED BALL" AS YOU WRITE.

    STOP. LOOK AT THE WORDS. CLOSE YOUR EYES. CAN YOU SEE THE WORDS IN YOUR MIND? PICTURE THE WORDS IN YOUR MIND. LOOK AGAIN. WHAT ARE THE WORDS?

2. NOW WRITE "RED BALL" BY YOURSELF.

3. I'LL SAY THE WORDS, YOU WRITE THEM.

4. I'LL TAKE ONE WORD AWAY. REMEMBER IT. LOOK AT THE OTHER WORD. WRITE THE MISSING WORD THAT GOES WITH THIS ONE. PUT IT WHERE IT BELONGS.

THE BALL IS BIG.
THE BOX IS SQUARE.
THE BOX WAS OLD.
THIS IS A GREEN TREE.
THE FUR IS SOFT.
THE LADY IS RICH.
THE POLICEMAN IS NICE.
THERE ARE FOUR BOYS.

THE GRAY HOUSE IS BIG, OLD, AND DIRTY.

THE OCEAN WAS BIG, COLD, WET, AND DARK.

IT WAS A PICTURE OF A BEAUTIFUL YELLOW ROSE.

Narration
Something happening
Something happening to someone
Someone doing something
Someone thinking
Something doing something

Intermixed description and narration

Exposition
Expressing an opinion
Expressing an idea

Reminder: Arrange sentences in gradually increasing complexity and length.

RAIN FELL FOR THREE DAYS.
THE RUNNER WAS TACKLED.
MARY WALKED QUICKLY TO THE WINDOW.
MARY WONDERED IF SHE WOULD WIN TOMORROW.
THE TRAIN SLOWED TO A STOP.

SLOWLY, THE OLD MAN WALKED ACROSS THE DRY GRASS.
THE HOT YELLOW SUN HUNG IN THE CLOUDLESS SKY.

THE MAN WAS WRONG.
LET'S GO TO THE STORE.

Writing Connected Sentences

Materials. Writing instruments, paper, pictures.

Criterion. Level V
Thirty correctly written instruction, narration, description, and exposition sentences combined in a minimum group of three each.

Purpose. To teach the written production of a series of sentences which are combined in a minimum group of three each.

Demonstration Sequence

1. Select various topics which might serve as beginning cues. Be sure to include the various writing forms: description, narration, and exposition. You might add the variable of instructions and directions to provide added sequencing ideas practice.

2. Model only as much as is minimally necessary. Give the topic and instruct the student to write some sentences about it.

3. Proceed at Levels III and IV, then instruct the student to make up his own topic.

Examples of topics

A GIRL NAMED MARY
THE GIRL IS NINE YEARS OLD.
SHE IS WEARING A DRESS.
MARY LIKES TO SWIM.

A DOG
BILLY IS MY DOG. HE IS OLD.
HE IS BROWN AND WHITE.

SAM
SAM IS MY UNCLE. HE WORKS HARD.
SAM IS VERY STRONG.

RAIN
I LIKE IT WHEN IT RAINS.
RAIN MAKES FLOWERS GROW.
RAIN GETS YOU WET.

BEING HAPPY
BEING HAPPY IS GOOD. I LIKE TO FEEL GLAD.
WE SMILE WHEN WE ARE HAPPY.

RUNNING
RUNNING IS GOOD FOR YOU.
IT MAKES YOU STRONG. SOMETIMES WE RUN FAST.

GETTING WATER
PICK UP THE GLASS. TURN ON THE WATER. HOLD THE GLASS UNDER THE WATER.

GO TO THE HALL
WALK TO THE DOOR. OPEN IT. WALK OUT INTO THE HALL.

Writing a "Story"

Gj

Materials. Writing instrument, paper.

Criterion. Level V
One complete three-paragraph "story" with no grammatical errors.

Purpose. To use the motor encoding and the cognitive functions in creating a coherent story line which includes some narration, exposition, and description.

Demonstration Sequence

1. Give the topic of the story and then, with the help of the student, write it. Begin with a brief, one-paragraph "story," gradually increasing the word choice complexity and length.

   The example provided is probably of higher syntactic level than your student can achieve at this point. Aim for that level of word choice, however.

   Correct all misspellings as they occur.

2. Stories may also be created with a basic theme of description, narration, or exposition. Keep these to one paragraph each at first.

3. An alternative activity might be to begin a story and have the student finish it.

1. *Examples*
   THE LOST RING
   MY AUNT NORA LOST HER EMERALD RING. ONE DAY, WHILE SHE WAS SLEEPING, A BLUE JAY FLEW IN THE WINDOW. THE BIRD SAW THE EMERALD RING ON THE DRESSER. IT HOPPED OVER AND PICKED IT UP. THEN, IT FLEW BACK OUT OF THE WINDOW. MY AUNT NORA NEVER SAW THE RING AGAIN.

   MARTHA
   MARTHA IS PRETTY. SHE TAKES LONG RIDES ON HER BIKE. SHE LIKES TO KEEP HEALTHY. WE SHOULD ALL BE AS HEALTHY AS MARTHA.

2. *Example:* Narration.
   THE HIKE
   BILL WALKED THROUGH THE FOREST. AT EACH STEP, HE COULD HEAR THE "CLUMP" OF HIS BOOTS ON THE TRAIL. THE SMELL OF THE TREES WAS EVERYWHERE. BILL TOOK A DEEP BREATH, SMILED, AND LOOKED AROUND HIM. HE WAS VERY HAPPY TO BE THERE.

3. *Example*
   FINISH THIS STORY.
   THE STRONG BOY
   JIMMY WAS VERY STRONG. HE COULD STAND ON HIS HANDS.

Appendixes

Word Finder

COMMONLY OCCURRING WORDS ACCORDING TO TOPIC
(Context Clusters)

BODY PARTS

Head	Eye	Teeth	Neck	Shoulder	Finger	Back	Ankle
Hair	Nose	Ear	Throat	Elbow	Thumb	Hip	Feet
Face	Mouth	Chin	Arm	Wrist	Fingernail	Leg	Foot
				Hand	Stomach	Knee	Toe

FAMILY MEMBERS

Woman, Mother	Man, Father Dad, Daddy	Baby
Mom, Mommy	Aunt	Girl, Sister
	Uncle	Boy, Brother

THINGS TO EAT

Peas	Potatoes	Orange	Cracker	Meat	Pancakes	Toast	Cookie
Carrots	Tomato	Banana	Sandwich	Milk	Eggs	Butter	Ice Cream
Lettuce	Fruit	Apple	Hamburger	Orange Juice	Salt and	Soda Pop	Candy
Corn	Grapes	Cheese	Hot Dog	Coffee	Pepper	Pie	Gum
			Soup	Bacon	Bread	Cake	Nut

EATING UTENSILS

Glass	Mug	Plate	Fork	Napkin
Cup	Bowl	Spoon	Knife	

CLOTHES — THINGS TO WEAR

Underwear	Suit	Watch	Dress	Shoe	Pajamas	Jacket	Cap
Shirt	Tie	Bracelet	Bathing Suit	Boot	Robe	Mittens	Hat
Pants	Belt	Ring	Sock	Slippers	Coat	Gloves	

ROOMS OF THE HOUSE

Kitchen	Living Room	Playroom	Closet	Laundry Room
Dining Room	Family Room	Bedroom	Bathroom	Basement

FURNITURE — THINGS IN HOUSE

Door	Floor	Phone	Lamp	Couch, Sofa	Table	Bedspread	Dresser
Window	Rug	Desk	Picture	Light	Chair	Blanket	Bathtub
Wall	Ashtray	Piano	Television	Cabinets	Stool	Pillow	Sink
				Refrigerator	Bed	Mirror	Toilet

THINGS TO PLAY WITH

Baseball	Kite	Blocks	Buggy	Skis	Wagon	Car	Games
Bat	Balloon	Tea Set	Teddy Bear	Sled	Tricycle	Truck	Horn
Ball	Block	Doll	Snowman	Skate	Bicycle	Train	Drum

ANIMALS

Rabbit	Sheep	Horse	Chicken	Bird	Frog	Bear	Monkey
(Bunny)	Pig	Dog	Rooster	Bug	Turtle	Deer	Lion
Mouse	Cow	Cat	Duck	Bee	Fish	Squirrel	Tiger
		Baby Chicks	Owl	Snake	Raccoon	Elephant	Giraffe

TRANSPORTATION — THINGS THAT GO

Tractor	Truck	Bus	Train	Cart	Bicycle
Car	Motorcycle	Airplane	Boat	Ship	Tricycle

THINGS TO USE

Toothbrush	Soap	Billfold	Glasses	Books	Scissors	Pan	Nail
Toothpaste	Comb	Money	Matches	Pen	Candle	Dishcloth	Hammer
Towel	Cane	(Coin)	Cigarette	Pencil	Clock	Broom	Ladder
Washcloth	Purse	Key	Radio	Paper	Bottle	Basket	Wheel
			Newspaper	Paint	Jar	Box	Camera

PEOPLE

Persons	Policeman	Mechanic	Milkman	Cowboy	Baseball	Football	Santa Claus
Doctor	Fireman	Plumber	Farmer	Basketball	Player	Player	Witch
				Player			

THINGS TO SEE OUTSIDE

Sunset	Snow	River	Trees	Feather	Circus	Church	Road
Sun	Rain	Ground	Leaf	Swing	Street	School	Farm
Moon	Beach	Mountains	Log	Grass	Streetlight	House	Barn
Stars	Ocean	Forest	Nest	Flower	Store	Gate	Haystack
							Scarecrow

ACTION WORDS

Brush	Fight	Play	Run	Cut	Listen	Frown	Turn on
Sleep	Kick	Climb	Walk	Crack	Wave	Smile	Put on
Stand up	Tie	Swim	Crawl	Cook	Point	Laugh	Pick up
Rock	Work	Throw	Hop	Burn	Knock	Talk	Bow
Sit down	Dig	Catch	Skip	Pour	Paint	Call	Push
Ride	Wash	Hide	Jump	Drink	Write	Blow	Pull
Drive	Lift	Slide	Slip	Eat	Read	Cough	Close
Fly	Chop	Swing	Fall	Stop	Sing	Sneeze	Open
Feel	Saw	Dance	Drop	Look	Cry	Turn	Give
							Pay

POLAR AND SHAPES

Big, Little	Hot, Cold	Heavy, Light	Round, Square	Cross	Square
Tall, Short	Few, Many	Fast, Slow	Circle	Curve	Triangle

MOST COMMONLY OCCURRING WORDS*

NOUNS

air	boat	cigarette	drop	friend	kite	monkey	pepper
airplane	body	circle	drum	frog	knee	month	persons
ankle	book	circus	duck	front	knife	moon	phone
answer	books	city	ear	fruit	ladder	morning	piano
apple	boot	clock	earth	games	lamp	mother	picture
arm	bottle	closet	eggs	garden	lane	motorcycle	pie
ashtray	bow	coat	eight	gate	laugh	mountains	pig
aunt	bowl	coffee	elbow	general	laundry room	mouse	pillow
baby	box	coins	elephant	giraffe	law	mouth	place
baby chicks	boy	comb	end	girl	lead	mug	plant
back	bracelet	company	eye	glass	leaf	nail	plate
bacon	bread	cook	face	glasses	leg	name	play
ball	broom	cookie	fair	gloves	length	napkin	playroom
balloon	brother	corn	family	gold	lettuce	neck	plumber
banana	brown	couch	family room	grapes	life	nest	policeman
baseball	bug	cough	farm	grass	lie	new	point
baseball player	buggy	country	farmer	ground	light	newspaper	potatoes
basement	bunny	course	father	gum	line	night	power
bank	bus	cover	fear	hair	lion	north	present
barn	butter	cow	feather	half	little	nose	purse
basket	cabinets	cowboy	feet	hamburger	living room	nothing	rabbit
basketball	cake	cracker	few	haystack	log	number	raccoon
basketball player	camera	cross	field	head	man	nut	radio
bat	can	cup	fight	heart	mark	ocean	rain
bathing suit	candle	curve	finger	help	many	one	reason
bathroom	candy	cut	fingernail	hill	matches	orange	refrigerator
bathtub	cane	dad	fire	hip	meat	orange juice	ring
beach	cap	daddy	fireman	home	mechanic	order	river
bear	car	dance	fish	hope	men	owl	road
bed	carrots	day	floor	horn	might	paints	robe
bedroom	cat	deer	flower	horse	mile	pajamas	rock
bedspread	cave	desk	fly	hot dog	milk	pan	roll
bee	chair	dining room	food	house	milkman	pancakes	room
belt	change	dishcloth	foot	hour	mind	pants	rooster
bicycle	cheese	doctor	football	ice cream	miss	paper	round
billfold	chicken	dog	football player	jacket	mirror	parts	rug
bird	child	doll	forest	jar	mittens	peas	sail
blanket	children	door	fork	key	mom	pen	salt
block	chin	dress	form	kitchen	mommy	pencil	sandwich
blocks	church	dresser	four	kind	money	people	Santa Claus

*According to Wepman & Hass.

scarecrow	sister	something	story	teddy bear	tomato	underwear	winter
school	skate	son	stove	teeth	tooth	voice	wish
scissors	skis	sound	street	television	toothbrush	wagon	witch
sea	sled	soup	streetlight	there	toothpaste	walk	woman
second	sleep	spoon	suit	thing	top	wall	wood
sheep	slide	spring	summer	throat	towel	war	word
ship	slippers	square	sun	tonight	town	wash	work
shirt	smile	squirrel	sunset	thumb	tractor	washcloth	would
shoe	snake	stars	sweet	tie	train	watch	wrist
shoulder	snow	state	swim	tiger	trees	water	year
show	snowman	step	swing	time	triangle	way	yellow
side	soap	stomach	system	today	tricycle	week	young
sight	sock	stone	table	toast	truck	well	
sink	soda pop	stool	talk	toe	turtle	wheel	
silver	sofa	store	tea set	toilet	uncle	window	

VERBS

add	cover	fly	know	move	ran	sing	told
ask	crack	follow	known	much	reach	sit	took
be	crawl	form	land	must	read	sit down	top
became	cross	found	laugh	name	reason	skip	try
been	cry	frown	lay	near	receive	sleep	turn
begin	cut	gave	lead	need	remain	slide	turn on
believe	dance	get	learn	open	remember	slip	true
blow	did	give	leave	order	rest	smile	use
bow	didn't	go	left	own	ride	sneeze	used
box	die	goes	let	paint	rock	sound	unite
bring	dig	going	lie	part	roll	speak	visit
build	do	ground	lift	pass	round	spring	voice
brush	does	grow	like	pay	run	stand	wait
burn	done	had	line	pick up	said	stand up	walk
buy	don't	has	listen	picture	sail	start	want
call	down	have	live	piece	save	state	war
came	dress	head	look	place	saw	stay	was
can	drink	hear	lost	plain	school	step	wash
care	draw	help	love	plant	second	stop	watch
carry	drive	hide	made	play	see	swim	water
catch	drop	hop	make	please	seem	swing	wave
change	eat	hope	mark	point	send	take	went
chop	fall	hurt	matter	pour	sent	tell	were
clean	fear	is	may	present	serve	talk	well
climb	feel	its	mean	pull	set	thank	while
close	field	jump	measure	push	ship	think	will
color	fight	keep	meet	put	should	thought	wind
come	fill	kick	might	put on	show	throw	wish
cook	find	knew	mind	rain	side	tie	work
cough	fire	knock	miss	raise	sight	till	would
							write

ADJECTIVES

a	blue	each	five	heavy	long	night	pay
after	both	early	four	high	lost	no	piece
all	brown	east	free	hot	low	north	plain
alone	by	end	fresh	hundred	many	off	poor
American	certain	enough	front	just	mean	old	power
an	clean	eight	full	kind	meet	once	present
another	clear	every	general	large	more	one	pretty
any	close	even	glad	last	most	only	quick
back	cold	fair	gold	late	Mr.	open	read
beautiful	cross	fall	good	later	Mrs.	other	red
bad	dark	far	got	lead	much	out	rich
best	dear	fast	great	left	must	over	right
better	deep	few	green	less	near	own	round
big	dirty	fine	happy	like	new	paper	same
black	down	first	hard	little	next	part	school

second	silver	sometime	still	ten	this	through	which
several	six	sound	strong	that	third	time	white
seven	small	south	such	the	those	top	whole
short	soft	spring	summer	then	thousand	true	wide
side	some	state	sweet	these	three	two	window
						very	winter
						war	work
						warm	yellow
						wash	young
						water	

ADVERBS

again	better	good	late	no	right	though	where
all	dear	great	later	north	same	through	which
almost	each	half	left	not	some	today	why
alone	enough	here	less	now	something	together	yet
along	even	high	light	off	sometime	true	
always	ever	hot	low	once	soon	until	
as	far	how	more	only	still	very	
away	fast	however	most	other	such	way	
back	free	just	next	out	then	well	
best	fall	large	never	over	there	when	

PRONOUNS

all	he	his	mine	our	them	us	you
another	her	I	my	she	these	we	your
both	herself	it	myself	some	this	what	
each	him	it's	one	that	they	which	
few	himself	me	other	their	those	who	

PREPOSITIONS

about	along	before	beside	down	inside	over	up
above	among	behind	between	during	into	past	upon
across	around	below	beyond	for	near	than	until
after	at	beneath	but	from	next	through	with
against	as	besides	by	in	of	throughout	within
					off	till	without
					on	to	
					opposite	toward	
					out	under	
					outside	underneath	

CONJUNCTIONS

also	if	so	until	without
and	like	than	when	yet
because	once	that	where	
both	or	though	while	
but	since	too	with	

INTERJECTIONS

ah!	don't!	oh!
aha!	go!	oho!
alas!	good!	ooo!
boo!	great!	off!
come!	ha-ha!	ouch!
eek!	(laughter)	out!
enough!	help!	
	no!	

WORDS RANK-ORDERED BY FREQUENCY OF USE
(5-Year-Olds)

is	with	them	old	saw	how	start	dress
and	got	book	more	same	someone	top	mouth
the	something	said	stand	those	chimney	shirt	wrong
a	girl	say	away	flower	sun	everybody	momma
that	had	open	nothing	guy	again	fix	always
he	get	sleep	fall	tell	head	been	doctor
to	think	came	cut	why	fire	chair	grow
not	can	another	would	guess	sleepy	took	money
there	about	put	where	black	lay	thought	statue
it	mother	does	off	person	outside	side	sad
I	see	thing	will	school	lion	stay	while
she	you	door	cloud	cave	found	piece	everything
they	or	for	snow	climb	kiss	kind	much
in	maybe	room	run	fell	hair	new	hole
man	boat	has	love	white	next	stuff	alligator
look	did	window	my	take	behind	bedroom	sick
was	when	else	play	mad	find	bat	someplace
go	end	no	hand	too	mountain	hat	number
do	have	big	right	watch	plow	read	truck
know	because	work	knife	turn	made	secret	daddy
on	come	well	around	way	call	every	lamp
one	other	live	am	might	wood	sky	boyfriend
all	try	any	feet	place	happen	child	sometimes
her	tree	their	we	table	shoot	pole	ear
like	water	woman	into	hug	fish	gone	ugly
this	sit	hold	rope	who	jump	even	hard
of	were	horse	by	tie	bush	yeah	long
then	want	day	garden	die	pocket	floor	hurt
are	dark	two	after	marry	now	bridge	need
lady	somebody	once	mean	story	ran	fight	face
so	went	husband	talk	done	along	through	steal
little	light	dead	lot	ship	ghost	ride	whole
at	walk	if	very	barn	name	only	almost
up	but	night	good	wife	me	really	hit
his	be	each	stair	left	leave	gun	except
down	here	time	anything	violin	bare	desk	robber
out	back	grass	over	morning	first	wonder	let
some	from	father	eat	duck	belt	ready	beach
what	could	picture	baby	nobody	bad	eye	bring
him	kill	rock	home	cross	building	world	keep
boy	just	real	bed	oh	tied	paper	under
cause	men	people	monster	hang	guitar	dog	wish
house	make	cry	these	together	wall	arm	

WORDS RANK-ORDERED BY FREQUENCY OF USE

(6-Year-Olds)

and	because	window	right	else	gun	rest	barn
is	can	live	too	baby	bug	woke	must
the	house	away	end	fish	children	help	us
he	might	walk	oh	way	dead	fix	money
a	mother	time	by	let	wife	eye	almost
to	girl	their	hard	kind-of	somewhere	stand	clothes
it	want	tree	very	asleep	left	never	only
she	got	put	dark	anything	fell	ground	forest
there	little	kill	any	everything	grave	three	stuff
they	know	real	rock	off	turn	grow	mountain
that	went	work	how	someone	morning	top	lay
was	have	picture	bed	who	bad	until	five
look	if	door	make	side	flower	car	sick
in	down	said	once	made	pretty	dog	dance
this	has	big	sleep	fall	under	fight	tired
not	just	men	find	eat	while	kept	near
man	with	two	hand	start	statue	table	garden
go	but	sit	lot	woman	am	happily	move
maybe	for	from	school	outside	plant	keep	yes
then	what	cause	watch	love	call	those	feel
well	you	people	old	me	kid	wrong	heard
I	does	no	run	an	violin	store	dad
her	were	these	snow	next	through	farm	stone
like	when	into	good	we	friend	swim	ready
so	see	home	say	monster	really	before	turtle
his	will	night	hair	rope	ever	listen	lake
of	back	room	now	should	year	bridge	police
on	other	tell	black	much	field	shot	face
or	play	horse	climb	husband	ran	hot	told
are	came	water	wall	wait	fire	together	blank
all	about	guy	after	white	ask	along	own
at	father	where	happen	place	behind	broke	paint
him	them	book	talk	food	doll	fast	hat
some	day	around	hold	took	thought	even	bring
lady	had	take	die	upon	nice	stair	star
think	could	cry	mean	story	better	lamp	pick
one	would	more	nothing	each	head	jump	ride
get	come	over	marry	grass	sad	lunch	bury
do	probably	light	happy	kind	brick	paper	animal
up	did	kiss	read	decide	guess	four	stop
out	boat	saw	again	both	child	knife	new
be	try	another	mad	my	wonder	step	whatever
something	thing	open	been	long	give	himself	cabin
boy	here	somebody	found	stay	hurt		

and	boy	over	school	water	grave	better	herself
the	little	think	climb	ask	us	hair	kiss
is	all	night	say	call	hat	nobody	woods
a	be	play	how	kind	ran	dream	near
he	when	put	after	stair	left	your	only
so	get	will	bed	husband	cave	lake	along
she	girl	my	tell	mad	someplace	eye	arm
to	some	woman	cause	rope	winter	building	doll
it	could	lot	take	pretty	graveyard	finally	surprised
was	down	live	too	rock	kept	forest	lay
there	with	thing	any	plow	bad	woke	learn
they	have	if	another	cut	dragon	done	fire
in	you	these	more	way	farm	keep	even
look	try	father	open	marry	ate	gone	new
not	were	violin	sort of	each	animal	sun	lamp
I	for	into	cry	hole	children	story	sister
this	mother	window	fish	hold	stand	white	gave
like	no	long	off	place	while	yeah	decide
man	know	we	good	anything	eat	snake	ground
then	want	start	told	never	hard	those	small
her	might	probably	guy	head	garden	lesson	change
one	just	their	let	money	okay	hug	music
go	came	by	who	through	three	hardly	pole
of	because	oh	hand	police	happy	ever	same
well	what	tree	dark	American	else	stuff	table
his	see	away	someone	mean	own	food	as
on	time	light	took	run	baby	monster	brother
got	them	maybe	found	read	dead	car	knew
went	once	around	kill	does	catch	move	ride
but	saw	where	somebody	kind-of	fix	enough	under
at	boat	snow	thought	hurt	stop	year	river
out	would	here	book	still	dinosaur	sad	chair
had	people	sit	next	use	bury	world	high
something	about	men	picture	scared	ready	barn	gold
said	other	two	stay	find	top	morning	fall
him	home	again	jump	fell	field	flower	sky
house	come	room	watch	outside	until	face	supper
back	very	me	friend	everybody	rabbit	much	before
up	big	sleep	now	every	shot	help	yes
lady	walk	from	die	been	almost	policeman	somewhere
do	real	make	turn	nothing	Indian	upon	star
did	has	door	horse	am	everything	sick	grow
day	right	end	why	jail	happen	fight	felt
are	can	made	nice	heard	love	doctor	store
or	work	old	talk	really			

The Criterion Placement Test (CPT), 177

The Cumulative Response Record (CRR), 185

The Language Script, 186

Certificate of Achievement, 187

Ordering Information
Criterion Placement Tests, Cumulative Response Forms, Sourcebook Language Scripts, and *Certificates of Achievement* are available for purchase by individuals, schools, and organizations.

Two-day Sourcebook training workshops are available.

For information regarding order forms and Sourcebook training workshops, please write:

Sourcebook Systems
P.O. Box 746
Ellensburg, WA 98926

Order Form

Mail this or a copy of this form to: **Sourcebook Systems
P.O. Box 746
Ellensburg, Washington 98926**

Date _____ Purchase order no. _____

Check appropriate box

☐ Organization   ☐ Individual   ☐ Please send workshop information.

Ship to or bill:

Name (attention of)_____

School or organization_____

City, state, zip_____

Visa or Master Charge no._____

Authorized signature_____

Orders from individuals and private organizations must include remittance plus 8% for postage and handling *OR* a Visa or Master Charge number. Other schools or organizations will be billed as requested.

Please allow four weeks for delivery.

Quantity	Item	Unit Price	Total
	Criterion Placement Test	$ .35 each	
	Cumulative Response Record (pad of 50)	1.50	
	Sourcebook Language Script (pad of 50)	1.50	
	Certificates of Achievement	.04 each	
		Sub Total	
		Taxes: 5.1% in State of WA	
		Postage and Handling Charge: 8% of subtotal	
		Total order	$

CRITERION PLACEMENT TEST
[C P T]

By W. J. Worthley, Ph.D.

NAME _____ Age: Yrs._____Months_____

Date Begun_____

LEVELS OF PRODUCTION

I. Clinician models.
Student is physically assisted.

II. Clinician produces.
Student produces simultaneously.

III. Clinician models.
Student imitates.

IV. Clinician cues.
Student produces.

V. Student produces spontaneously.

NOTATIONS: ✓ = Activity in process   ✓ = Criterion passed

O = Criterion failed   ✓ = Limited criterion passed

SECTION A BASIC SKILLS

	LEVELS				
	I	II	III	IV	V
Set A a Becoming aware of sound. Attending to sound.	—	—	—	—	—
A b Producing rhythms.	—	—	—	—	—
A c Visual motor organization. Cutting and coloring.	—	—	—	—	—
A d Producing non-meaningful sounds.	—	—	—	—	—
A e Following directions presented verbally and/ or gesturally.	—	—	—	—	—
A f Producing speech melody patterns.	—	—	—	—	—
A g Imitating environmental sounds. Onomatopoeia.	—	—	—	—	—
A h Matching forms, sizes, and pictures.	—	—	—	—	—
A i Sorting forms, sizes, and pictures.	—	—	—	—	—
A j Visual-motor association. Pairing according to function.	—	—	—	—	—

1.

	LEVELS				
	I	II	III	IV	V

A k   Visual motor sequencing. Completing an action sequence.

A l   Comprehending "same" vs. "different".

SECTION B RECEPTIVE VOCABULARY BUILDING

Set B a   Identifying pictures and/or objects by pointing.

B b   Associating objects with pictures.

B c   Recognizing objects or pictures presented aurally.

B d   Identifying verbs by pointing.

B e   Making "yes-no" judgments.

B f   Discriminating nouns and verbs by pointing. Negation.

SECTION C EXPRESSIVE SYNTAX — WORDS AND PHRASES

Set C a   Naming objects and pictures. Nouns.

C b   Producing common expressions.

C c   Naming pictures and objects. Vocabulary expansion.

C d   Identifying actions. Verbs.

C e   Auditory decoding and listening. Recognizing sounds.

C f   Auditory closure. Word completion.

C g   Sequential visual memory. Remembering names, nouns.

C h   Arranging words into classes.

C i   Learning noun phrases. Article plus noun.

C j   Visual-motor organization. Learning numbers, conceptualizing counting.

C k   Conceptualizing categories. Plurals.

C l   Identifying colors. Conceptualizing adjectives.

C m   Making yes-no judgments. Conceptualizing "yes" and "no".

2.

		LEVELS			
	I	II	III	IV	V

C n   Learning noun phrases. Noun plus adjective. Adjective plus noun.

C o   Understanding relationships. Prepositions.

C p   Learning verb phrases. Subject plus verb.

C q   Learning adverb phrases. Verb plus adverb.

C r   Identifying characteristics by sight and touch. Adjectives.

C s   Learning noun phrases. Quantifier plus noun. Plurals.

C t   Identifying persons. Pronouns "I" and "you".

C u   Learning verb phrases. Verb plus object.

C v   Using nouns and possessive pronouns. Conceptualizing possession.

C w   Learning verb phrases. Verb plus particle, preposition, pronoun.

C x   Learning predicative phrases. Demonstrative plus possessive pronouns. Full to substitute form transformations.

C y   Learning designative phrases. Plurals. Interrogatives. locator, demonstrator, identifier plus noun.

SECTION D EXPRESSIVE SYNTAX — SENTENCES

Set D a   Building sentences. Auditory sequential memory.

D b   Auditory sequential memory. Remembering word sequences.

D c   Grammatic closure and sequential memory. Sentence completion.

D d   Grammatic closure. Sentence completion.

D e   Building beginning sentences. Subject + verb + noun object.

D f   Conceptualizing negatives.

D g   Learning "is" in present indicative. Carrier phrase + noun.

3.

	I	II	III	IV	V

D h   Learning "is" with an adjective.
Carrier phrase + complement.

D i   Learning "is" with "ing".
Carrier phrase + present participle "ing" verb.

D j   Learning to use pronouns with "is".

D k   Learning "is" and "are". Using pronouns and nouns.
Proun + is + person's name + noun/pronoun.

D l   Using adjectives as predicate complements.
Pronoun/article + noun + verb + adjective complement.

D m   Expanding the use of "is".
Noun phrase + verb + noun phrase.
Article + noun object + is + prepositional phrase.
Pronoun adverb + is + possessive pronoun + adjective + noun.

D n   Making two sentences one sentence. Making one sentence two sentences. Coordinate transformations.
Pronoun + verb + article + noun.
Article + noun + verb + adjective.
Pronoun + verb + article + adjective + noun.

D o   Producing expanded sentences using "is" and other subjects, verbs, prepositions, and objects of the preposition.
Article + subject + verb + preposition + article + object of preposition.

D p   Learning "am, are, was, were". Using pronouns, adjectives and verbs.
Pronoun + verb + adjective/verb/pronoun.

D q   Building sentences. "Wh" questions. Interrogatives.

D r   Learning to use pronouns with verbs. "Want-see have-has."

4.

		LEVELS			
	I	II	III	IV	V

D s   Learning to use verbs. Past, present, future tense.
Noun + verb + adjective + adverb.

D t   Learning to use verbs. Actor-action sentences.

D u   Learning "ed" verb endings plus past tense.

D v   Learning to use verbs. Past tense.

D w   Learning verbal sentences.
Verb + particle + noun phrase and/or prepositional phrase.

D x   Expanding sentence forms. Transformations of order.

SECTION E   COMMUNICATION SKILLS — COGNITIVE ANALYSIS

Set E a   Using sentences in context. Conversation. Telling a story.

E b   Auditory organizing. Word associations.

E c   Visual-auditory association. "Tell me all you can about".

E d   Associating words.

E e   Associating ideas presented orally. "What is it?" "What is happening?"

E f   Using auditory memory. Answering questions.

E g   Auditory vocal sequencing. Giving directions, instructions.

E h   Associating ideas presented aurally. Problem solving.

E i   Making mental judgments. "Alike". "Different"

E j   Associating ideas. Alike-different comparisons.

E k   Associating words. "Which doesn't belong?"

E l   Auditory decoding-encoding. Associating ideas presented aurally. "What's wrong with it?"

E m   Verbal association. Answering questions.

5.

SECTION F   READING

	LEVELS			
I	II	III	IV	V

Set F a   Visual closure. Object/picture identification.

F b   Visual association. Consonant recognition.

F c   Visual association. Combining consonants with vowels and diphthongs.

F d   Visual organizing. Sound blending. Word building.

F e   Visual closure. Word perception.

F f   Visual association. Word and picture identification.

F g   Visual association. Word recognition.

F h   Visual association. Reorganizing written phrases.

F i   Visual association. Reorganizing written sentences.

F j   Visual organizing. Reading.

SECTION G   WRITING — SPELLING

Set G a   Visual motor sequencing. Manually duplicating an ordered sequence.

G b   Visual closure. Completing form drawings.

G c   Visual memory. Making simple drawings.

G d   Motor encoding. Draw a _____.

G e   Writing the letters of the alphabet.

G f   Visual-auditory sequential memory. Spelling.

G g   Writing words.

G h   Writing sentences.

G i   Writing connected sentences.

G j   Writing a "story".

6.

SELF-ORIGINATED SETS

	LEVELS			
I	II	III	IV	V

7.

VERBAL EXPRESSION OUTPUT

ADMINISTRATION(S)

Date_____Date_____Date_____

Mean Length of Response (MLR) _____ _____ _____

Number of One Word Responses (N1W) _____ _____ _____

Mean of Five Longest Responses (M5L) _____ _____ _____

SENTENCE TYPES (Percent of each occurring from total)

Date_____Date_____Date_____

A. Incomplete #_____%_____ #_____%_____ #_____%_____

B. Functionally Complete -
    Structurally Incomplete _____ _____ _____ _____ _____ _____

C. Simple Sentence without Phrase _____ _____ _____ _____ _____ _____

D. Simple Sentence with Phrase _____ _____ _____ _____ _____ _____

E. Compound and Complex _____ _____ _____ _____ _____ _____

TOTAL _____ 100% _____ 100% _____ 100%

STRUCTURAL COMPLEXITY SCORE _____ _____ _____

FREQUENCY OF OCCURRENCE AS PARTS OF SPEECH, ETC. (Percent of each occurring from total)

Date_____Date_____Date_____

Article #_____%_____ #_____%_____ #_____%_____

Noun _____ _____ _____ _____ _____ _____
Pronoun _____ _____ _____ _____ _____ _____
Adjective _____ _____ _____ _____ _____ _____

Verb _____ _____ _____ _____ _____ _____

Infinitive _____ _____ _____ _____ _____ _____

Adverb _____ _____ _____ _____ _____ _____

Preposition _____ _____ _____ _____ _____ _____

Conjunction _____ _____ _____ _____ _____ _____

Interjection _____ _____ _____ _____ _____ _____

Negative _____ _____ _____ _____ _____ _____

Interrogative _____ _____ _____ _____ _____ _____

TOTAL _____ 100% _____ 100% _____ 100%

8.

CUMULATIVE RESPONSE RECORD
[C.R.R.]
By William Justin Worthley, Ph.D.

...ME _____

...GINNING DATE _____ DISMISSAL DATE _____ SN. LTH. _____ # SNS. /WK. _____ # IN GR. _____

RESPONSES				SN. #	SET(S)	%	CLINICAL NOTES (Use reverse side if necessary)

...Harris 39352-C

...OTATIONS:

− = Correct but no verbal reinforcer

/ = Correct plus ''good''

0 = Incorrect

% = Percent correct per session

✓ = Criterion test passed

✓ = Limited criterion passed

O = Criterion test failed

SOURCEBOOK LANGUAGE SCRIPT

By William Justin Worthley, Ph.D.

Page _____ of _____

NAME	SENTENCE TYPE	ARTICLE	NOUN	PRONOUN	ADJECTIVE	VERB	INFINITIVE	ADVERB	PREPOSITION	CONJUNCTION	INTERJECTION	NEGATIVE	INTER-ROGATIVE	RESPONSE LENGTH

Sentence Types	A	B	C	D	E
TOTALS					

Certificate of Achievement

THIS CERTIFIES THAT

HAS SATISFACTORILY COMPLETED THE FOLLOWING ASSIGNMENT.

SIGNED

SPEECH SPECIALIST _____

TEACHER _____

PARENT/GUARDIAN _____

MONITOR _____

Materials

EXAMINE A SET

In the upper left-hand corner the materials recommended as the working components of the set are indicated. Obtain as many of these as possible prior to the beginning of the school year or professional activity. The private possession of a substantial number of practical and directly applicable therapeutic items contributes greatly to the therapist's confidence. Of course, most of these materials are readily obtainable as supplies in any school district. Others may be produced as a group project or during any convenient free time.

Of paramount importance is the portability, appearance, and resilience of the container(s) that will house the accumulated materials. It is wise to wait until you have assembled all the items you expect to be using. Examine them in terms of amount and the categories into which they apparently arrange themselves. You will probably decide on a group of containers of varying sizes. If you are one of those fortunate persons who does not move from school to school and has a permanent room, you may still want to have containers readily available, in case you wish to hold in-service or other demonstrations outside.

PICTURES

The basic group of pictures should be cut from magazines and mounted on 8½" × 11" colored construction paper. These may be as simple or complex as you desire. Include any highly visual subjects and activities which might generate the form of language production sought after at any particular time. If you have the resources, various groups of pictures may be produced, to include both single items and multiple and varying topics.

Refer to recent educational materials catalogs. These list commercially produced sets of language pictures. Any within your resources should be obtained, as they provide a dimension to picture presentation which you might otherwise not have. Different pictures of the same objects may then be combined.

OBJECTS

(Refer to the Context Clusters in the Word Finder, Appendix I)

Talk to friends who have children who have outgrown their toys. Visit any thrift shop in the vicinity. The objective is to accumulate a collection of toys and other things that can be used as stimulus—object items:

The same noun (e.g., cars), but of varying sizes and colors
Items of clothing
Complete place setting
Movement and nonmovement toys

Sound-Producing Toys

Noisemakers: whistle, triangle, drum, etc.
Blocks of different colors
Geometric forms: wooden and cut-out
Doll house equipped as completely as possible
Boy and girl doll (dressed)
Some identical object pairs
Balloons
Construction paper of various colors

Other Therapeutic Tools

Geometric form outlines
Letters, numbers
Crayons
4" × 5" and/or 5" × 8" cards
Wide-tipped felt pen, chalk, pencils
8½" × 11" paper for tracing
8½" × 11" paper for writing
Cut-out coloring book
White cloth squares, 1' × 1'
Flannel board (black felt-covered) or separate small flannel
  boards for each person
Flash cards with sandpaper on the back
Cassette tape recorders
Graded story books: lowest possible reading level to high
  school reading level
Highly visual illustrated books

You might wish to produce new sets that are tailored specifically to your student. If you have developed therapeutic ideas that do not appear in the *Sourcebook*, this format provides a convenient means whereby your creative efforts may be worked into the system. Produce as many sets as you wish. Insert them where they logically belong. Add the listing of the set(s) on page 7 of the *Criterion Placement Test*.

Set

Materials.   **Criterion.**   **Purpose.**

Demonstration Sequence

Bibliography

Nature of Language   195
Development of Language   197
Assessment of Language   200
Language-Related Tests   201
Nature of Aphasia   202
Aphasic Disorders   203
Assessment of Aphasia   203
Habilitation of Aphasia   204
Emotionally Disturbed   204
Cerebral Palsy   205
Mental Retardation   205
Therapeutics   206
General References   208

Bibliography

NATURE OF LANGUAGE

Alston, W. P. *Philosophy of Language.* Englewood Cliffs, N.J.: Prentice-Hall, 1964.

Anisfeld, M., and Gordon, M. On the psychophonological structure of English inflectional rules. *Journal of Verbal Learning and Verbal Behavior* 1:973, 1968.

Archer, E. J. The Psychological Nature of Concepts. In H. J. Klausmeier and C. W. Harris (eds.), *Analyses of Concept Learning.* New York: Academic, 1966.

Bangs, T. E. Communication. In T. E. Bangs, *Language and Learning Disorders of the Pre-academic Child: With Curriculum Guide.* New York: Appleton-Century-Crofts, 1968. Pp. 6—24.

Bangs, T. E. Intelligence, In *Language and Learning Disorders.* Pp. 25—39.

Berry, M. F. Operational Mechanisms. In M. F. Berry, *Language Disorders of Children: The Bases and Diagnoses.* New York: Appleton-Century-Crofts, 1969. Pp. 47—86.

Berry, M. F. Operational Systems, In *Language Disorders.* Pp. 47—86.

Bever, T. G., Lackner, J., and Kirk, R. The underlying structure sentence is the primary unit of speech perception. *Perception and Psychophysics* 5:255, 1969.

Braine, M. D. S. The ontogeny of English phrase structure: The first phase. *Language* 39:1, 1963.

Brannon, J. B. A comparison of syntactic structures in the speech of three- and four-year-old children. *Language and Speech* 11:171, 1968.

Brown, R. Language and Categories. In J. S. Bruner, J. J. Goodnow, and G. A. Austin (eds.), *A Study of Thinking.* New York: Science Editions, 1962.

Brown, R. How Shall a Thing Be Called? In R. Brown (ed.), *Psycholinguistics.* New York: Free Press, 1970. Pp. 3—15.

Brown, R. Linguistic Determinism and the Part of Speech. In R. Brown (ed.), *Psycholinguistics.* New York: Free Press, 1970. Pp. 16—27.

Brown, R., Black, A. H., and Horowitz, A. E. Phonetic Symbolism in Natural Languages. In R. Brown (ed.), *Psycholinguistics.* New York: Free Press, 1970. Pp. 258—273.

Brown, R., Fraser, C., and Bellugi, U. Explorations in Grammar Evaluation. In R. Brown (ed.), *Psycholinguistics.* New York: Free Press, 1970. Pp. 56—74.

Brown, R., and Gilman, A. The Pronouns of Power and Solidarity. In R. Brown (ed.), *Psycholinguistics.* New York: Free Press, 1970. Pp. 302—335.

Brown, R., and Lenneberg, E. H. A Study in Language and Cognition. In R. Brown (ed.), *Psycholinguistics.* New York: Free Press, 1970. Pp. 235—357.

Brown, R., and McNeill, D. The "Tip of the Tongue" Phenomenon. In R. Brown (ed.), *Psycholinguistics.* New York: Free Press, 1970. Pp. 274—301.

Chapman, R. S. Some Simple Ways of Talking About Normal Language and Communication. In J. E. McLean, D. E. Yoder, and R. L. Schiefelbusch (eds.), *Language Intervention With the Retarded.* Baltimore: University Park Press, 1972. Pp. 17—32.

Chomsky, N. Categories and Relations in Syntactic Theory. In N. Chomsky, *Aspects of the Theory of Syntax.* Cambridge, Mass.: MIT Press, 1965. Pp. 63—127.

Chomsky, N. Deep Structures and Grammatical Transformations, In *Aspects of the Theory of Syntax.* Pp. 128—147.

Chomsky, N. Methodological Preliminaries, In *Aspects of the Theory of Syntax.* Pp. 3—62.

Chomsky, N. Some Residual Problems, In *Aspects of the Theory of Syntax.* Pp. 148—192.

Cooper, F. S. How is Language Conveyed by Speech? In J. F. Kavanagh and I. G. Mattingly (eds.), *Language by Ear and by Eye.* Cambridge, Mass.: MIT Press, 1972. Pp. 25—46.

Corcoran, D. *Pattern Recognition.* Middlesex, Engl.: Penguin, 1971.

Danks, J. Grammaticalness and meaningfulness in the comprehension of sentences. *Journal of Verbal Learning and Verbal Behavior* 8:687, 1969.

Deese, J. The Biological and Social Context of Language. In J. Deese, *Psycholinguistics.* Boston: Allyn and Bacon, 1970. Pp. 115—135.

Deese, J. Meaning, In *Psycholinguistics.* Pp. 83—114.

Deese, J. The Nature of Language, In *Psycholinguistics.* Pp. 1—34.

Denny-Brown, D. The Physiological Basis of Perception and Speech. In L. Halpern (ed.), *Problems of Dynamic Neurology.* Jerusalem: Dept. Nerv. Dis., Rothschild Hadassah University Hospital and Hebrew University Hadassah Medical School, 1963.

Engler, L., and Haden, E. Status of Utterance. *Acta Linguistica Hafniensia International Journal of General Linguistics* 9:25, 1965.

Engler, L., and Hannah, E. P. Juncture phenomena and the segmentation of linguistic corpus. *Language and Speech* 10:228, 1967.

Fay, W. H. The challenge of personal pronouns. *Journal of Learning Disabilities* 5:299, 1972.

Fillmore, C. J. The Case for Case. In E. Bach and R. T. Harms (eds.), *Universals in Linguistic Theory.* New York: Holt, Rinehart, and Winston, 1968.

Fodor, J. A., and Garrett, M. Some Reflections on Competence and Performance. In J. Lyons and R. J. Wales (eds.), *Psycholinguistic Papers· The Proceedings of the 1966 Edinburgh Conference.* Edinburgh: Edinburgh University Press, 1966.

Fodor, J. A., and Garrett, M. Some syntactic determinants of sentential complexity. *Perception and Psychophysics* 2:289, 1967.

Fodor, J. A., Garrett, M., and Bever, T. G. Some syntactic determinants of sentential complexity: II. Verb structure. *Perception and Psychophysics* 3:453, 1968.

Frith, U., and Hermelin, B. The role of visual and motor cues for normal, subnormal, and autistic children. *Journal of Child Psychology and Psychiatry* 10:153, 1969.

Gruber, J. S. Topicalization in child language. *Foundations of Language* 3:37, 1967.

Halle, M. Phonology in Generative Grammar. In J. A. Fodor and J. J. Katz (eds.), *The Structure of Language.* Englewood Cliffs, N.J.: Prentice-Hall, 1964. Pp. 334—352.

Halliday, M. A. K. Language Structure and Language Function. In J. Lyons (ed.), *New Horizons in Linguistics.* New York: Penguin, 1970.

Hamilton, H., and Deese, J. Comprehensibility and subject-verb relations in complex sentences. *Journal of Verbal Learning and Verbal Behavior* 10:163, 1971.

Hasan, R. Syntax and Semantics. In J. Morton (ed.), *Biological and Social Factors in Psycholinguistics.* London: Logos, 1971.

Healy, A., and Miller, G. The relative contribution of nouns and verbs to sentence acceptability and comprehensibility. *Psychonomic Science* 24:94, 1971.

Hebb, D. O., Lambert, W. E., and Tucker, G. R. Language, thought and experience. *Modern Language Journal* 55:212, 1971.

Hill, A. *Introduction to Linguistic Structures.* New York: Harcourt, Brace and World, 1958.

Hirsch, I. J. Audition in Relation to Perception of Speech. In E. C. Carterette (ed.), *Speech, Language and Communication.* Vol. 3. Brain Function. Berkeley, Calif.: University of California Press, 1966.

Hockett, C. F. *A Course in Modern Linguistics.* New York: Macmillan, 1958.

Hockett, C. F. Animal "Languages" and Human Language. In J. N. Spuhler (ed.), *The Evolution of Man's Capacity for Culture.* Detroit: Wayne State University Press, 1959.

Hockett, C. F. The origin of speech. *Scientific American* 3:88, 1960.

Hopper, R. Expanding the notion of competence. *The Speech Teacher* 20:29, 1971.

Ingram, D. Transitivity in child language. *Language* 47:888, 1971.

Ingram, D. The Relationship Between Comprehension and Production. In R. L. Schiefelbusch and L. L. Lloyd (eds.), *Language Perspectives: Acquisition, Retardation, and Intervention.* Baltimore: University Park Press, 1974. Pp. 313—334.

Jacobs, R. A., and Rosenbaum, P. *English Transformational Grammar.* Lexington, Mass.: Blaisdell, 1968.

Jakobson, R., Fant, C. G. M., and Halle, M. *Preliminaries to Speech Analysis: The Distinctive Features and Their Correlates.* Cambridge, Mass.: MIT Press, 1969.

Jakobson, R., and Halle, M. *Fundamentals of Language.* S'-Gravenhage, The Hague: Mouton, 1956.

Joos, M. *The English Verb: Form and Meanings.* Ann Arbor, Mich.: University of Wisconsin Press, 1964.

Judson, A. J., Cofer, C. N., and Gelfand, S. Reasoning as an associative process: II. "Direction" in problem solving as a function of prior reinforcement of relevant responses. *Psychological Reports* 2:501, 1956.

Kagan, J. A Developmental Approach to Conceptual Growth. In H. J. Klausmeier and C. W. Harris (eds.), *Analysis of Concept Learning.* New York: Academic, 1966.

Kendler, H. H., and D'Amato, M. F. A comparison of reversal shifts and nonreversal shifts in human concept formation behavior. *Journal of Experimental Psychology* 49:165, 1955.

Kendler, T. S., and Kendler, H. H. Reversal and nonreversal shifts in kindergarten children. *Journal of Experimental Psychology* 58:56, 1959.

Kendler, T. S., Kendler, H. H., and Wells, D. Reversal and nonreversal shifts in nursery school children. *Journal of Comparative and Physiological Psychology* 53:83, 1960.

Klima, E. S., and Bellugi, U. Syntactic Regularities in the Speech of Children. In J. Lyons and R. J. Wales (eds.), *Psycholinguistic Papers: The Proceedings of the 1966 Edinburgh Conference.* Edinburgh: Edinburgh University Press, 1966.

Kohlberg, L., Yaeger, J., and Kjertholm, H. Private Speech Four studies and a review of theories. *Child Development* 39:691, 1968.

Laffal, J. Pathological and Normal Language. New York: Lieber-Atherton, 1965.

Lecours, A. R., and Lhermitte, F. Phonemic paraphasias: Linguistic structures and tentative hypotheses. *Cortex* 5:193, 1969.

Lees, B. The grammar of English nominalization. *International Journal of Applied Linguistics* 26:1, 1960.

Lewis, M. M. *Infant Speech: A Study of the Beginnings of Language.* Atlantic Highlands, N.J.: Humanities Press, 1951.

Liberman, A. M. The grammars of speech and language. *Cognitive Psychology* 1:301, 1970.

Liberman, A. M., Cooper, F. S., Harris, K. S., MacNeilage, F. F., and Studdert-Kennedy, M. Some Observations on a Model for Speech Perception. In W. Waltham-Dunn (ed.), *Models for the Perception of Speech and Visual Form.* Cambridge, Mass.: MIT Press, 1967. Pp. 68—87.

Liberman, A. M., Cooper, F. S., Shankweiler, D. P., and Studdert-Kennedy, M. Perception of the speech code. *Psychological Review* 74:431, 1967.

Lieberman, P. *Intonation, Perception and Language.* Cambridge, Mass.: MIT Press, 1967.

Lieberman, P. *Speech Acoustics and Perception.* Indianapolis, Ind.: Bobbs-Merrill, 1972.

Liles, B. L. *An Introductory Transformational Grammar.* Englewood Cliffs, N.J.: Prentice-Hall, 1971.

Loban, W. D. *The Language of Elementary School Children.* National Council of Teachers of English Research Report Number 1. Urbana, Ill.: University of Illinois Press, 1963.

Luria, A. R. *The Role of Speech in the Regulation of Normal and Abnormal Behavior.* New York: Liveright, 1961.

McConnell, F., Love, R. J., and Clark, B. Language Disorders and Language Deviations. In S. Dickson (ed.), *Communication Disorders: Remedial Principles and Practices.* Glenview, Ill.: Scott, Foresman, 1974. Pp. 57—63.

Maclay, H., and Osgood, C. E. Hesitation phenomena in spontaneous English speech. *Word* 15:19, 1959.

Maclay, H., and Sleator, M. Responses to language: Judgment of grammaticalness. *International Journal of American Linguistics* 26:275, 1960.

McNeill, D. Linguistic Appendix. In D. McNeill, *The Acquisition of Language: The Study of Developmental Psycholinguistics.* New York: Harper & Row, 1970. Pp. 144—164.

McNeill, D. Methodology and Methodological Issues, In *Acquisition of Language.* Pp. 5—14.

McNeill, D. Transformations, In *Acquisition of Language.* Pp. 81—102.

McNeill, D. Universals in Child Language, In *Acquisition of Language.* Pp. 57—79.

McNeill, D. Developmental Psycholinguistics. In F. Smith, and G. Miller (eds.), *The Genesis of Language.* Cambridge, Mass.: MIT Press, 1966.

McReynolds, L. V., and Engmann, D. L. An Experimental Analysis of the Relationship of Subject and Object Noun Phrases. In L. V. McReynolds (ed.), *Developing Systematic Procedures for Training Children's Language.* American Speech and Hearing Association Monographs, No. 18. 1974. Pp. 30—46.

Malinowski, B. The Problem of Meaning in Primitive Languages. In C. K. Ogden, and I. A. Richards (eds.), *The Meaning of Meaning.* London: Routledge and Kegan Paul, 1949.

Mattingly, I. G. Reading, the Linguistic Process, and Linguistic Awareness. In J. F. Kavanagh, and I. G. Mattingly (eds.), *Language by Ear and by Eye.* Cambridge, Mass.: MIT Press, 1972. Pp. 133—148.

Menyuk, P. Syntactic structures in the language of children. *Child Development* 34:407, 1963.

Menyuk, P. Syntactic rules used by children from pre-school through first grade. *Child Development* 35:533, 1964.

Menyuk, P. Some Theoretical Considerations, In P. Menyuk, *Sentences Children Use.* Cambridge, Mass.: MIT Press, 1969. Pp. 1—22.

Messer, S. Implicit phonology in children. *Journal of Verbal Learning and Verbal Behavior* 6:609, 1967.

Messing, E. S. Auditory Perception: What Is It? In J. L. Arena (ed.), *Successful Programming: Many Points of View.* Proceedings of the Fifth Annual Conference of the Association for Children with Learning Disabilities. San Rafael, Calif.: Academic Therapy Publications, 1969.

Miller, G. A. Some preliminaries to psycholinguistics. *American Psychologist* 20:15, 1965.

Miller, G. A., McKean, K., and Slobin, D. The exploration of transformations by sentence matching. *American Psychologist* 17:748, 1962.

Morton, J. What Could Possibly Be Innate? In J. Morton (ed.), *Biological and Social Mechanisms in Language.* London: Logos, 1971.

O'Connor, N., and Hermelin, B. Visual analogies of verbal operations. *Language and Speech* 8:197, 1965.

Olson, D. R. Language and thought: Aspects of a cognitive theory of semantics. *Psychological Review* 77:257, 1970.

Osgood, C. E., and Sebeok, T. A. (eds.). *Psycholinguistics: A Survey of Theory and Research Problems.* Bloomington, Ind.: Indiana University Press, 1965.

Peck, B. A compendium of patterned language. *Journal of the Oregon Speech and Hearing Association* 10:2, 1971.

Perozzi, J. A., and Kunze, L. H. Relationship between speech sound discrimination skills and language abilities of kindergarten children. *Journal of Speech and Hearing Research* 14:382, 1971.

Premack, D. A functional analysis of language. *Journal of the Experimental Analysis of Behavior* 14:107, 1970.

Premack, D. Language in chimpanzee? *Science* 172:808, 1971.

Quine, W. V. O. *Word and Object.* Cambridge, Mass.: MIT Press, 1960.

Rees, N. S. Noncommunicative functions of language in children. *Journal of Speech and Hearing Disorders* 38:98, 1973.

Roberts, P. *English Syntax.* New York: Harcourt, Brace and World, 1964.

Savin, H., and Perchonock, E. Grammatical structure and the immediate recall of English sentences. *Journal of Verbal Learning and Verbal Behavior* 4:348, 1965.

Schiefelbusch, R. L. Summary. In R. L. Schiefelbusch and L. L. Lloyd (eds.), *Language Perspectives: Acquisition, Retardation, and Intervention.* Baltimore: University Park Press, 1974.

Schlesinger, I. M. Relational Concepts Underlying Language. In R. L. Schiefelbusch and L. L. Lloyd (eds.), *Language Perspectives: Acquisition, Retardation, and Intervention.* Baltimore: University Park Press, 1974. Pp. 129—151.

Searle, J. R. *Speech Acts: An Essay in the Philosophy of Language.* London: Cambridge University Press, 1970.

Shiffrin, R. M., and Atkinson, R. C. Storage and retrieval processes in long-term memory. *Psychological Review* 76:179, 1969.

Sinclair-DeZwart, H. Developmental Psycholinguistics. In D. Elkind, and J. H. Flavell (eds.), *Studies in Cognitive Development: Essays in Honor of Jean Piaget.* New York: Oxford University Press, 1965.

Skinner, B. F. *Verbal Behavior.* New York: Appleton-Century-Crofts, 1957.

Staats, A. W. Speech as a Response. In A. W. Staats, *Learning, Language, and Cognition.* New York: Holt, Rinehart and Winston, 1968. Pp. 53—65.

Stevens, K. Segments, Features and Analyses and Syntheses. In J. F. Kavanagh, and I. G. Mattingly (eds.), *Language by Ear and by Eye.* Cambridge, Mass.: MIT Press, 1972. Pp. 47—52.

Stolz, W. Some experiments with queer sentences. *Language and Speech* 12:203, 1969.

Studdert-Kennedy, M., Liberman, A. M., Harris, K. S., and Cooper, F. S. The motor theory of speech perception: A replay to Lane's critical review. *Psychological Review* 77:234, 1970.

Templin, M. C. *Certain Language Skills in Children: Their Development and Interrelationships.* (Child Welfare Monographs, No. 26.) Minneapolis, Minn.: University of Minnesota Press, 1957.

Thomas, O. *Transformational Grammar and the Teacher of English.* New York: Holt, Rinehart and Winston, 1965.

Thorne, J. P. On Hearing Sentences. In J. Lyons and R. J. Wales (eds.), *Psycholinguistic Papers.* Edinburgh: Edinburgh University Press, 1966.

Wang, M. Influence of linguistic structure on comprehensibility and recognition. *Journal of Experimental Psychology* 85:83, 1970.

Waryas, C., and Ruder, K. On the limitations of language comprehension procedures and an alternative. *Journal of Speech and Hearing Disorders* 39:44, 1974.

Williams, F., and Naremore, R. C. On the functional analysis of social class differences in modes of speech. *Speech Monographs* 36:77, 1969.

Yngve, V. H. A model and an hypothesis for language structure. *Proceedings of the American Philosophical Society* 104:444, 1960.

DEVELOPMENT OF LANGUAGE

Bellugi, U. Development of Language in the Normal Child. In J. E. McLean, D. E. Yoder, and R. L. Schiefelbusch (eds.), *Language Intervention With the Retarded.* Baltimore: University Park Press, 1972. Pp. 33—41.

Berko, J. The child's learning of English morphology. *Word* 14:150, 1958.

Berry, M. F. The Child Develops Language. In M. F. Berry, *Language Disorders of Children: The Bases and Diagnoses.* New York: Appleton-Century-Crofts, 1969. Pp. 156—185.

Berry, M. F. Longitudinal Study of Verbal and Nonverbal Behaviors, In *Language Disorders of Children.* Pp. 189—253.

Berry, M. F. Neural Substrates of Language Development, In *Language Disorders of Children.* Pp. 9—46.

Berry, M. F. Psychological Parameters of Language Learning. In *Language Disorders of Children.* Pp. 113—155.

Bever, T. G. The Cognitive Basis for Linguistic Structures. In J. R. Hayes (ed.), *Cognition and the Development of Language.* New York: Wiley, 1970.

Bever, T. G. The Influence of Speech Performance on Linguistic Structure. In G. B. F. D'Arcais and W. J. M. Levelt (eds.), *Advances in Psycholinguistics.* Amsterdam: North-Holland, 1970.

Bloom, L. *Language Development: Form and Function in Emerging Grammars.* (Research Monograph No. 59.) Cambridge, Mass.: MIT Press, 1970.

Bloom, L. Talking, Understanding, and Thinking. In R. L. Schiefelbusch and L. L. Lloyd (eds.), *Language Perspectives: Acquisition, Retardation, and Intervention.* Baltimore: University Park Press, 1974. Pp. 285—311.

Bowerman, M. F. Discussion Summary: Developments of Concepts Underlying Language. In R. L. Schiefelbusch and L. L. Lloyd (eds.), *Language Perspectives: Acquisition, Retardation, and Intervention.* Baltimore: University Park Press, 1974. Pp. 191—209.

Brown, R. The development of wh questions in child speech. *Journal of Verbal Learning and Verbal Behavior* 7:279, 1968.

Brown, R. The First Sentences of Child and Chimpanzee. In R. Brown (ed.), *Psycholinguistics.* New York: Free Press, 1970. Pp. 208—231.

Brown, R., and Bellugi, U. Three Processes in the Child's Acquisition of Syntax. In R. Brown (ed.), *Psycholinguistics.* New York: Free Press, 1970. Pp. 75—99.

Brown, R., Cazden, C., and Bellugi, U. The Child's Grammar from One to Three. In R. Brown (ed.), *Psycholinguistics.* New York: Free Press, 1970. Pp. 100—154.

Brown, R., and Fraser, C. The Acquisition of Syntax. In U. Bellugi and R. Brown (eds.), *The Acquisition of Language.* Society for Research in Child Development Monograph No. 29. Chicago: University of Chicago Press, 1964.

Brown, R., Fraser, C., and Bellugi, U. Explorations in Grammar Evaluation. In U. Bellugi and R. Brown (eds.), *The Acquisition of Language.* Society for Research in Child Development Monograph No. 29. Chicago: University of Chicago Press, 1964. Pp. 79–92.

Brown, R., and Hanlon, C. Derivational Complexity and Order of Acquisition in Child Speech. In R. Brown (ed.), *Psycholinguistics.* New York: Free Press, 1970. Pp. 155–207.

Butterfield, E. C., and Cairns, G. F. Discussion Summary: Infant Reception Research. In R. L. Schiefelbusch and L. L. Lloyd (eds.), *Language Perspectives: Acquisition, Retardation, and Intervention.* Baltimore: University Park Press, 1974. Pp. 75–102.

Carrow, M. A. The development of auditory comprehension of language structure in children. *Journal of Speech and Hearing Disorders* 33:99, 1968.

Cazden, C. B. *Environmental Assistance to the Child's Acquisition of Grammar.* Doctoral dissertation. Boston: Harvard University Press, 1965.

Cazden, C. B. The acquisition of noun and verb inflections. *Child Development* 39:433, 1968.

Chalfant, J. C., and Flathouse, V. E. Auditory and Visual Learning. In H. R. Myklebust (ed.), *Progress in Learning Disabilities.* New York: Grune & Stratton, 1971. Vol. II.

Chapman, R. S. Discussion Summary: Developmental Relationship Between Receptive and Expressive Language. In R. L. Schiefelbusch and L. L. Lloyd (eds.), *Language Perspectives: Acquisition, Retardation, and Intervention.* Baltimore: University Park Press, 1974. Pp. 335–344.

Church, J. The Ontogeny of Language. In H. Moltz (ed.), *The Ontogeny of Vertebrate Behavior.* New York: Academic, 1971.

Clark, E. V. On the acquisition of the meaning of before and after. *Journal of Verbal Learning and Verbal Behavior* 10:266, 1971.

Clark, E. V. Some Aspects of the Conceptual Basis for First Language Acquisition. In R. L. Schiefelbusch and L. L. Lloyd (eds.), *Language Perspectives: Acquisition, Retardation, and Intervention.* Baltimore: University Park Press, 1974. Pp. 105–128.

Deese, J. Linguistic Competence and Performance, In J. Deese, *Psycholinguistics.* Boston: Allyn and Bacon, 1970. Pp. 35–51.

Deese, J. Linguistic Development, In *Psycholinguistics.* Pp. 53–81.

deVilliers, P., and deVilliers, J. Early judgments of semantic and syntactic acceptability. *Journal of Psycholinguistic Research* 1:287, 1972.

Donaldson, M., and Wales, R. J. On the Acquisition of Some Relational Terms. In J. R. Hayes (ed.), *Cognition and the Development of Language.* New York: Wiley, 1970.

Edelheit, H. The relationship of language development to problem-solving ability. *Journal of the American Psychoanalytical Association* 19:145, 1971.

Eimas, P. D. Linguistic Processing of Speech by Young Infants. In R. L. Schiefelbusch and L. L. Lloyd (eds.), *Language Perspectives: Acquisition, Retardation, and Intervention.* Baltimore: University Park Press, 1974. Pp. 55–73.

Eisenson, J., and Ogilvie, M. Delayed or Retarded Language Acquisition and Development. In J. Eisenson and M. Ogilvie, *Speech Correction in the Schools.* New York: Macmillan, 1971. Pp. 175–192.

Ervin, S. M. Imitation and Structural Change in Children's Language. In E. Lenneberg (ed.), *New Directions in the Study of Language.* Cambridge, Mass.: MIT Press, 1964.

Ervin, S. M., and Miller, W. Language Development. In Second Yearbook of NSSE, I: *Child Psychology.* Chicago: University of Chicago Press, 1963.

Ervin-Tripp, S. Language Development. In L. W. Hoffman and M. L. Hoffman, *Review of Child Development Research.* New York: Russell Sage Foundation, 1966.

Ervin-Tripp, S. Discourse Agreement: How Children Answer Questions. In J. R. Hayes (ed.), *Cognition and the Development of Language.* New York: Wiley, 1970.

Fischer, S. Acquisition of conditioned rules. *Quarterly Progress Report 96, Research Laboratory of Electronics.* Cambridge, Mass.: MIT Press, 1970. Pp. 179–180.

Freedman, D. A. Congenital and perinatal sensory deprivation: Some studies in early development. *American Journal of Psychiatry* 127:115, 1971.

Gleitman, L., Gleitman, H., and Shipley, E. The emergence of the child as grammarian. *Cognition* 1:137, 1972.

Gollin, E. S., and Saravo, A. A Developmental Analysis of Learning. In J. Hellmuth (ed.), *Cognitive Studies,* Vol. 1. New York: Brunner/Mazel, 1970.

Guess, D., Sailor, W., Rutherford, G., and Baer, D. M. An experimental analysis of linguistic development: The productive use of the plural morpheme. *Journal of Applied Behavior Analysis* 1:297, 1968.

Hass, W. A. On the Heterogeneity of Psychological Processes in Syntactic Development. In C. S. Lavatelli (ed.), *Language Training in Early Childhood Education.* University of Illinois Press, 1972. Pp. 49–59.

Hayes, J. R. (ed.). *Cognition and the Development of Language.* New York: Wiley, 1970.

Hopper, R., and Naremore, R. C. *Children's Speech: A Practical Introduction to Communication Development.* New York: Harper & Row, 1973.

Hopper, R., and Naremore, R. C. Child Speech as a Biological Process, In *Children's Speech: A Practical Introduction.* Pp. 8–19.

Hopper, R., and Naremore, R. C. Development of Pragmatics, In *Children's Speech: A Practical Introduction.* Pp. 58–71.

Hopper, R., and Naremore, R. C. Development of Semantics, In *Children's Speech: A Practical Introduction.* Pp. 51–57.

Hopper, R., and Naremore, R. C. Development of the Sound System, In *Children's Speech: A Practical Introduction.* Pp. 23–33.

Hopper, R., and Naremore, R. C. Development of Syntax: What Really Happened Behind the Transformational Tree? In *Children's Speech: A Practical Introduction.* Pp. 34–50.

Hopper, R., and Naremore, R. C. How Children Learn to Communicate, In *Children's Speech: A Practical Introduction.* Pp. 85–96.

Hopper, R., and Naremore, R. C. Of Children and Speech Clinics, or "Is My Baby Normal?" In *Children's Speech: A Practical Introduction.* Pp. 127–134.

Hopper, R., and Naremore, R. C. School, Communication, and Minority-Group Children, In *Children's Speech: A Practical Introduction.* Pp. 114–126.

Hopper, R., and Naremore, R. C. Teaching Communication to Children, In *Children's Speech: A Practical Introduction.* Pp. 97–113.

Ingram, D. The Acquisition of Questions and Its Relation to Cognitive Development in Normal and Linguistically Deviant Children: A Pilot Study. In Committee on Linguistics, *Papers and Reports on Child Language Development.* Stanford, Calif.: Stanford University Press, 1972.

James, S., and Miller, J. Children's awareness of semantic constraints in sentences. *Child Development* 44:69, 1973.

Kendler, T. S. Development of Mediating Responses in Children. In J. C. Wright and J. Kagan (eds.), *Basic Cognitive Processes in Children.* (Monograph of Social Research and Child Development No. 28.) Chicago: University of Chicago Press, 1963. Pp. 33–48.

Koeningsknecht, R. A. Statistical Information on Developmental Sentence Analysis. In L. Lee, *Developmental Sentence Analysis.* Evanston: Northwestern University Press, 1974. Pp. 222–268

Lee, L. L. Background Information on Grammatical Structure. In L. L. Lee, *Developmental Sentence Analysis.* Evanston, Ill.: Northwestern University Press, 1974. Pp. 3–56.

Lee, L. L. Comparison of Developmental Sentence Analysis with Brown's Developmental Stages, In *Developmental Sentence Analysis.* Pp. 202–221.

Lee, L. L. Developmental Sentence Analysis: The Selection of Appropriate Teaching Goals, In *Developmental Sentence Analysis.* Pp. 176–201.

Lee, L. L. Developmental Sentence Scoring: The Quantification of Syntactic Growth Within Complete Sentences, In *Developmental Sentence Analysis.* Pp. 132–175.

Lee, L. L. Developmental Sentence Types: The Classification of Pre-Sentence Utterances, In *Developmental Sentence Analysis.* Pp. 82–131.

Leopold, W. F. *Speech Development of a Bilingual Child.* Vol. 1. Evanston, Ill.: Northwestern University Press, 1939.

Lewis, M. M. *How Children Learn to Speak.* New York: Basic Books, 1959.

McCarthy, D. A. Language Development in Children. In L. Carmichael (ed.), *Manual of Child Psychology.* New York: Wiley, 1954. Pp. 492–630.

McConnell, F., Love, R. J., and Clark, B. S. The Normal Development of Language. In S. Dickson (ed.), *Communication Disorders: Remedial Principles and Practices.* Glenview, Ill.: Scott, Foresman, 1974. Pp. 52–57.

McNeill, D. *The Acquisition of Language: The Study of Developmental Psycholinguistics.* New York: Harper & Row, 1970.

McNeill, D. The Contribution of Experience, In *The Acquisition of Language.* Pp. 103–112.

McNeill, D. The Creation of Language by Children. In J. Lyons and R. J. Wales (eds.), *Psycholinguistic Papers.* Edinburgh: Edinburgh University Press, 1966.

McNeill, D. The Pattern of Early Speech, In *The Acquisition of Language.* Pp. 15–36.

McNeill, D. Semantic Development, In *The Acquisition of Language.* Pp. 113–128.

Marquardt, T. P., and Saxman, J. H. Language comprehension and auditory discrimination in articulation deficient kindergarten children. *Journal of Speech and Hearing Research* 15:382, 1972.

Menyuk, P. Comparison of grammar of children with functionally deviant and normal speech. *Journal of Speech and Hearing Research* 7:109, 1964.

Menyuk, P. *Sentences Children Use.* Cambridge, Mass.: MIT Press, 1969.

Menyuk, P. Base Structure in Sentences, In *Sentences Children Use.* Pp. 23–66.

Menyuk, P. Grammatical Competence, In *Sentences Children Use.* Pp. 110–144.

Menyuk, P. Summary and Conclusions, In *Sentences Children Use.* Pp. 145–158.

Menyuk, P. Transformational Structures in Sentences, In *Sentences Children Use.* Pp. 67–109.

Menyuk, P. *The Acquisition and Development of Language.* Englewood Cliffs, N.J.: Prentice-Hall, 1971.

Menyuk, P. *The Development of Speech.* Indianapolis, Ind.: Bobbs-Merrill, 1972.

Menyuk, P. Early Development of Receptive Language: From Babbling to Words. In R. L. Schiefelbusch and L. L. Lloyd (eds.), *Language Perspectives: Acquisition, Retardation, and Intervention.* Baltimore: University Park Press, 1974. Pp. 213–235.

Miller, W., and Ervin, S. The Development of Grammar in Child Language. In U. Bellugi and R. Brown (eds.), *The Acquisition of Language.* Society for Research in Child Development Monograph No. 29. Chicago: University of Chicago Press, 1964.

Morehead, D., and Ingram, D. The Development of Base Syntax in Normal and Linguistically Deviant Children. In *Papers and Reports on Child Language Development.* Stanford, Calif.: Stanford University Press, 1970.

Morehead, D. M., and Morehead, A. From Signal to Sign: A Piagetian View of Thought and Language During the First Two Years. In R. L. Schiefelbusch and L. L. Lloyd (eds.), *Language Perspectives: Acquisition, Retardation, and Intervention.* Baltimore: University Park Press, 1974. Pp. 153–190.

Morse, P. A. Infant Speech Perception: A Preliminary Model and Review of the Literature. In R. L. Schiefelbusch and L. L. Lloyd (eds.), *Language Perspectives: Acquisition, Retardation, and Intervention.* Baltimore: University Park Press, 1974. Pp. 19–53.

Mowrer, O. H. Speech development in the young child: The autism theory of speech development and some clinical applications. *Journal of Speech and Hearing Disorders* 17:263, 1952.

Mowrer, O. H. Hearing and speaking: An analysis of language learning. *Journal of Speech and Hearing Disorders* 23:143, 1958.

Mysak, E. *Speech Pathology and Feedback Theory.* Springfield, Ill.: Thomas, 1966.

Rampp, D. L. (ed.). *Proceedings of the First Annual Memphis State University Symposium on Auditory Processing and Learning Disabilities.* Las Vegas Hilton, Las Vegas, July 10–15, 1972.

Rebelsky, F. G., Starr, R., and Luria, Z. Language Development: The First Four Years. In Y. Brackbill (ed.), *Infancy and Early Childhood.* New York: Free Press, 1967.

Reese, H. W. Verbal mediation as a function of age level. *Psychological Bulletin* 59:502, 1962.

Risley, T. R., Hart, B. M., and Doke, L. Operant Language Development: The Outline of a Therapeutic Technology. In R. L. Schiefelbusch (ed.), *Language of the Mentally Retarded.* Baltimore: University Park Press, 1972. Pp. 107–123.

Rosenberger, S., Stoddard, L. T., and Sidman, M. Sample-Matching Techniques in the Study of Children's Language. In R. L. Schiefelbusch (ed.), *Language of the Mentally Retarded.* Baltimore: University Park Press, 1972. Pp. 211–229.

Ruder, K. F. Psycholinguistic Viewpoint of the Language Acquisition Process. In R. L. Schiefelbusch (ed.), *Language of the Mentally Retarded.* Baltimore: University Park Press, 1972. Pp. 3–18.

Sadkin, B. The development of complexity in the language of first, third, and fifth grade boys. Kansas State University Master's thesis, 1966.

Shipley, E. F., Smith, C. S., and Gleitman, L. R. A study in acquisition of language: Free responses to commands. *Language* 45:322, 1969.

Sigel, I. Language of the Disadvantaged: The Distancing Hypothesis. In C. S. Lavatelli (ed.), *Language Training In Early Childhood Education.* Urbana, Ill.: University of Illinois Press, 1972. Pp. 60–76.

Simon, C. T. The Development of Speech. In L. E. Travis (ed.), *Handbook of Speech Pathology.* New York: Appleton-Century-Crofts, 1957. Pp. 3–43.

Slobin, D. I. Universals of Grammatical Development in Children. In G. B. F. D'Arcais and W. J. M. Levelt (eds.), *Advances in Psycholinguistics.* Amsterdam: North-Holland, 1970.

Spradlin, J. E. Discussion Summary: Development of Receptive Language. In R. L. Schiefelbusch and L. L. Lloyd (eds.), *Language Perspectives: Acquisition, Retardation, and Intervention.* Baltimore: University Park Press, 1974. Pp. 269–281.

Staats, A. W. Communication: A Pluralistic Learning Conception. In A. W. Staats, *Learning, Language, and Cognition.* New York: Holt, Rinehart and Winston, 1968. Pp. 119–131.

Staats, A. W. The Experimental-Longitudinal Study of Cognitive Learning, In *Learning, Language, and Cognition.* Pp. 264–346.

Staats, A. W. Hierarchical Child Development, the Basic Behavioral Repertoire and Conceptions of Human Motivation and Imitation, In *Learning, Language, and Cognition.* Pp. 383–469.

Staats, A. W. Integrated Learning Theory and Complex Language Interactions, In *Learning, Language, and Cognition.* Pp. 85–118.

Staats, A. W. Laboratory Study on Reading Learning in Children, In *Learning, Language, and Cognition.* Pp. 219–263.

Staats, A. W. Language Learning and Linguistics and Additional Aspects of Language and Thought, In *Learning, Language, and Cognition.* Pp. 154–192.

Sweeney, S. The importance of imitation in the early stages of speech acquisition: A case report. *Journal of Speech and Hearing Disorders* 38:490, 1973.

Templin, M. C. Certain Language Skills in Children: Their Development and Interrelationships. (Child Welfare Monographs, No. 26.) Minneapolis, Minn.: University of Minnesota Press, 1957.

Winitz, H. The Development of Speech and Language in the Normal Child. In R. W. Rieber and R. S. Brubaker (eds.), *Speech Pathology.* Amsterdam: North-Holland, 1966. Pp. 42–76.

Witkin, B. R. Auditory perception: Implications for language development. *Language, Speech, and Hearing Services in Schools* 2:31, 1971.

ASSESSMENT OF LANGUAGE

Adams, S. M. D. A descriptive linguistic investigation of language problems in preschool children. Southern Illinois University Doctoral Dissertation, 1968.

Bangs, T. E. Assessment Tools. In T. E. Bangs, *Language and Learning Disorders of the Pre-academic Child: With Curriculum Guide.* New York: Appleton-Century-Crofts, 1968. Pp. 40–70.

Bangs, T. E. Techniques of Assessing and Reporting, In *Language and Learning Disorders.* Pp. 71–91.

Bellugi-Klima, U. Some Language Comprehension Tests. In C. S. Lavatelli (ed.), *Language Training In Early Childhood Education.* University of Illinois Press, 1972. Pp. 157–169.

Berry, M. F. Appendixes. In M. F. Berry, *Language Disorders of Children. The Bases and Diagnoses.* New York: Appleton-Century-Crofts, 1969. Pp. 371–426.

Berry, M. F. Diagnostic Testing of Oral Language, In *Language Disorders of Children.* Pp. 254–276.

Berry, M. F. Testing Abilities Associated with Language Learning, In *Language Disorders of Children.* Pp. 277–304.

Bloom, L. M. A comment on Lee's Developmental sentence types: A method for comparing normal and deviant syntactic development. *Journal of Speech and Hearing Disorders* 32:294, 1967.

Carrow, E. Assessment of Speech and Language in Children. In J. E. McLean, D. E. Yoder, and R. L. Schiefelbusch (eds.), *Language Intervention With the Retarded.* Baltimore: University Park Press, 1972. Pp. 52–88.

Church, J. Techniques for the Differential Study of Cognition in Early Childhood. In J. Hellmuth (ed.), *Cognitive Studies,* Vol. 1. New York: Brunner/Mazel, 1970.

Danks, J., and Glucksberg, S. Psychological scaling of linguistic properties. *Language and Speech* 13:118, 1970.

Darley, F. L. *Diagnosis and Appraisal of Communication Disorders.* Englewood Cliffs, N.J.: Prentice-Hall, 1964.

Eisenson, J. Comment on Kleffner: More on children with language disorders. *Journal of Speech and Hearing Disorders* 38:542, 1973.

Engler, L. F., Hannah, E. P., and Longhurst, T. M. Linguistic analysis of speech samples: A practical guide for clinicians. *Journal of Speech and Hearing Disorders* 38:192, 1973.

Fluharty, N. B. The design and standardization of a speech and language screening test for use with preschool children. *Journal of Speech and Hearing Disorders* 39:75, 1974.

Girardeau, F. L., and Spradlin, J. E. An Introduction to the Functional Analysis of Speech and Language. In *A Functional Analysis Approach to Speech and Language* (American Speech and Hearing Association Monograph No. 14.) Washington, D.C.: American Speech and Hearing Association, 1970.

Hedrick, D. L., and Prather, E. M. A Behavioral System for Assessing Language Development. In R. L. Schiefelbusch (ed.), *Language of the Mentally Retarded.* Baltimore: University Park Press, 1972. Pp. 143–168.

Johnson, W., Darley, F. L., and Spriestersbach, D. C. *Diagnostic Methods in Speech Pathology.* New York: Harper & Row, 1963.

Koeningsknecht, R. A., and Lee, L. L. Validity and reliability of developmental sentence scoring: A method for measuring syntactic development in children's spontaneous speech. Presented at the Annual Convention of the American Speech and Hearing Association, Chicago, 1971.

Kunze, L. H. Program for training in behavioral observation. (American Speech and Hearing Association Monograph No. 9.) 1967. Pp. 473–476.

Lee, L. L. Developmental sentence types: A method for comparing normal and deviant syntactic development. *Journal of Speech and Hearing Disorders* 31:311, 1966.

Lee, L. L. *Developmental Sentence Analysis: A Grammatical Assessment Procedure for Speech and Language Clinicians.* Evanston, Ill.: Northwestern University Press, 1974.

Lee, L. L. Taking a Language Sample in a Clinical Setting, In *Developmental Sentence Analysis.* Pp. 57–81.

Lee, L., and Canter, S. Developmental sentence scoring: A clinical procedure for evaluating syntactic development in children's spontaneous speech. *Journal of Speech and Hearing Disorders* 36:315, 1971.

Longhurst, T. M. Linguistic analysis of children's speech: A comparison of four procedures. *Journal of Speech and Hearing Disorders* 38:240, 1973.

McConnell, F., Love, R. J., and Clark, B. S. Evaluation Principles and Procedures. In S. Dickson (ed.), *Communication Disorders: Remedial Principles and Practices.* Glenview, Ill.: Scott, Foresman, 1974. Pp. 63–84.

Merklein, R. A., and Briskey, R. J. Audiometric findings in children referred to a program for language disorders. *Volta Review* 64:294, 1962.

Monsees, E., and Berman, C. Speech and language screening in a summer Headstart program. *Journal of Speech and Hearing Disorders* 33:121, 1968.

Nunnally, J. C. Individual Differences in Word Usage. In S. Rosenberg (ed.), *Directions in Psycholinguistics.* New York: Macmillan, 1965.

Premack, D. On the assessment of language competence in the chimpanzee. *Behavior of Non-Human Primates* 4:185, 1971.

Sanders, L. J. *Procedure Guides for Evaluation of Speech and Language Disorders in Children.* Danville, Ill.: Interstate Printers & Publishers, 1972.

Sanders, L. J. Evaluation of Language in Children, In *Procedure Guides for Evaluation.* Pp. 29–50.

Sharf, D. J. Some relationships between measures of early language development. *Journal of Speech and Hearing Disorders* 37:64, 1972.

Staats, A. W. A general apparatus for the investigation of complex learning in children. *Behaviour Research and Therapy* 6:45, 1968.

LANGUAGE-RELATED TESTS

Ammons, R. B., and Ammons, C. H. *The Quick Test*. 1962. Psychological Test Specialists, P.O. Box 1441, Missoula, MT. 59801.
A test of receptive ability.

Ammons, R. B., and Ammons, H. S. *Full-Range Picture Vocabulary Test*. 1948. Psychological Test Specialists, P.O. Box 1441, Missoula, MT. 59801.
Assesses receptive vocabulary.

Ammons, R. B., and Holmes, J. C. The full-range picture vocabulary test: III. Results for pre-school population. *Child Development* 20:5, 1949.

Beery, K. E. *Developmental Test of Visual-Motor Integration*. 1967. Follett Publishing Company, 1010 W. Washington Blvd., Chicago, IL. 60607.
Assesses visual perception and motor coordination; a test for "educational assessment."

Bender, L. *Bender Motor Gestalt Test*. 1946. The American Orthopsychiatric Association.
The purpose of this test is "to explore retardation, regression, loss of function and organic brain defects in both adults and children . . . "

Burgemeister, B. B., Blum, L. H., and Lorge, I. *Columbia Mental Maturity Scale*. 1954. World Book Company, Yonkers-on-Hudson, N.Y.
A test of intelligence.

Bzoch, K. R., and League, R. *Receptive-Expressive Emergent Language Scale*. 1971. Tree of Life Press, 1309 N. E. 2nd St., P.O. Box 447, Gainesville, FL. 32601.
An interview test that provides a receptive language age, expressive language age, and a combined language age. Age periods range from zero to 36 months.

Carrow, E. *Test for Auditory Comprehension of Language*. 1973. Learning Concepts, 2501 N. Lamar, Austin, TX. 78705.
A receptive test of auditory comprehension. Assesses vocabulary and grammar (syntax).

Cattell, R. B. *Culture-Fair Intelligence Test (Culture-Free Intelligence Test): Scale 1*. 1950. Western Psychological Services, 12031 Wilshire Blvd., Los Angeles, CA. 90025.
Assesses "general ability" in areas such as "selecting named objects" and "following directions."

Crabtree, M. *The Houston Test for Language Development* 1958. Margaret Crabtree, Ed.D., 10133 Bassoon, Houston, TX.
For use with children from 6 to 36 months. Assesses receptive and expressive abilities.

DeRenzi, E., and Vignolo, L. A. The token test: A sensitive test to detect receptive disturbance in aphasia. *Brain* 85:665, 1962.

Doll, E. A. *Vineland Social Maturity Scale*. Revised 1965. American Guidance Service, Publisher's Building, Circle Pines, MN. 55014.
Tests "growth in social responsibility" by assessing "self-help, self-direction, locomotion, occupation, communication, and social relations."

Dunn, L. M. *Peabody Picture Vocabulary Test*. 1965. American Guidance Service, Publisher's Building, Circle Pines, MN. 55014.
A test of receptive abilities involving vocabulary identification; a language age and mental age are obtained from the scores.

Eisenson, J. *Examining for Aphasia*. 1954. The Psychological Corporation, 304 East 45th St., New York, N.Y. 10017.
A test to determine the level of difficulty in the receptive and expressive modes.

Elizur, A. *Elizur Test of Psycho-Organicity for Children and Adults*. 1969. Western Psychological Services, 12031 Wilshire Blvd., Los Angeles, CA. 90025.
Diagnoses brain conditions and shows impairment in the visual and/or auditory areas.

Feldman, M. J., and Drasgow, J. *The Visual-Verbal Test*. 1959. Western Psychological Services, 12031 Wilshire Blvd., Los Angeles, CA. 90025.
Assesses "aspects of conceptual thought in schizophrenics."

Flowers, A., Costello, M. R., and Small, V. *Flowers-Costello Tests of Central Auditory Abilities*. 1970. Perceptual Learning Systems, P.O. Box 4209, Dearborn, MI. 48126.
Investigates the existence of auditory perceptual disorders that may interfere with normal language acquisition.

Foster, R., Giddan, J. J., and Stark, J. *Assessment of Children's Language Comprehension*. 1969. Consulting Psychologists' Press, 577 College Ave., Palo Alto, CA. 94306.
Receptive test of language comprehension. The child identifies increasingly longer word groups.

Frankenburg, W. K., Dodds, J. B., and Fandal, A. W. *Denver Developmental Screening Test*. Revised 1970.
Investigates developmental problems in the following areas: personal—social, fine motor—adaptive, language, and gross motor.

Frostig, M., Lefever, W., and Whittlesey, J. R. B. *Marianne Frostig Developmental Test of Visual Perception*. Revised 1966. Consulting Psychologists' Press, 577 College Ave., Palo Alto, CA. 94306.
Assesses visual perception and reveals impairment related to brain damage, emotional disturbances, and slow development rates.

Goldman, R., Fristoe, M., and Woodcock, R. *Goldman-Fristoe-Woodcock Test of Auditory Discrimination*. 1970. American Guidance Service, Publisher's Building, Circle Pines, MN. 55014.
Tests speech—sound discrimination ability that may be important to language acquisition.

Goodenough, M., and Harris, D. B. *Goodenough-Harris Drawing Test Manual*. 1963. Harcourt, Brace, & World, 757 Third Ave., New York, N.Y. 10017.
Indicates the presence of brain dysfunction.

Graham, F. K., and Kendall, B. S. *Memory-For-Designs Test*. 1946. Psychological Test Specialists, P.O. Box 1441, Missoula, MT. 59801.
For identifying brain-disordered individuals.

Haeusserman, E. *Educational Evaluation of Preschool Children*. 1962. Grune & Stratton, 757 Third Ave., New York, N.Y. 10017.
An interview test to investigate physical development and intellectual development (language behavior).

Halstead, W. *Halstead Aphasia Test*. 1955. Education Industry Service, 975 East 60th St., Chicago, IL. 60650.
Test of aphasia — provides a determination of severity. Assesses reading, articulation, picture identification, and arithmetic ability.

Harris, D. B. *Goodenough-Harris Drawing Test Manual*. 1963. Harcourt, Brace & World, 757 Third Ave., New York, N.Y. 10017.
"The Drawing Test may supply important additional evidence of severe intellectual and conceptual retardation."

Haworth, M. R. *The Primary Visual Motor Test*. 1970. Grune & Stratton, 757 Third Ave., New York, N.Y. 10017.
Assesses visual motor abilities in preschool and primary grades. Because of correlations found between this test and chronological age and mental age, this test could serve "as a nonverbal means of estimating developmental levels for deaf and speech handicapped children."

Hedrick, D. L., and Prather, E. M. *Sequenced Inventory of Language Development Test*. 1977. Child Development and Mental Retardation Center, University of Washington, Seattle, WA. 98105.
Tests receptive and expressive abilities, both by interview and directly.

Jastak, J. F., and Jastak, S. R. *The Wide Range Achievement Test*. 1965. Guidance Associates, Wilmington, DE.

Kahn, T. *Kahn Test of Symbol Arrangement.* 1956. Psychological Test Specialists, P.O. Box 11, Grand Forks, N.D. 58201.

Kirk, S. A., McCarthy, J. J., and Kirk, W. D. *Illinois Test of Psycholinguistic Abilities.* 1968. Board of Trustees of the University of Illinois.
Assesses twelve functions of psycholinguistic ability at the representational and automatic levels.

Lee, L. *Northwestern Syntax Screening Test.* 1971. Northwestern University Press, 1735 Benson Ave., Evanston, IL. 60201.
A screening test of receptive and expressive abilities in the areas of speech sounds, vocabulary, and syntax. Can be used with children between 3 and 8 years of age.

Leiter, R. G. *The Leiter International Performance Scale.* 1969. Stoelting Company, 424 N. Homan Ave., Chicago, IL. 60624.
Entails matching block designs, pictures, genus, and numbers with figures. A mental age is obtained.

McCarthy, D. *McCarthy Scales of Children's Abilities.* 1972. The Psychological Corporation, New York, N.Y. 10017.
Shows "general intellectual level" on six scales: verbal, perceptual performance, quantitative, general cognitive, memory, and motor. Designed for children from 2½ to 8½ years old.

Mecham, M. J. *Verbal Language Development Scale.* 1958. American Guidance Service, Publisher's Building, Circle Pines, MN. 55014.
An "informant-interview method" is used. The score is changed into a "Language Age."

Mecham, M. J., Jex, J. L., and Jones, J. D. *Utah Test of Language Development,* revised, 1969. Communication Research Associates, P.O. Box 11012, Salt Lake City, UT.
Assesses verbal language skill in receptive and expressive areas.

Miller, J. F., and Yoder, D. E. *The Miller-Yoder Test of Grammatical Comprehension (The MY Test).* 1972. Madison, WI.
An experimental test with limited distribution.

Mills, R. E. *Learning Methods Test.* 1955. The Mills Center, 1512 E. Broward Blvd., Fort Lauderdale, FL.
Determines a child's ability to "learn new words under different teaching procedures."

Miner, L. E. Scoring procedures for the length-complexity index: A preliminary report. *Journal of Communication Disorders* 2:224, 1969.

Murray, H. A. *Thematic Apperception Test.* 1943. Harvard University, Cambridge, MA. 02138.

Myklebust, H. R. *Picture Story Language Test for Diagnosis of Disorders in Written Language.* 1965. Grune & Stratton, 361 Park Ave. South, New York, N.Y. 10016.
Can be used "as a diagnostic instrument for the study of children with language disorders and other types of learning disabilities."

Otis, A. S., and Lennon, R. T. *Otis-Lennon Mental Ability Test.* 1967. Harcourt, Brace & World, 757 Third Ave., New York, N.Y. 10017.
Assesses "general mental ability" by "measuring the pupil's facility in reasoning and in dealing abstractly with verbal, symbolic, and figural test content sampling a broad range of cognitive abilities." Designed for grades K—12.

Porch, B. *Porch Index of Communicative Ability: Theory and Development.* 1967. Consulting Psychologists' Press, 577 College Ave., Palo Alto, CA. 93406.
A test of aphasia developed by a consulting psychologist.

Raven, J. C. *The Colored Progressive Matrices.* 1956. The Psychological Corporation, 304 East 45th St., New York, N.Y. 10017.

Rogers, W. *Picture Articulation and Language Screening Test (PALST).* 1972. Word Making Productions, Salt Lake City, UT.

Sarno, M. T. The functional communication profile: Manual of directions. *Rehabilitation Monograph 42.* New York Univ. Med. Ctr., Inst. Rehab. Med., 1969.

Schuell, H. *Minnesota Test For Differential Diagnosis of Aphasia.* 1965. University of Minnesota, Minneapolis, MN. 55455.
Investigates "auditory disturbances, visual and reading disturbances, speech and language disturbances, visuomotor and writing disturbances, and disturbances of numerical relations and arithmetic processes."

Schuell, H. A short examination for aphasia. *Neurol.* (Minneap.) 7:625, 1957.

Sklar, M. *Sklar Aphasia Scale.* 1966. Western Psychological Services, 12031 Wilshire Blvd., Los Angeles, CA. 90025.
Designed to show types of language disorders resulting from brain damage. Assesses "auditory verbal comprehension, reading comprehension, oral expression, and graphic production."

Slingerland, B. H. *Slingerland Screening Tests for Identifying Children with Specific Language Disability.* Revised, 1970. Educators Publishing Service, Cambridge, MA. 02138.
Identifies children with learning disabilities that affect "reading, writing and spelling."

Slosson, R. L. *The Slosson Drawing Coordination Test for Children and Adults.* 1967. Slosson Educational Publications, 140 Pine St., East Aurora, N.Y. 14052.
Helps "to identify individuals with various forms of brain dysfunction or perceptual disorders where eye—hand coordination is involved."

Slosson, R. L. *Slosson Intelligence Test for Children and Adults.* 1963. Slosson Educational Publications, 140 Pine St., East Aurora, N.Y. 14052.
An individual test of intellectual functioning.

Slosson, R. L. *Slosson Oral Reading Test.* 1963. Slosson Educational Publications, 140 Pine St., East Aurora, N.Y. 14052.

Valett, R. E. *Valett Developmental Survey of Basic Learning Abilities.* 1966. Consulting Psychologists' Press, 577 College Ave., Palo Alto, CA. 94306.
Assesses the following abilities: "motor integration and physical development, tactile discrimination, auditory discrimination, visual—motor coordination, visual discrimination, language development and verbal fluency, and conceptual development."

Van Alstyne, D. *Van Alstyne Picture Vocabulary Test.* 1961. Harcourt, Brace & World, 757 Third Ave., New York, N.Y. 10017.
A test of receptive abilities based upon picture vocabulary identification. Indicates mental ability in the range of 2 to 7 years.

Wechsler, D. *Wechsler Preschool and Primary Scale of Intelligence.* 1967. The Psychological Corporation, 304 East 45th St., New York, N.Y. 10017.
A two-part test that assesses verbal and performance areas.

Wepman, J. M., and Jones, L. V. *The Language Modalities Test for Aphasia.* 1961. Education Industry Service, 975 East 60th St., Chicago, IL. 60650.
A film strip is used to test reading, speaking, writing, spelling, and arithmetic abilities. Articulation abilities are also tested. A manual giving directions for administering and scoring the test (*Studies in Aphasia: An Approach to Testing*) is also available from the distributor.

Wolski, W. *The Michigan Picture Language Inventory.* 1962. University of Michigan, Ann Arbor, MI. 48104.

NATURE OF APHASIA

Biorn-Hansen, V. Social and emotional aspects of aphasia. *Journal of Speech and Hearing Disorders* 22:53, 1957.

Efron, R. Temporal perception, aphasia, and deja vu. *Brain* 86:403, 1963.

Eisenson, J. The Young Aphasic Child. In M. F. Berry and J. Eisenson (eds.), *Speech Disorders: Principles and Practices of Therapy*. New York: Appleton-Century-Crofts, 1956.

Eisenson, J. *Aphasia in Children*. New York: Harper & Row, 1972.

Eisenson, J., and Ingram, D. Childhood aphasia: An updated concept based on recent research. *Papers and Reports on Child Language Development*. Stanford, Calif.: Stanford University Press, 1972.

Goodglass, H., Quadfasel, F. G., and Timberlake, W. J. Phrase length and the type of severity of aphasia. *Cortex* 1:133, 1964.

Hodgins, E. *Episode: Report on the Accident Inside My Skull*. New York: Atheneum, 1964.

Johns, D. F., and Darley, F. L. Phonemic variability in apraxia of speech. *Journal of Speech and Hearing Research* 13:556, 1970.

Leicester, J., Sidman, M., Stoddard, L. T., and Mohr, J. P. The nature of aphasic responses. *Neuropsychologia* 9:141, 1971.

Lhermitte, F., Lecours, A. R., and Bertaux, D. Activation and Seriation of Linguistic Units in Aphasic Transformations. In L. D. Proctor (ed.), *Biocybernetics of the Central Nervous System*. Boston: Little, Brown, 1969. Pp. 389–418.

Lowe, A. D., and Campbell, R. A. Temporal discrimination in aphasoid and normal children. *Journal of Speech and Hearing Research* 8:313, 1965.

Luria, A. R. Factors and Forms of Aphasia. In A. V. S. de Reuck and M. O'Connor (eds.), *Disorders of Language* (a Ciba Foundation Symposium). Boston: Little, Brown, 1964.

Luria, A. R., and Tsvetkova, L. S. The mechanism of "dynamic aphasia." *Foundations of Language, International Journal of Language and Philosophy* 4:296, 1968.

Malone, R. Expressed attitudes of families of aphasics. *Journal of Speech and Hearing Disorders* 34:146, 1969.

Martin, A. D. Some objections to the term *apraxia of speech*. *Journal of Speech and Hearing Disorders* 39:53, 1974.

Pincas, A. Linguistics and aphasia. *Journal of the Australian College of Speech Therapy* 15:20, 1965.

Sarno, M., and Levita, E. Natural course of recovery in severe aphasia. *Archives of Physical Medicine and Rehabilitation* 52:175, 1971.

Schlanger, B., Arnold, B., Brotkin, R., Kilpatrick, I., and Miller, R. Relationship between the communicative functioning of aphasics and performance on varied tasks. Presented at the Annual Convention of American Speech and Hearing Association, Washington, D.C., 1966.

Schuell, H. M. Aphasic difficulties understanding spoken language. *Neurology* 3:176, 1953.

Schwebel, M. C., and Brookshire, R. H. Aphasia complicated by hypercalcemia. *Journal of Speech and Hearing Disorders* 37:542, 1972.

Spreen, O. Psycholinguistic aspects of aphasia. *Journal of Speech and Hearing Research* 11:467, 1968.

Strauss, A. A., and McCarus, E. N. A linguist looks at aphasia in children. *Journal of Speech and Hearing Disorders* 23:54, 1958.

Weiner, P. S. The perceptual level functioning of dysphasic children. *Cortex* 5:440, 1969.

Weiner, P. S. The perceptual level functioning of dysphasic children: A follow-up study. *Journal of Speech and Hearing Research* 15:423, 1972.

Zangwill, O. L. Intelligence in Aphasia. In A. V. S. de Reuck and M. O'Connor (eds.), *Disorders of Language* (a Ciba Foundation Symposium). Boston: Little, Brown, 1964. Pp. 261–275.

APHASIC DISORDERS

Bangs, T. E. *Language and Learning Disorders of the Pre-academic Child*. New York: Appleton-Century-Crofts, 1968.

Benton, A. L. Developmental aphasia and brain damage. *Cortex* 1:40, 1964.

Fay, W. H. Childhood echolalia in delayed psychotic and neuropathologic speech patterns. *Folia Phoniatrica* 18:68, 1966.

Fay, W. H. Childhood echolalia: A group study of late abatement. *Folia Phoniatrica* 19:297, 1967.

Fay, W. H., and Butler, B. V. Echolalia, IQ, and the developmental dichotomy of speech and language systems. *Journal of Speech and Hearing Research* 11:365, 1968.

Goetzinger, C. Effects of small perceptive losses on language and on speech discrimination. *Volta Review* 64:408, 1962.

Griffith, R., and Ritvo, E. Echolalia: Concerning the dynamics of the syndrome. *Journal of the American Academy of Child Psychiatry* 6:184, 1967.

Hardy, W. G. On language disorders in young children: A reorganization of thinking. *Journal of Speech and Hearing Disorders* 8:3, 1965.

Johnson, D. J., and Myklebust, H. R. *Learning Disabilities: Educational Principles and Practices*. New York: Grune & Stratton, 1967.

Kleffner, F. R. Hearing losses, hearing aids, and children with language disorders. *Journal of Speech and Hearing Disorders* 38:232, 1973.

Lenneberg, E. H. Understanding language without ability to speak: A case report. *Journal of Abnormal and Social Psychology* 65:419, 1962.

Lenneberg, E. H. Language disorders in childhood. *Harvard Educational Review* 34:152, 1964.

Leonard, L. B. What is deviant language? *Journal of Speech and Hearing Disorders* 37:427, 1972.

Lerner, J. W. *Children with Learning Disabilities*. Boston: Houghton Mifflin, 1971.

Rees, N. S. Auditory processing factors in language disorders: The view from Procrustes' bed. *Journal of Speech and Hearing Disorders* 38:304, 1973.

Stark, J., Rosenbaum, R. L., Schwartz, D., and Wisan, A. The nonverbal child: Some clinical guidelines. *Journal of Speech and Hearing Disorders* 38:59, 1973.

Weiner, P. S. A language-delayed child at adolescence. *Journal of Speech and Hearing Disorders* 39:202, 1974.

ASSESSMENT OF APHASIA

Boller, F., and Vignolo, L. A. Latent sensory aphasia in hemisphere damaged patients: An experimental study with the Token Test. *Brain* 89:815, 1966.

Critchley, M. Articulatory defects in aphasia. *Journal of Laryngology and Otolaryngology* 66:1, 1952.

Darley, F. L. The classification of output disturbances in neurologic communication disorders. Presented in the dual session on Aphasia: Input and output disturbances in speech and language processing, at the Annual Convention of the American Speech and Hearing Association, Chicago, 1969.

Darley, F. L., Aronson, A. E., and Brown, J. R. Differential diagnostic patterns of dysarthria. *Journal of Speech and Hearing Research* 12:246, 1969.

Denny-Brown, D. The nature of apraxia. *Journal of Nervous and Mental Disease* 126:9, 1958.

Needham, L. S., and Swisher, L. P. A comparison of three tests of auditory comprehension for adult aphasics. *Journal of Speech and Hearing Disorders* 37:123, 1972.

Orgass, B., and Poeck, K. Clinical validation of a new test for aphasia: An experimental study on the Token Test. *Cortex* 2:222, 1966.

Stark, J. A. Comparison of the performance of aphasic children on three sequencing tests. *Journal of Communication Disorders* 1:31, 1967.

Swisher, L. P., and Sarno, M. T. Token Test scores of three matched patient groups: Left brain damaged with aphasia; right brain damaged without aphasia; non-brain damaged. *Cortex* 5:264, 1969.

Taylor, M. L. A measurement of functional communication in aphasia. *Archives of Physical Medicine and Rehabilitation* 46:101, 1965.

HABILITATION OF APHASIA

Anderson, T., Boureston, N., and Greenberg, F. *Rehabilitation predictors in completed stoke.* Final report to the U. S. Soc. Rehab. Service. Minneapolis: Kenny Rehabilitation Institute, American Rehabilitation Foundation, 1971.

Berman, M., and Peelle, L. Self-generated cues: A method for aiding aphasic and apractic patients. *Journal of Speech and Hearing Disorders* 32:372, 1967.

Darley, F. L. The efficacy of language rehabilitation in aphasia. *Journal of Speech and Hearing Disorders* 37:3, 1972.

Davis, N., and Leach, E. Scaling aphasics' error responses. *Journal of Speech and Hearing Disorders* 37:305, 1972.

Gardiner, B. J., and Brookshire, R. H. Effects of unisensory and multisensory presentation of stimuli upon naming by aphasic subjects. *Language and Speech* 15:342, 1972.

Gray, B. B., and Fygetakis, L. Mediated language acquisition for dysphasic children. *Behaviour Research and Therapy* 6:263, 1968.

Holland, A. L. *Current trends in aphasia rehabilitation.* (American Speech and Hearing Association Monographs, No. 11.) 1969. Pp. 3–7.

Holland, A. L., and Levy, C. B. Syntactic Generalization in Aphasics as a Function of Relearning an Active Sentence: Some Preliminary Findings. In J. W. Black and E. G. Jancosek (eds.), *Proceedings of the Conference on Language Retraining for Aphasics.* Ohio State University Research Foundation, 1968. Pp. 205–217.

Howes, D. Application of the Word-Frequency Concept to Aphasia. In A. V. S. de Reuck and M. O'Connor (eds.), *Disorders of Language (Ciba Foundation Symposium).* Boston: Little, Brown, 1964. Pp. 47–75.

Johns, D. F. Treatment of apraxia of speech. Presented at the Annual Convention of the American Speech and Hearing Association, New York, 1970.

Kolman, I., and Shimizu, H. Recovery from aphasia as monitored by AER audiometry. *Journal of Speech and Hearing Disorders* 37:414, 1972.

Morley, J. J. Applying linguistics to speech and language therapy for aphasics. *Language Learning* 10:135, 1960.

Rosenbek, J. C., Lemme, M. L., Ahern, M. B., Harris, E. H., and Wertz, R. T. A treatment for apraxia of speech in adults. *Journal of Speech and Hearing Disorders* 38:462, 1973.

Salvatore, A. P. Use of a baseline probe technique to monitor the test responses of aphasic patients. *Journal of Speech and Hearing Disorders* 37:471, 1972.

Sarno, M. T., Silverman, M., and Sands, E. Speech therapy and language recovery in severe aphasia. *Journal of Speech and Hearing Research* 13:607, 1970.

Scargill, M. H. Modern linguistics and recovery from aphasia. *Journal of Speech and Hearing Disorders* 19:507, 1954.

Shankweiler, D., and Harris, K. An experimental approach to the problem of articulation in aphasia. *Cortex* 2:277, 1966.

Turnblom, M., and Myers, J. Group discussion programs with the families of aphasic patients. *Journal of Speech and Hearing Disorders* 17:393, 1952.

Wepman, J. M. A conceptual model for the processes involved in recovery from aphasia. *Journal of Speech and Hearing Disorders* 18:4, 1953.

Wepman, J. M. Aphasia therapy: A new look. *Journal of Speech and Hearing Disorders* 37:203, 1972.

West, R. W., and Ansberry, M. Disorders of Symbolization and Language. In R. W. West and M. Ansberry, *The Rehabilitation of Speech.* New York: Harper & Row, 1968.

EMOTIONALLY DISTURBED

Benassi, V. Imitation and functional speech in autistic children: A reply to Hartung. *Journal of Speech and Hearing Disorders* 37:421, 1972.

Bettelheim, B. *The Empty Fortress: Infantile Autism and the Birth of Self.* New York: Free Press, 1967.

Bostow, D. E., and Bailey, J. Modification of severe disruptive and aggressive behavior using brief time out and reinforcement procedures. *Journal of Applied Behavior Analysis* 2:31, 1969.

Bryson, C. Q. Systematic identification of perceptual disabilities in autistic children. *Perceptual and Motor Skills* 31:239, 1970.

Bryson, C. Q. Short-term memory and cross-modal information processing in autistic children. *Journal of Learning Disabilities* 5:25, 1972.

Cantrell, R. P., Hayes, W. A., and Bricker, W. A. Programmed Learning and Reversal Sets for "Autistic" Children: A Pilot Study. In H. C. Haywood (ed.), *Abstracts of Peabody Studies in Mental Retardation,* Vol. 4. 1968.

Carrier, J. K. Application of functional analysis and a non-speech response mode to teaching language. Kansas Center for Research in Mental Retardation and Human Development, Report No. 7. Parsons, Kansas, 1973.

Churchill, D. W. The relation of infantile autism and early childhood schizophrenia to developmental language disorders of childhood. *Journal of Autism and Childhood Schizophrenia* 2:182, 1972.

Colby, K. M., and Smith, D. C. Computer as Catalyst in The Treatment of Nonspeaking Autistic Children. In J. H. Masserman (ed.), *Current Psychiatric Therapies.* New York: Grune & Stratton, 1971.

Fay, W. H. On the basis of autistic echolalia. *Journal of Communication Disorders* 2:38, 1969.

Fay, W. H. On normal and autistic pronouns. *Journal of Speech and Hearing Disorders* 36:242, 1971.

Fay, W. H. On the echolalia of the blind and of the autistic child. *Journal of Speech and Hearing Disorders* 38:478, 1973.

Goldfarb, W. Self-awareness in schizophrenic children. *Archives of General Psychiatry* 8:47, 1963.

Goldfarb, W. *Childhood Schizophrenia.* Cambridge, Mass.: Harvard University Press, 1969.

Hartung, J. Establishing verbal imitation skills and functional speech in autistic children: A rebutal to Benassi. *Journal of Speech and Hearing Disorders* 37:422, 1972.

Hermelin, B. Recent Psychological Research. In J. K. Wing (ed.), *Early Childhood Autism.* New York: Pergamon, 1966.

Hermelin, B., and O'Connor, N. Effects of sensory input and sensory dominance on severely disturbed, autistic children and on subnormal controls. *British Journal of Psychology* 55:201, 1964.

Hermelin, B., and O'Connor, N. Visual imperception in psychotic children. *British Journal of Psychology* 56:455, 1965.

Hermelin, B., and O'Connor, N. *Psychological Experiments with Autistic Children.* New York: Pergamon, 1970.

Hewett, F. M. Teaching speech to an autistic child through operant conditioning. *American Journal of Orthopsychiatry* 35:927, 1965.

Keeler, W. R. Autistic Patterns and Defective Communication in Blind Children with Retrolental Fibroplasia. In P. H. Hoch and J. Zubin (eds.), *Psychopathology of Communication.* New York: Grune & Stratton, 1958.

Kirby, F. D., and Toler, H. C. Modification of pre-school isolate behavior: A case study. *Journal of Applied Behavior Analysis* 3:309, 1970.

Kugelmass, I. N. *The Autistic Child.* Springfield, Ill.: Thomas, 1970.

Lovaas, I. A Program for the Establishment of Speech in Psychotic Children. In H. Sloan and B. MacAulay (eds.), *Operant Procedures in Remedial Speech and Language Training.* Boston: Houghton Mifflin, 1968.

Lovaas, I., Berberich, J., Perloff, B., and Schaeffer, B. Acquisition of imitative speech by schizophrenic children. *Science* 151:705, 1966.

McGrew, W. C., and Craig, J. M. An auditory integrational problem with associated language disability in an adult mental patient. *Journal of Speech and Hearing Disorders* 38:374, 1973.

McLean, L. P., and McLean, J. E. A language training program for nonverbal autistic children. *Journal of Speech and Hearing Disorders* 39:186, 1974.

Marshall, N. R., and Hegrenes, J. R. Programmed communication therapy for autistic mentally retarded children. *Journal of Speech and Hearing Disorders* 35:70, 1970.

Marshall, N. R., and Hegrenes, J. R. The use of written language as a communication system for an autistic child. *Journal of Speech and Hearing Disorders* 37:258, 1972.

Ottinger, D. R., Sweeney, N., and Loew, L. H. Visual discrimination learning in schizophrenic and normal children. *Journal of Clinical Psychology* 21:251, 1965.

Pronovost, W., Wakstein, M. P., and Wakstein, D. J. A longitudinal study of the speech behavior and language comprehension of fourteen children diagnosed atypical or autistic. *Exceptional Children* 33:19, 1966.

Rodrique, E. The Analysis of a Three-Year-Old Mute Schizophrenic. In M. Klein, P. Heimann, and R. E. Money-Kyrle (eds.), *New Directions in Psycho-Analysis.* New York: Basic Books, 1957.

Roth, F., Veth, E., Garrett, T., Rosenbaum, R., and Wisan, A. The use of a video-taped model to expand language forms in an autistic child. Presented at the New York State Speech and Hearing Association, Ellenville, N.Y., 1972.

Rousey, C. L., and Toussieng, P. W. Contributions of a speech pathologist to the psychiatric examination of children. *Mental Hygiene* 48:566, 1964.

Rutter, M., and Bartak, L. Causes of infantile autism. *Journal of Autism and Childhood Schizophrenia* 1:20, 1971.

Rutter, M., Greenfield, D., and Lockyer, L. A five to fifteen year follow-up study of infantile psychosis: II. Social and behavioral outcome. *British Journal of Psychiatry* 113:1183, 1967.

Savage, V. A. Childhood autism: A review of the literature with particular reference to the speech and language structure of the autistic child. *British Journal of Disorders of Communication* 3:75, 1968.

Schell, R., Stark, J., and Giddan, J. Development of language behavior in an autistic child. *Journal of Speech and Hearing Disorders* 32:51, 1967.

Schopler, E. Visual versus tactile receptor preference in normal and schizophrenic children. *Journal of Abnormal and Social Psychology* 71:108, 1966.

Stengel, E. Speech Disorders and Mental Disorders. In A. V. S. de Reuck and M. O'Connor (eds.), *Disorders of Language* (a Ciba Foundation Symposium). Boston: Little, Brown, 1964. Pp. 285–292.

Sulzbacher, S., and Costello, J. A Behavioral Strategy for Language Training of a Child with Autistic Behaviors. *Journal of Speech and Hearing Disorders* 35:256, 1970.

Weiner, P. S. The emotionally disturbed child in a speech clinic: Some considerations. *Journal of Speech and Hearing Disorders* 33:158, 1968.

Yudkovitz, E., and Rottersman, J. A case study example of the implications of a developmental feedback approach to the modification of speech and language disorders in schizophrenic children. *Psychosocial Process* 2:145, 1973.

Yudkovitz, E., and Rottersman, J. Language therapy in childhood schizophrenia: A case study of a monitoring and feedback approach. *Journal of Speech and Hearing Disorders* 38:520, 1973.

CEREBRAL PALSY

Cruickshank, W. M. *Cerebral Palsy: Its Individual and Community Problems.* New York: Syracuse University Press, 1966.

Denhoff, E. *Cerebral Palsy — The Preschool Years: Diagnosis, Treatment and Planning.* Springfield, Ill.: Thomas, 1967.

Denhoff, E., and Robinault, I. P. *Cerebral Palsy and Related Disorders.* New York: McGraw-Hill, 1960.

Fitch, J. L. Treatment of a case of cerebral palsy with hearing impairment. *Journal of Speech and Hearing Disorders* 37:373, 1972.

Goldberg, H., and Fenton, J. (eds.), *Aphonic communication for those with cerebral palsy: Guide for the development and use of a conversation board.* Report. New York: United Cerebral Palsy Associations of New York State (undated).

Hagen, C., Porter, W., and Brink, J. Nonverbal communication: An alternate mode of communication for the child with severe cerebral palsy. *Journal of Speech and Hearing Disorders* 38:448, 1973.

Halpern, H., Darley, F. L., and Brown, J. R. Differential language and neurologic characteristics in cerebral involvement. *Journal of Speech and Hearing Disorders* 38:162, 1973.

McDonald, E. T., and Chance, B. *Cerebral Palsy.* Englewood Cliffs, N.J.: Prentice-Hall, 1964.

McDonald, E. T., and Schultz, A. R. Communication boards for cerebral-palsied children. *Journal of Speech and Hearing Disorders* 38:73, 1973.

Mysak, E. D. Cerebral Palsy Speech Syndromes. In L. E. Travis (ed.), *Handbook of Speech Pathology and Audiology.* New York: Appleton-Century-Crofts, 1971.

Sayre, J. M. Communication for the non-verbal cerebral palsied. *Cerebral Palsy Review* 24:3, 1963.

Westlake, H. *A System for Developing Speech with Cerebral Palsy Children.* Chicago: National Society for Crippled Children and Adults, 1961.

MENTAL RETARDATION

Baer, D. M., Guess, D., and Sherman, J. A. Adventures in Simplistic Grammar. In R. L. Schiefelbusch (ed.), *Language of the Mentally Retarded.* Baltimore: University Park Press, 1972. Pp. 93–105.

Bloom, L. Semantic Features in Language Development. In R. L. Schiefelbusch (ed.), *Language of the Mentally Retarded.* Baltimore: University Park Press, 1972. Pp. 19–33.

Bricker, W. A. A Systematic Approach to Language Training. In R. L. Schiefelbusch (ed.), *Language of the Mentally Retarded.* Baltimore: University Park Press, 1972. Pp. 75–92.

Cromer, R. F. Receptive Language in the Mentally Retarded: Processes and Diagnostic Distinctions. In R. Schiefelbusch and L. L. Lloyd (eds.), *Language Perspectives: Acquisition, Retardation, and Intervention.* Baltimore: University Park Press, 1974. Pp. 237–267.

Garstecki, D. C., Borton, T. E., Stark, E. W., and Kennedy, B. T. Speech, language, and hearing problems in the Laurence-Moon-Biedl syndrome. *Journal of Speech and Hearing Disorders* 37:407, 1972.

Guess, D., Sailor, W., and Baer, D. M. To Teach Language to Retarded Children. In R. L. Schiefelbusch and L. L. Lloyd (eds.), *Language Perspectives: Acquisition, Retardation, and Intervention.* Baltimore: University Park Press, 1974. Pp. 529–563.

Hass, W. A., and Hass, S. K. Syntactic Structure and Language Development in Retardates. In R. L. Schiefelbusch (ed.), *Language of the Mentally Retarded.* Baltimore: University Park Press, 1972. Pp. 35–51.

Kent, L. R., Klein, D., Falk, A., and Guenther, H. A Language Acquisition Program for the Retarded. In J. E. McLean, D. E. Yoder, and R. L. Schiefelbusch (eds.), *Language Intervention With the Retarded.* Baltimore: University Park Press, 1972. Pp. 151–190.

Lloyd, L. L., and Fulton, R. T. Audiology's Contribution to Communications Programming with the Retarded. In J. E. McLean, D. E. Yoder, and R. L. Schiefelbusch (eds.), *Language Intervention with the Retarded.* Baltimore: University Park Press, 1972. Pp. 111–129.

Matthews, J. Speech problems of the mentally retarded. In L. E. Travis (ed.), *Handbook of Speech Pathology.* New York: Appleton-Century-Crofts, 1957. Pp. 531–551.

Miller, J. F., and Yoder, D. E. An Ontogenetic Language Teaching Strategy for Retarded Children. In R. L. Schiefelbusch and L. L. Lloyd (eds.), *Language Perspectives: Acquisition, Retardation, and Intervention.* Baltimore: University Park Press, 1974. Pp. 505–528.

Naremore, R. C., and Dever, R. B. Language performance of educable mentally retarded and normal children at five age levels. *Journal of Speech and Hearing Research* 18:82, 1975.

Schiefelbusch, R. L. (ed.), *Language of the Mentally Retarded.* Baltimore: University Park Press, 1972.

Schiefelbusch, R. L., Bair, H. V., Spradlin, J. E., Siegel, G. M., Horowitz, F. D., Harkins, J. P., and Copeland, R. H. Language studies of mentally retarded children. *Journal of Speech and Hearing Disorders* (Suppl. 10), 1963.

Siegel, G. M. Three Approaches to Speech Retardation. In R. L. Schiefelbusch (ed.), *Language of the Mentally Retarded.* Baltimore: University Park Press, 1972. Pp. 127–141.

Yoder, D. E., and Miller, J. F. What We May Know and What We Can Do: Input Toward a System. In J. E. McLean, D. E. Yoder, and R. L. Schiefelbusch (eds.), *Language Intervention With the Retarded.* Baltimore: University Park Press, 1972. Pp. 89–107.

Zeamon, D., and House, B. J. The Role of Attention in Retardate Discrimination Learning. In N. R. Ellis (ed.), *Handbook of Mental Deficiency.* New York: McGraw-Hill, 1963.

THERAPEUTICS

Albright, J. S., and Albright, R. W. The role of linguistics in speech and hearing therapy. *Language Learning* 9:51, 1959.

Anderson, R., Miles, M., and Matheny, P. *Communicative Evaluation Charts.* Cambridge, Mass.: Educators Publishing Service, 1963.

Austin, J. L. *How to Do Things with Words.* New York: Oxford University Press, 1962.

Baer, D. M., Peterson, R. F., and Sherman, J. A. *Building an Imitative Repertoire by Programming Similarity Between Child and Model as Discriminative Reinforcement.* Minneapolis: Society for Research in Child Development, 1965.

Bandura, A., and Harris, M. B. Modification of syntactic style. *Journal of Experimental Child Psychology* 3:341, 1966.

Bangs, T. E. Adapting the Curriculum Guide: Children in a Pre-Academic Setting. In T. E. Bangs, *Language and Learning Disorders of the Pre-academic Child: With Curriculum Guide.* New York: Appleton-Century-Crofts, 1968. Pp. 166–187.

Bangs, T. E. Appendix, In *Language and Learning Disorders.* Pp. 337–393.

Bangs, T. E. A Pre-Academic Curriculum Guide, In *Language and Learning Disorders.* Pp. 191–333.

Bangs, T. E. Teaching Principles and Techniques, In *Language and Learning Disorders.* Pp. 117–133.

Becker, W., Engelmann, S., and Thomas, D. *Teaching: A Course in Applied Psychology.* Palo Alto: Science Research Associates, 1971. Pp. 40–45.

Bierman, M. The operant conditioning of verbal behavior and its relevance to syntax. Harvard University Bachelor's Thesis, 1964.

Bloom, L. Why not pivot grammars? *Journal of Speech and Hearing Disorders* 36:40, 1971.

Bricker, W. A., and Bricker, D. D. A program of language training for the severely language handicapped child. *Exceptional Child* 37:101, 1970.

Bricker, W. A., and Bricker, D. D. An Early Language Training Strategy. In R. L. Schiefelbusch and L. L. Lloyd (eds.), *Language Perspectives: Acquisition, Retardation, and Intervention.* Baltimore: University Park Press, 1974. Pp. 431–468.

Borus, J. F., Greenfield, S., Spiegel, B., and Daniels, G. Establishing imitative speech employing operant techniques in a group setting. *Journal of Speech and Hearing Disorders* 38:533, 1973.

Brown, R., Fraser, C., and Bellugi, U. Control of Grammar in Imitation, Comprehension, and Production. In R. Brown (ed.), *Psycholinguistics.* New York: Free Press, 1970. Pp. 28–55.

Butterfield, E. C., and Belmont, J. M. The Role of Verbal Processes in Short-Term Memory. In R. L. Schiefelbusch (ed.), *Language of the Mentally Retarded.* Baltimore: University Park Press, 1972. Pp. 231–247.

Carrier, J. K., Jr. Application of Functional Analysis and a Nonspeech Response Mode to Teaching Language. In L. V. McReynolds (ed.), *Developing Systematic Procedures for Training Children's Language.* (American Speech and Hearing Association Monographs, No. 18.) 1974. Pp. 47–95.

Cazden, C. B. Language Programs for Young Children: Notes from England and Wales. In C. S. Lavatelli (ed.), *Language Training in Early Childhood Education.* Urbana, Ill.: University of Illinois Press, 1972. Pp. 119–153.

Cowan, P. A., Weber, J., Hoddinott, B. A., and Klein, J. Mean length of spoken response as a function of stimulus, experimenter, and subject. *Child Development* 38:191, 1967.

Cruickshank, W. M., Bentzen, F. A., Ratzenburg, F. H., and Tannhouser, M. T. *A Teaching Method for Brain-Injured and Hyperactive Children.* Syracuse, N.Y.: Syracuse University Press, 1961.

Davis, G. A. Linguistics and language therapy: The sentence construction board. *Journal of Speech and Hearing Disorders* 38:205, 1973.

Dixon, C., and Curry, B. Some thoughts on the communication board. *Cerebral Palsy Journal* 26:12, 1965.

Dunn, L. M., and Smith, J. O. *Peabody Language Development Kit.* Circle Pines, Minn.: American Guidance Service, 1967.

Efron, R. Comments in response to Hirsh, I. J., Information Processing in Input Channels for Speech and Language: The Significance of Serial Order of Stimuli. In C. H. Millikan and F. L. Darley (eds.), *Brain Mechanisms Underlying Speech and Language.* New York: Grune & Stratton, 1967.

Ervin-Tripp, S. Imitation and Structural Changes in Children's Language. In E. H. Lenneberg (ed.), *New Directions in the Study of Language.* Cambridge, Mass.: MIT Press, 1964.

Feallock, B. Communication for the non-verbal individual. *American Journal of Occupational Therapy* 12:60, 1958.

Fitzgerald, E. *Straight Language for the Deaf.* Washington, D.C.: Volta Bureau, 1954.

Frailberg, S. Intervention in infancy: A program for blind infants. *Journal of Child Psychiatry* 10:381, 1971.

Fraser, C., Bellugi, U., and Brown, R. W. Control of grammar in imitation, comprehension, and production. *Journal of Verbal Learning and Verbal Behavior* 2:121, 1963.

Fry, E. *Teaching Machines and Programmed Instruction.* New York: McGraw-Hill, 1963. Pp. 37–67.

Gottsleben, R. H., Tyack, D., and Buschini, G. Three case studies in language training: Applied linguistics. *Journal of Speech and Hearing Disorders* 39:213, 1974.

Hahn, E. Communication in the therapy session: A point of view. *Journal of Speech and Hearing Disorders* 25:18, 1960.

Hahn, E. Indications for direct, non-direct and indirect methods in speech correction. *Journal of Speech and Hearing Disorders* 26:230, 1961.

Hedrick, D. L., Christman, M. A., and Augustine, L. Programming for the antecedent event in therapy. *Journal of Speech and Hearing Disorders* 38:339, 1973.

Hill, S. D., Campagna, J., Long, D., Munch, J., and Naecker, S. An exploratory study of the use of two response key boards as a means of communication for the severely handicapped child. *Perceptual and Motor Skills* 26:699, 1968.

Holland, A. Some applications of behavioral principles to clinical speech problems. *Journal of Speech and Hearing Disorders* 32:11, 1967.

Holland, A. Language therapy for children. Presented at conference of the Southern California Speech and Hearing Association, Los Angeles, 1971.

Horton, K. B. Infant Intervention and Language Learning. In R. L. Schiefelbusch and L. L. Lloyd (eds.), *Language Perspectives: Acquisition, Retardation, and Intervention.* Baltimore: University Park Press, 1974. Pp. 469–491.

Ingram, D. The Acquisition of the English Verbal Auxiliary and Copula in Normal and Linguistically Deviant Children. In L. V. McReynolds (ed.), *Developing Systematic Procedures for Training Children's Language.* (American Speech and Hearing Association Monographs, No. 18.) 1974. Pp. 5–14.

Jones, M. L. Electrical communication devices. *American Journal of Occupational Therapy* 6:3, 1971.

Keith, R. L. *Speech and Language Rehabilitation.* Danville, Illinois: Interstate Printers & Publishers, 1972.

Larson, T. Communication for the non-verbal child. *Academic Therapy* 6:3, 1971.

Lavatelli, C. S. A Systematized Approach to Language Teaching: The Tucson Method. In C. S. Lavatelli (ed.), *Language Training in Early Childhood Education.* Urbana, Ill.: University of Illinois Press, 1972. Pp. 101–118.

Lavoy, R. W. Rick's communicator. *Exceptional Children* 23:338, 1957.

Leach, E. Interrogation: A model and some implications. *Journal of Speech and Hearing Disorders* 37:33, 1972.

Leonard, L. B. Teaching by the rules. *Journal of Speech and Hearing Disorders* 38:174, 1973.

Lynch, L., and Tobin, A. The development of language-training programs for postrubella hearing impaired children. *Journal of Speech and Hearing Disorders* 38:15, 1973.

McConnell, F., Love, R. J., and Clark, B. S. Principles and Methods of Language Remediation. In S. Dickson (ed.), *Communication Disorders: Remedial Principles and Practices.* Glenview, Ill.: Scott, Foresman, 1974. Pp. 84–103.

McLean, J. E., Yoder, D. E., and Schiefelbusch, R. L. *Language Intervention with the Retarded: Some Strategies.* Baltimore: University Park Press, 1972.

McReynolds, L. V. Contingencies and consequences in speech therapy. *Journal of Speech and Hearing Disorders* 35:12, 1970.

McReynolds, L. V. Application of Systematic Procedures in Clinical Environments. In L. V. McReynolds (ed.), *Developing Systematic Procedures for Training Children's Language.* (American Speech and Hearing Association Monographs, No. 18.) 1974. Pp. 131–140.

McReynolds, L. V. Introduction to Developing Systematic Procedures, In *Developing Systematic Procedures.* Pp. 1–4.

McReynolds, L. V. Verbal sequence discrimination training for language impaired children. *Journal of Speech and Hearing Disorders* 32:249, 1967.

McReynolds, L. V. Reinforcement Procedures for Establishing and Maintaining Echoic Speech by a Nonverbal Child. In F. L. Girardeau and J. E. Spradlin (eds.), *A Functional Analysis Approach to Speech and Language.* (American Speech and Hearing Association Monographs, No. 14.) 1970. Pp. 60–66.

Marshall, N. R., and Hegrenes, J. R. A Communication Therapy Model for Cognitively Disorganized Children. In J. E. McLean, D. E. Yoder, and R. L. Schiefelbusch (eds.), *Language Intervention with the Retarded: Developing Strategies.* Baltimore: University Park Press, 1972. Pp. 130–150.

Martin, E. W. Client centered therapy as a theoretical orientation for speech therapy. (American Speech and Hearing Association Monographs, No. 5.) 1963. Pp. 576–578.

Martin, E. W., and Roberts, K. H. Grammatical factors in sentence retention. *Journal of Verbal Learning and Verbal Behavior* 5:211, 1966.

Matheny, A. P. Pathological echoic responses in a child: Effect of environmental mand and tact control. *Journal of Experimental Child Psychology* 6:624, 1968.

May, F. *Teaching Language as Communication to Children.* Columbus, Ohio: Bobbs-Merrill, 1967.

Miller, J., and Carpenter, C. Electronics for communication. *American Journal of Occupational Therapy* 28:20, 1964.

Miller, J. F., and Yoder, D. E. A Syntax Teaching Program. In J. E. McLean, D. E. Yoder, and R. L. Schiefelbusch (eds.), *Language Intervention with the Retarded.* Baltimore: University Park Press, 1972. Pp. 191–211.

Milstead, J. R. Modification of echolalic speech in a blind, behaviorally-deficient child using parental contingency management. *Journal of Communication Disorders* 5:275, 1972.

Monsees, E. K. *Structured Language for Children with Special Language Learning Problems.* Washington, D.C.: Children's Hearing and Speech Center, Children's Hospital of the District of Columbia, 1972.

Moore, D. R. Language Research and Preschool Language Training. In C. S. Lavatelli (ed.), *Language Training In Early Childhood Education.* Urbana, Ill.: University of Illinois Press, 1972. Pp. 3–48.

Moore, O. K., and Anderson, A. R. The Response Environment Project. In R. D. Hess and R. M. Bear (eds.), *Early Education.* Chicago: Aldine, 1968. Pp. 171–190.

Morehead, D. M., and Johnson, M. Piaget's theory of intelligence applied to the assessment and treatment of linguistically deviant children. *Stanford Papers Reports on Child Language Development* 4:143, 1972.

Muma, J. Language Intervention: Two Questions and Ten Techniques, In *Language Speech and Hearing Services in Schools.* (American Speech and Hearing Association Monographs, No. 5.) 1971.

Nelson, R. O., and Evans, I. M. The combination of learning principles and speech therapy techniques in the treatment of non-communicating children. *Journal of Child Psychology and Psychiatry and Allied Disciplines* 9:111, 1968.

Painter, G. A Tutorial Language Program for Disadvantaged Infants. In C. S. Lavatelli (ed)., *Language Training in Early Childhood Education.* Urbana, Ill.: University of Illinois Press, 1972. Pp. 79—100.

Palmer, M. F. Studies in clinical techniques: II. A home program. *Journal of Speech and Hearing Disorders* 12:157, 1951.

Perfetti, C. A. Sentence retention and the depth hypothesis. *Journal of Verbal Learning and Verbal Behavior* 8:101, 1969.

Peterson, H. A. A case report of speech and language training for a two-year-old laryngectomized child. *Journal of Speech and Hearing Disorders* 38:275, 1973.

Peterson, R. Imitation: A Basic Behavioral Mechanism. In H. Sloane and B. MacAulay (eds.), *Operant Procedures in Remedial Speech and Language Training.* Boston: Houghton Mifflin, 1968.

Premack, D. Toward empirical behavior laws: I. Positive reinforcement. *Psychological Review* 66:219, 1959.

Premack, D., and Premack, A. J. Teaching Visual Language to Apes and Language-Deficient Persons. In R. L. Schiefelbusch and L. L. Lloyd (eds.), *Language Perspectives: Acquisition, Retardation, and Intervention.* Baltimore: University Park Press, 1974. Pp. 347—376.

Rees, N. S. Bases of decision in language training. *Journal of Speech and Hearing Disorders* 37:283, 1972.

Rice, C. E. Perceptual enhancement in the early blind? *Psychological Record* 19:1, 1969.

Risley, T. Learning and lollipops. *Psychology Today* 1:28, 1968.

Ruder, K. F., and Smith, M. D. Issues in Language Training. In R. L. Schiefelbusch and L. L. Lloyd (eds.), *Language Perspectives: Acquisition, Retardation, and Intervention.* Baltimore: University Park Press, 1974. Pp. 565—605.

Ruder, K. F., Smith, M. D., and Hermann, P. Effect of Verbal Imitation and Comprehension on Verbal Production of Lexical Items. In L. V. McReynolds (ed.), *Developing Systematic Procedures for Training Children's Language.* (American Speech and Hearing Association Monographs, No. 18.) 1974. Pp. 15—29.

Schultz, M. C. The bases of speech pathology and audiology: What are appropriate models? *Journal of Speech and Hearing Disorders* 37:118, 1972.

Schultz, M. C., and Carpenter, M. A. The bases of speech pathology and audiology: Selecting a therapy model. *Journal of Speech and Hearing Disorders* 38:395, 1973.

Siegel, G. M. Vocal conditioning in infants. *Journal of Speech and Hearing Disorders* 34:3, 1969.

Slobin, D. I., and Welsh, C. A. Elicited Imitation as a Research Tool in Developmental Psycholinguistics. In C. S. Lavatelli (ed.), *Language Training In Early Childhood Education.* Urbana, Ill.: University of Illinois Press, 1972. Pp. 170—185.

Staats, A. W. Classical Conditioning and Emotional (Attitudinal) Word Meaning. In A. W. Staats, *Learning, Language, and Cognition.* New York: Holt, Rinehart and Winston, 1968. Pp. 10—40.

Staats, A. W. Complex Verbal S-R Mechanisms and Concept Learning. In A. W. Staats, *Learning, Language, and Cognition.* New York: Holt, Rinehart and Winston, 1968. Pp. 132—153.

Stremel, K., and Waryas, C. A Behavioral-Psycholinguistic Approach to Language Training. In L. V. McReynolds (ed.), *Developing Systematic Procedures for Training Children's Language.* (American Speech and Hearing Association Monographs, No. 18.) 1974. Pp. 96—130.

Taylor, O. L., and Anderson, C. B. Neuropsycholinguistics and Language Retraining. In J. W. Black and E. G. Jancosek (eds.), *Proceedings of the Conference on Language Retraining for Aphasics.* Columbus, Ohio: Ohio State University Research Foundation, 1968. Pp. 3—18.

Turton, L. J. Discussion Summary: Early Language Intervention. In R. L. Schiefelbusch and L. L. Lloyd (eds.), *Language Perspectives: Acquisition, Retardation, and Intervention.* Baltimore: University Park Press, 1974. Pp. 493—501.

Van Riper, C. *Teaching Your Child to Talk.* New York: Harper & Row, 1950.

GENERAL REFERENCES

Backus, O., and Beasley, J. *Speech Therapy with Children.* Boston: Houghton Mifflin, 1951.

Bangs, T. E. *Language and Learning Disorders of the Preacademic Child: With Curriculum Guide.* New York: Appleton-Century-Crofts, 1968.

Berry, M. F. *Language Disorders of Children: The Bases and Diagnoses.* New York: Appleton-Century-Crofts, 1969.

Berry, M. F., and Eisenson, J. *Speech Disorders.* New York: Appleton-Century-Crofts, 1956.

Black, M. *The Labyrinth of Language.* New York: New American Library, 1968.

Brown, B. *A First Language.* Cambridge, Mass.: Harvard University Press, 1973.

Brown, R. *Words and Things.* New York: Free Press, 1958.

Brown, R. *Psycholinguistics.* New York: Free Press, 1970.

Bruner, J. S., Goodnow, J. J., and Austin, G. A. *A Study of Thinking.* New York: Science Editions, 1962.

Bruner, J. S., Olver, R., and Greenfield, P. *Studies in Cognitive Growth.* New York: Wiley, 1966.

Cassirer, E. *An Essay on Man.* New Haven: Yale University Press, 1944.

Chomsky, N. *Syntactic Structures.* The Hague: Mouton, 1957.

Chomsky, N. *Aspects of the Theory of Syntax.* Cambridge, Mass.: MIT Press, 1965.

Chomsky, N. *Language and Mind.* New York: Harcourt, Brace and World, 1968.

Church, J. *Language and the Discovery of Reality.* New York: Random House, 1961.

Copi, I. M. *Introduction to Logic* (3rd ed.). New York: Macmillan, 1968.

Cruickshank, W. M. (ed.). *Psychology of Exceptional Children and Youth.* Englewood Cliffs, N.J.: Prentice-Hall, 1955.

Deese, J. *Psycholinguistics.* Boston: Allyn and Bacon, 1970.

DeVito, J. A. *The Psychology of Speech and Language.* New York: Random House, 1970.

Dickson, S. (ed.). *Communication Disorders: Remedial Principles and Practices.* Glenview, Ill.: Scott, Foresman, 1974.

Eisenson, J., and Ogilvie, M. *Speech Correction in the Schools.* New York: Macmillan, 1971.

Erikson, E. H. *Insight and Responsibility.* New York: Norton, 1964.

Fries, C. C. *The Structure of English.* New York: Harcourt, Brace and World, 1952.

Furth, H. G. *Piaget and Knowledge.* Englewood Cliffs, N.J.: Prentice-Hall, 1969.

Gleason, H. A., Jr. *An Introduction to Descriptive Linguistics* (rev. ed.). New York: Holt, Rinehart and Winston, 1961.

Inhelder, B., and Piaget, J. *The Early Growth of Logic in the Child.* New York: Harper & Row, 1964.

Jakobson, R. *Child Language, Aphasia and Phonological Universals.* The Hague: Mouton, 1968.

Kirk, S. A., and Kirk, W. D. *Psycholinguistic Learning Disabilities: Diagnosis and Remediation.* Urbana, Ill.: University of Illinois Press, 1971.

Lavatelli, C. S. (ed.). *Language Training in Early Childhood Education.* Chicago: University of Illinois Press, 1972.

Lenneberg, E. H. *Biological Foundations of Language.* New York: Wiley, 1967.

Lewis, M. M. *Language and the Child.* London: National Foundation for Educational Research, 1969.

Luria, A. R. *Higher Cortical Functions in Man.* New York: Basic Books, 1966.

Luria, A. R. *The Mind of a Mnemonist.* New York: Basic Books, 1968.

McGinnis, M. A. *Aphasic Children: Identification and Education by the Association Method.* Washington, D.C.: Alexander Graham Bell Association for the Deaf, 1963.

McNeill, D. *The Acquisition of Language: The Study of Developmental Psycholinguistics.* New York: Harper & Row, 1970.

Mecham, M. J., Berko, M. J., Berko, F. G., and Palmer, M. F. *Communication Training in Childhood Brain Damage.* Springfield, Ill.: Thomas, 1969.

Menyuk, P. *Sentences Children Use.* Cambridge, Mass.: MIT Press, 1969.

Moffett, J. *Teaching the Universe of Discourse.* Boston: Houghton Mifflin, 1968.

Piaget, J. *Play, Dreams, and Imitation in Childhood.* New York: Norton, 1962.

Rieber, R. W., and Brubaker, R. S. (eds.). *Speech Pathology.* Amsterdam: North-Holland, 1966.

Salus, P. *Linguistics.* Indianapolis, Ind.: Bobbs-Merrill, 1969.

Schiefelbusch, R. L., and Lloyd, L. L. (eds.). *Language Perspectives: Acquisition, Retardation, and Intervention.* Baltimore: University Park Press, 1974.

Schuell, H., Jenkins, J. J., and Jimenez-Pabon, E. *Aphasia in Adults: Diagnosis, Prognosis, and Treatment.* New York: Hoeber Medical Division, Harper & Row, 1964.

Schultz, M. C. *An Analysis of Clinical Behavior in Speech and Hearing.* Englewood Cliffs, N.J.: Prentice-Hall, 1972.

Slobin, D. I. *Psycholinguistics.* Glenview, Ill.: Scott, Foresman, 1971.

Staats, A. W. *Learning, Language and Cognition: Theory, Research, and Method for the Study of Human Behavior and Its Development.* New York: Holt, Rinehart and Winston, 1968.

Streng, A. *Syntax, Speech and Hearing.* New York: Grune & Stratton, 1972.

Terwilliger, R. F. *Meaning and Mind: A Study in the Psychology of Language.* New York: Oxford University Press, 1968.

Travis, L. E. *Handbook of Speech Pathology.* New York: Appleton-Century-Crofts, 1957.

Vygotsky, L. S. *Thought and Language.* Cambridge, Mass.: MIT Press, 1962.

Weir, R. *Language in the Crib.* The Hague: Mouton, 1962.

Wepman, J., and Hass, W. *A Spoken Word Count.* Los Angeles: Western Psychological Services, 1969.

West, R. W., and Ansberry, M. *The Rehabilitation of Speech* (4th ed.). New York: Harper & Row, 1968.

Williams, F. (ed.). *Language and Poverty: Perspectives on a Theme.* Skokie, Ill.: Rand McNally, 1970.

Order Form

Mail this or a copy of this form to: **Sourcebook Systems**
P.O. Box 746
Ellensburg, Washington 98926

Date _____   Purchase order no. _____

Check appropriate box
☐ Organization   ☐ Individual   ☐ Please send workshop information.

Ship to or bill:

Name (attention of)_____

School or organization_____

City, state, zip_____

Visa or Master Charge no. _____

Authorized signature _____

Orders from individuals and private organizations must include remittance plus 8% for postage and handling *OR* a Visa or Master Charge number. Other schools or organizations will be billed as requested.

Please allow four weeks for delivery.

Quantity	Item	Unit Price	Total
	Criterion Placement Test	$ .35 each	
	Cumulative Response Record (pad of 50)	1.50	
	Sourcebook Language Script (pad of 50)	1.50	
	Certificates of Achievement	.04 each	
		Sub Total	
		Taxes: 5.1% in State of WA	
		Postage and Handling Charge: 8% of subtotal	
		Total order	$